THE TOUCH
OF TRANSCENDENCE

THE TOUCH
OF TRANSCENDENCE

A Postcolonial Theology of God

MAYRA RIVERA

Westminster John Knox Press
LOUISVILLE • LONDON

Scripture quotations from the New Revised Standard Version of the Bible are copyright © 1989 by the Division of Christian Education of the National Council of the Churches of Christ in the U.S.A. and are used by permission.

Marjorie Agosín's poem "Napa" is originally published in *An Absence of Shadows*. Translated by Celeste Kostopulos-Cooperman, Cola Franzen, and Mary G. Berg. Fredonia, New York: White Pine Press, 1998. Copyright © 1998 by Marjorie Agosín. Translations copyright © 1988, 1998 by Cola Franzen, 1992, 1998 by Celeste Kostopulos-Cooperman, and 1998 by Mary G. Berg. It is used herein with the permission of White Pine Press.

Book design by Drew Stevens

First edition
Published by Westminster John Knox Press
Louisville, Kentucky

This book is printed on acid-free paper that meets the American National Standards Institute Z39.48 standard. ♾

PRINTED IN THE UNITED STATES OF AMERICA

07 08 09 10 11 12 13 14 15 16—10 9 8 7 6 5 4 3 2 1

Library of Congress Cataloging-in-Publication Data

Rivera, Mayra.
    The touch of transcendence : a postcolonial theology of God / Mayra Rivera.—1st ed.
        p. cm.
    Includes bibliographical references.
    ISBN 978-0-664-23073-9 (alk. paper)
    1. Transcendence of God.   2. God (Christianity)   3. Postcolonialism.
    4. Christian sociology.   I. Title.
    BT124. 5.R58   2007
    231'.4—dc22   2006048911

In loving memory
of my mother, Cuqui

Contents

Preface

Divine transcendence is a theological idiom referring to God's otherness. It is also a controversial concept, of which progressive contemporary theologies are rightly suspicious. Transcendence is often associated
with hierarchical distance. Thus, the most common images and concepts
that Christians have used to describe divine transcendence convey the idea
that God's otherness entails separation from creation. This assumption
has negative implications for our visions of God and the created world
because it sets up real difference as antithetical to close relationships.

Perhaps the claim that modern attempts to imagine God's otherness
have often produced disappointing results should not surprise us, for
dominant modern cultures have had serious difficulties dealing with
otherness in general. Contemporary critiques of dominant Western
thought consistently denounce the cultural tendency to privilege sameness over difference, which has led to deficient models of relationship
with those identified as Others. For instance, the world is commonly
imagined as clearly divided between "us" and "the Others." The "Others"
are expected to assimilate into an overarching sameness ("us") or to
remain excluded from "our" community. In practice, we have too often
failed to respect otherness and live peacefully and responsibly with our
differences. The limitations of our models of interhuman difference
stem from our difficulties envisioning divine otherness.

This book examines the challenges of imagining God's otherness
by engaging recent theologies of God as well as theoretical sources
about otherness which analyze the shortcomings of prevalent models
of interhuman difference and propose constructive alternatives. These

perspectives interlace in this constructive theology of God, grounding its critical and affirmative moves.

The Touch of Transcendence stages a dialogue between theological and nontheological discussions about transcendence to uncover not only its problems, but also its promises for theologies concerned with social justice. What would divine transcendence look like if we revised our conceptions of difference? What if we no longer assumed that difference entails separation? What if transcendence were not understood as that which radically distances God from creatures, but rather as a theological concept that makes differences significant, especially our differences from one another?

Through its engagement with contemporary theological models of transcendence espoused by radical orthodoxy and Latin American liberation theology as well as with models of inter-human difference from philosophical, feminist, and postcolonial sources, this book develops a model of *relational transcendence*—one that affirms not only the irreducible difference of God from all creatures, but the complex differences among creatures as well.

*****

This book has been called forth by many *others*. Their multiplicity transcends the limits of this page, where I can name only a few who have persistently and singularly touched this text. I am thankful to the Drew community for its hospitality and intellectual nurture. This work is especially indebted to Catherine Keller's perceptive and informed guidance, consistently offered in the spirit of her theology—"tuning relation to possibility." I am grateful to Virginia Burrus for pertinent challenges in matters of ancient and contemporary worldviews, which she uniquely combines with forthright pragmatic advice in the how-to's of scholarly research and writing. Otto Maduro's questions have been provocative and engaging, and have kept me mindful of the importance of saying it "como pa' Juan Pedro." I thank Fernando Segovia for his mentorship and scholarly challenges. My friends at Drew offered helpful challenges and suggestions, and solidarity in joy and distress—my thanks to Michael Nausner, Sigridur Gudsmarsdottir, Mario Costa, Seung Gap Lee, Soo Kim, and Luke Higgins, and to Anna Mercedes and Krista Hughes who also offered editorial advice. Anne Joh and Inese Radzins gave me valuable feedback. Marion Grau has shared precious insights through all phases of the project. I am also thankful to the Pacific School of Religion, where I have recently found my academic home. I warmly thank Dean Mary Donovan Turner for her support. My thanks to Eugene McMullan, a talented graduate student at the GTU, for his careful proofreading.

I gratefully acknowledge the Hispanic Theological Initiative for the economic support that their scholarship provided through my doctoral program as well as for offering the space in which to develop my relations with many Latina/o scholars. Among those scholars, I am especially grateful to Ángel Méndez, whose commitment to radical orthodoxy made him a keen conversation partner. Ulrike Guthrie patiently read through the earliest drafts of this manuscript. My thanks to Jon Berquist and Dan Braden from WJK for their support and diligence.

And I thank my family and friends for their trust and support. Rebecca, Caco, Meche, Chucho, Chalo, Chal, Vicky, Lillian, Oscar, and Nancy sprinkled the journey with love and humor. With and because of José Carlos, Andrea, Mónica, and Raquel, this book has been felt, thought, written, set aside, and rewritten. In my relation to their wonderful singularity I encounter the glory of God.

CHAPTER 1

Introduction

"God is transcendent." Most theologians would agree with this statement, but what do we mean by it? At first glance, the answer seems obvious. "Transcendent" signifies that which is beyond normal physical experience, apart, above, unlimited by materiality. "Divine transcendence" thus indicates God's aloftness, separation, independence, and immateriality—in short, his super/iority. These associations are indeed the most common for the term "transcendence" and the reason it has acquired the reputation of being a tool of patriarchal and imperial self-legitimation. For decades, progressive theologians have objected to the validation of hierarchical rule that attends such a concept of the deity. Theologians have also been concerned about the ways in which allusions to transcendence tend to orient religious life away from the pursuit of social transformation, promoting instead the individualistic aspiration to attain a positive otherworldly existence. When claimed as the basis of a superior, unquestionable knowledge owned by some, on the other hand, transcendence has often served to legitimize decidedly ungodly actions. Feminist theologians have further challenged the image of the separate immaterial God for its collusion with the subordination of women and the devastation of creation, choosing instead to emphasize the "immanence" of God. While most theologies do not reject divine transcendence, the numerous suspicions about the term have not been dispelled.

These well-known critiques of the notion of transcendence should not be ignored. Yet I find myself drawn to a different approach. Instead of focusing on the hierarchical and separatist images with which transcendence is laden, and thus implicitly admitting them as normative, I want to delve into an ancient intuition that lies hidden beneath these battered images. Wary, and a bit weary, of the usual formulations for transcendence—beyond being, beyond time, beyond creation, beyond materiality—I have opted instead to being with the simple assertion that God is irreducibly Other, always *beyond* our grasp. But not beyond our touch. How we might imagine this otherness is not what this study presumes, but the vision the book strives to develop. This book seeks to stir up conventional certainties and enable different understandings of "transcendence" to emerge. It hopes, ultimately, to remobilize the passion and the wisdom of a Christian love for the inappropriable divine Other as theological resources for rethinking our relationship with human others.[1]

The Touch of Transcendence offers a vision of transcendence within creation and between creatures: a relational transcendence. In order to liberate the potential of the notion of transcendence for reconceiving interhuman relations, we must resist its pervasive associations with otherworldliness. It is crucial to bring transcendence in contact with the concrete realities of our world—where we encounter and "touch upon" one another. "Touching upon," as feminist philosopher Luce Irigaray defines it, means a "touching which respects the other," that never aims at appropriating or capturing.[2] The book's title intends to highlight the intimacy of transcendence—a transcendence in the flesh of others whom we touch, but may never fully grasp.

The aim of this work is theological. I seek to offer a constructive formulation of divine transcendence in the conviction that Christianity has important resources for envisioning ethical relationships between human beings. Our images of the divine Other shape our constructions of human otherness. An apparent structural relation exists between imagining our relation to the human Other and to God as wholly Other: God can be perceived as an extreme instance of interhuman difference. Yet I will further assert that the relation between human and divine otherness goes beyond the structural. Theologically God's transcendence is inseparable from theological anthropology—that is, from theological notions of what a human being is and, as a consequence, of the meaning of interhuman differences. I ground in Christian theology my affirmation that the cosmos, and thus human beings, are rooted in the divine. Indeed, the cosmos is inconceivable devoid of the divine life force. Moreover, it is always and only within creation that the divine Other is encountered. Although moving toward a theological cosmology, this work focuses on the ways in which transcendence is encountered among human creatures.

It may thus be conceived as an elaboration of Irenaeus's familiar definition: "Gloria Dei vivens homo" (the glory of God is the human being fully alive).[3] This metaphor of "glory" will lure forward this entire book. What does it mean to encounter the "glory of God" in another human being? How does it affect our conceptions of the human person and of relations across differences? What images of God's transcendence are conducive to relations that promote the fullness of life for all creatures?

The book begins by engaging the explicitly theological discourses of "radical orthodoxy" theologians John Milbank and Catherine Pickstock, and liberation theologian Ignacio Ellacuría. The theological insights that arise from those engagements are then developed through a series of readings of the philosophical works of Emmanuel Levinas and Enrique Dussel, the feminist contributions of Luce Irigaray, and postcolonial texts by Gayatri Chakravorty Spivak. If this work's constructive theological proposal unfolds from the interaction with multiple nontheological texts it is partly because the cosmology that it espouses affirms the theological significance of human relations as much as the ethical import of theology. Its interdisciplinary approach is also a necessity dictated by the subject matter. The notion of transcendence has always been as much philosophical as theological, bearing the traces of one discipline when it appears in the other.

The present engagement honors the glory of the otherness to which transcendence testifies, even as the book seeks to release its potential for promoting ethical relations. This study therefore works constructively at the interstices between theology and theoretical discourses about the ethics of difference, where notions of transcendence and interhuman otherness interweave. Although they represent different academic disciplines, all of the discourses explored in this study share the conviction that notions of radical alterity are crucial for ethics. Through my interaction with them, I hope to show how alternative understandings of interhuman difference can lead to a theological reconstruction of the idea of divine transcendence, one that can resist patriarchal and imperialist assumptions while affirming not only the irreducible difference of God from all creatures, but the differences among creatures as well.

This inquiry is thus a variation on liberation and feminist engagements with the doctrine of God. Like liberation theologies, including feminist ones, this book places the concern for right relations with other human beings at the center of the doctrinal discussion, refusing the disjunction between theology and ethics. It also builds upon feminist theologies' meticulous analysis of the correlation between prevalent images of divine transcendence and patriarchal ideals. This theology shares feminist awareness of the power of doctrine to shape communities and direct their praxis; it assents to Elizabeth Johnson's sharp refrain: "The symbol of God functions."[4] And because the symbol functions, this work strives to offer not only a critique of the dominant imaginary, but also an alternative vision that may nurture ethical action. This vision incarnates as a cosmology inspired by that feminist genre where theology becomes self-consciously metaphorical in its attempt to "convert" the imaginary.[5] It nevertheless differs from those remarkable feminist contributions in that, rather than concentrating on the link between the embodiment of creatures and the immanence of God, it emphasizes the inextricability of God's transcendence and the transcendence of the human Other.

THE WHOLLY OTHER

In contemporary Christian theology, the idea of transcendence is associated with the "wholly Other" as described by Karl Barth, perhaps the most influential theologian of the twentieth century. Writing in the aftermath of World War I, at a historical turning point when the optimism of Enlightenment humanism in the dominant cultures of the West had been shattered by monstrous violence, Barth rejected grounding of theology in culture. God is not defined by the cultural and political principles of our societies, and theologies that elevate the human being to divinity have dangerous social consequences. God is wholly Other, Barth proclaimed. "If I have a system," he wrote, "it is limited to the recognition of what Kierkegaard called the 'infinite qualitative distinction' between time and eternity, and to my regarding this as possessing negative as well as positive significance: 'God is in heaven, thou art on earth.'"[6] This qualitative distinction meant for Barth that the reality of God shattered all human cognitive schemes and rendered human understanding of God as ignorance. Thus God relativizes all human constructions: God is ultimately irreducible to our images of God.

This book agrees with the spirit of Barth's critique: God is beyond our grasp. This is indeed the point of departure for this theology of relational transcendence. The fact that the term "wholly Other" appears throughout this text, even in the nontheological writings cited in it, shows the persistent significance of Barth's critiques. But Barth's wholly Other was not only irreducible to human concepts, but also absolutely separate from them. God and humanity are separated by a gulf that is only bridged by Christ.[7] The metaphor that Barth uses to describe the relationship between God and creation highlights that detachment in terms that reveal the tensions with the vision espoused in this work. Jesus intersects the plane of created existence "vertically, from above." Even that intersection is hesitant. "In the resurrection the new world of the Holy Spirit touches the old world of the flesh, but *touches it as a tangent touches a circle, that is, without touching it.*"[8]

In this touch, which does not quite touch, God remains "detached" while effecting the "dissolution of [human] distinction." Human solidarity is based on the assumption that the glory of God is lacking in each and every one of us, and thus "all distinctions between men are seen to be trivial."[9] We may sympathize with Barth's critiques of hierarchies of his times, but the dissolution of distinction has revealed itself to be a fraught strategy that confuses homogeneity with solidarity. This work argues that divine transcendence does not need to dissolve or even subordinate created differences. Indeed a relational transcendence touches creatures, embracing their irreducible differences.

TRANSCENDENCE IN THE WESTERN IMAGINARY

The notion of transcendence evokes both spatial and temporal dimensions of "beyond." On the one hand, transcendence is commonly associated with spatial distance; that which transcends us is most frequently imagined and represented as being spatially distant from us. In its verb form, on the other hand, it alludes to change in time as well as place. "To transcend" means to move beyond the same—either as physical displacement above and beyond existing limits, or as transformation, becoming something new. In common theological parlance, these two dimensions intersect: God is conceived as both the distant Other and sometimes also as the reality toward which persons or history move: the driving force of personal and collective transformation. In nontheological discourses, notions of transcendence may appear without explicit references to God, and yet alluding to a reality distinct from the world (or the self) that nonetheless drives its movement beyond. The ideas of such influential figures of Western modernity as G. W. F. Hegel and Karl Marx provide well-known examples of secularized versions of transcendence.

Whether the term "transcendence" is explicitly invoked or not, the Western imaginary retains the versions of the disembodied controlling power that theism commonly associates with transcendence. Consider the following image of globalized capitalism. On the cover of an issue of *Time* magazine devoted to new trends in global corporate management, a telling image is offered. The globe is at the center. Surrounding it are a number of hands. All seem to support the floating globe or control its movements, but none touch it. A critical separation is maintained between "management" and the "managed." The actual story inside is congruent with this picture. One of the benefits of globalization, we are told, is that technology allows the managers of global corporations to remain in the comfort and convenience of their cities while managing interests in faraway countries. Their hands do not have to touch, nor their lungs breathe the material realities of, the worlds (in) which their economic interests produce. Yet they see and control.

Feminist theologians have long noted the intersections between the conceptions of power as controlling and distant, such as the one just described, and images of divine transcendence. They have further noted that these ideas of transcendent power are based on a cosmic dualism that produces a variety of binaries, thus shaping our ideas about power, materiality, and human differences, particularly those pertaining to gender. Just as traditional notions of transcendence open a rift between the created realm and God, that rift travels through the created realm opening a metaphysical gap between, on the one hand, transcendence/immateriality/progress/intelligibility/independence/Man/God, and, on the other, immanence/materiality/stagnation/sensibility/dependence/Woman/Nature.[10] This dualistic framework entails an oppositional view of gender difference, where women are associated with an immanence conceived as the opposite of transcendence.

In *Beyond God the Father*, a foundational text for feminist theology, Mary Daly challenged the confinement implied in the association of women with stagnation and reclaimed transcendence for women.[11] Her critique followed the classic analysis of feminist philosopher Simone de Beauvoir, in which she observed that "what peculiarly signalizes the situation of woman is that she—a free and autonomous being like all human creatures—nevertheless finds herself living in a world where men compel her to assume the status of the Other." This "woman" is construed as a negative image of the male subject. Confined within the fixed boundaries of patriarchal definitions, she is denied excess. According to de Beauvoir, defining woman as a defective man, patriarchy "propose[s] to stabilize her as object." Such objectification dooms woman to immanence "since her transcendence is to be overshadowed and forever transcended by another ego (conscience) which is essential and sovereign."[12]

To challenge the objectification of women that results from the prevalent definitions of transcendence also requires questioning its theological versions. Daly contended that theologies tend to "hypostasize transcendence," that is, to describe transcendence as the "nature" of a being. Thus these theologies objectify God. Transcendence is not a characteristic of a divine being, Daly argued. Instead, it has a dynamic meaning: transcendence is a verb. Transcendence, she asserted, is the unfolding of God, an event in which women participate.[13] As divine transcendence is released from objectification, women are liberated from the doomed immanence to which patriarchal societies have condemned them. But Daly's depiction of transcendence (like de Beauvoir's) retained aspects of its prevalent images, namely those of separation and independence, which other feminists have subsequently found problematic.[14]

The association of transcendence with separation and independence mirrors the ideals of a masculinist culture that envisions the becoming of subjectivity as overcoming the constraints of materiality (and the body), the demands of relationships with the community, the distractions of affection, and the unpredictable effects of others in the self. All these traits define what Catherine Keller called in her early work "the separative self."[15] Striving toward this ideal, the subject must deny the influences that others have in it. This can only be achieved by domination, for "[o]nly by subduing and possessing the Other can [the self] feel truly in possession of itself." The success of this gesture, however, depends on what it hides: the subject's dependence on others to carry the burdens said ego refuses. Keller's analysis focuses on the functioning of these ideals within patriarchal societies: "Woman, as man's most intimately threatening and yet most comfortingly controlled Other, is there to fill his lack . . . of intimate connections. . . ."[16] Yet this analysis also illuminates the dynamics between the First and Third World economies. Pursuing progress without restraint, the First World asserts its control and possession of the Third World, which carries the burden of the physical labor and ecological devastation, all while the First World refuses the vulnerability of intimate connections, interdependence, and mutuality.[17]

As the maximum expression of freedom from the constraints of materiality, transcendence is often assumed to be a synonym for immateriality. This conflation makes transcendence highly problematic for feminist theologians, for as Rosemary Radford Ruether succinctly states: "the disembodied nature of the . . . divine . . . has served as a linchpin of the Western masculinist symbolic."[18] A view of transcendence as independence or separation from matter and flesh depends upon consigning embodiment to a lower realm, which in turn leads to the subordination of women, whose reproductive functions are generally assumed to place them closer to nature. Nature and body are thus depicted as the inferior "others" of the male-associated principles of rational order, progress, and culture. Epistemologically, immaterial images of God lead to the sundering of the sensible, associated with the flesh, from the intelligible, associated with rational divine order. The critique of dualistic metaphysics—including body/soul, matter/spirit, intelligible/sensible, as well as their divine correlates—is thus a persistent theme in feminist theology, and a central concern for a constructive theology of divine transcendence.[19]

Abstracted from matter, an immaterial transcendence is out of touch with the rhythms of bodily life—a disjuncture that affects views of embodiment, gender, and sexuality, as well as of capitalist production. Thus we find a critique of disembodied transcendence not only among feminists, but also among important critics of capitalism. Walter Benjamin identified a detached conception of historical progress as a key fallacy of industrialization; his analysis of the tenets and implications of this view of transformation further illuminates the material implications of the concept of immaterial, detached transcendence. Transformation as progress, Benjamin explained, is an abstraction, removed from persons and nature, a "progression through a homogeneous, empty time."[20] Progress implies the movement of "mankind itself" as opposed to advances in human "ability and knowledge." Depicted as "something boundless," progress assumes the "infinite perfectibilility" of humankind. Indeed, progress has been "regarded as irresistible, something that automatically pursued a straight or spiral course."[21] This displacement through empty time was unaffected by bodies or nature. To contrast the "new conception of labor," which "amounts to the exploitation of nature," with the "exploitation of the proletariat," betrays a "naïve complacency," Benjamin protested.[22] The ecological crisis that our generation can no longer ignore sadly confirms the vulnerability shared by humans and nonhumans under the fallacy of unrestricted progress.

There is, of course, nothing "natural" about this idea of progress. The imposition of homogeneous universal time required for the routines of industrialization was accomplished through practices intended to forcefully break the links between Native Peoples and their lands.[23] This "massive social abstraction of time from the recalcitrant local rhythms of daily life" further entailed a separation between public time/space from the private "feminized domestic space temporalized by economically trivial rituals."[24] Embodied time is thus confined to the private spheres of domesticity, setting free from space and matter a public (masculinized) time—the time of uninhibited production and detached transcendence.

Transcendence has also frequently meant an implicit privilege of heights—a fact that is seldom addressed in critiques of that notion. That which is transcendent is imagined as above; to transcend is to move up. This valuation of erection colludes with a geopolitical "scale of being," where Northern countries are imagined as closer to cosmological heights, and thus closer to God, than those in the South. This tendency is evident in linguistic expressions, such as "going south," meaning plummeting into the depths of stagnation.[25] As abstract as the term "transcendence" may seem, its depictions are seldom devoid of spatial references that represent and legitimize sociopolitical hierarchies. A theology of transcendence must thus uncover the inscriptions of spatial metaphors in contemporary geopolitical hierarchies. "Space needs to be made visible by foregrounding its ideological content, to illustrate how it can be made to hide consequences, how relations of power and discipline are inscribed into the apparently innocent spatiality of our environment."[26]

The secularized pictures of transcendence that these critiques target reflect and legitimize the value structures of our society and have colluded with the projects of colonization and its civilizing principles as well as with patriarchal domination. There are, however, valuable aspects of the notion of transcendence that are not merely absent from these hierarchical images, but are actually suppressed by them. Hierarchical caricatures of transcendence depend on hypercertainties supported by claims to absolute knowledge, totalizing systems that foreclose the openness, excess, and irreducibility that transcendence implies, for appeals to a realm beyond the grasp of normative subjects, systems of thought, and social structures would threaten the certainties on which these hierarchies depend. Transcendence is thus relegated to an invisible realm and thus effectively prevented from touching our daily lives.

I have referred above to the patriarchal representation of woman as a defective man, which discursively assimilates and essentializes her as subordinate. The fact that she exceeds the parameters of patriarchal metaphysics, that she is irreducible to it—beyond it—is denied. Colonialism and imperialism similarly operate under this type of denial; there must be nothing beyond that the colonizer would not seek to grasp—no person, no land, no Other who could not on principle be appropriated into its own projects.[27] The following example makes this remarkably explicit. In the context of the Protestant missions that accompanied (and coincided with) the U.S. invasion and occupation of Puerto Rico in 1898, a missionary writes the following directive: "To *know the mind of God* is the first requisite of the missionary, but next to that he must come to *knowledge of the mind of the people* over whom he shall be placed by the Holy Spirit."[28] In the colonial context in which this statement was uttered, "knowledge" hardly disguises its links to the aims of power and control. Knowledge here is an attempt to grasp, to comprehend, to gain control over people. That the production of knowledge was a key strategy of colonial domination has been a central claim of postcolonial criticism. What the missionary's statement makes surprisingly clear is the intricate relation between colonial strategies of objectification and control over others, and an objectifying vision of God; the claim "to know the mind of God" is considered the foundation of the claim to know (and rule over) the subjected Other. A space is opened by this appeal to God, the supreme Other, in the subordination of the human Other, and from that space this work calls forth a reconsideration of transcendence.

A CALL FROM BEYOND

"Beyond" signifies spatial distance, marks progress, promises the future, but our initmation of exceeding the barrier or boundary—the very act of going *beyond*—are unknowable, unrepresentable, without a return to the "present" which, in the process of repetition, becomes disjunct and displaced.

—*Homi Bhabha*, The Location of Culture[29]

Postcolonial thinkers resist the totalizing tendencies of modern Western thought. They trace the production of systems—philosophical or sociopolitical—that claim to represent the whole and leave no place for otherness. It is not surprising if today we find among these critics of the modern claims to universality a renewed attention to a beyond. "It is the trope of our times to locate the question of culture in the realm of *beyond*."[30] Thus Homi Bhabha begins his introduction to the book that has become an icon of postcolonial theory: *The Location of Culture*. That the peculiar ethos of a "present"—"for which there seems to be no proper name other than the current and controversial shiftiness of the prefix 'post': *postmodernism, postcolonialism, postfeminism*—is captured for Bhabha by the trope of "beyond" reveals more than the well-known disillusions of contemporary culture. It also points to its hope to transcend its shortcomings.[31]

The relationship between this theoretical allusion to the beyond and theological notions of transcendence will only emerge gradually through this study. For now I will only call attention to a notable encounter between theology and the postmodern questioning of totalizing systems and their denial of the "beyond." The work of poststructuralist philosopher Jacques Derrida has provoked those concerned with God-talk. Derrida's work carefully traces how texts and systems of knowledge produce (rather than simply discover) all-encompassing foundations—a project that is ultimately impossible. To create the illusion of totality, those systems suppress anything or anyone that does not fit: they deny there is anything beyond.

Derrida's critique has included theological systems (what he calls onto-theology, or a theology of being). Some theologians have interpreted these critiques as proof that Derrida, and the deconstructive philosophy that he exemplifies, are nihilistic and inherently atheistic. Ironically, other theologians have "accused" Derrida of practicing negative theology. Derrida refuted both accusations. Yet he later conceded a certain affinity between deconstruction and negative theology. Negative theology works out of an intense awareness that language and symbols cannot possibly grasp God. God exceeds all representation; God is beyond our images of God. Negative theologians thus seek to uncover the limits of our speech about the infinite. Like negative theology, deconstruction seeks to uncover the limits of systems of knowledge and representation—theological or non-theological—by identifying the presence of something Other than the system.[32] Deconstructive readings certainly challenge the totalizing gestures of theological texts and systems, but the significance of these engagements is not reducible to an argument against theism. Indeed, after all his challenges to onto-theology, Derrida's texts remain suggestively haunted by allusions to the wholly Other, alterity, the beyond.

References to "the Other" run through Derrida's extensive corpus, not always in connection to philosophical or theological uses of the (divine) wholly Other. Yet the influence of Emmanuel Levinas on Derrida's work, and through him on postmodern thought, makes deconstruction particularly susceptible to the haunting of the divine Other. For Levinas the Other is the site of encounter with the (divine) wholly Other, as we will see in chapter 4. Derrida keeps God at a safe philosophical distance, and yet he has posed crucial questions for theological thought in a postmodern era and stirred creative discussions within both fields.[33]

One of Derrida's tantalizing statements stimulated the enquiries that led to this book. In the context of his reading of Kierkegaard's *Fear and Trembling*, an analysis of Abraham's sacrifice, Derrida writes, "If God is completely other, the figure or name of the wholly other, then every other (one) is every (bit) other. *Tout autre est tout autre.*" Derrida contends, in typical deconstructive mode, that this formula disturbs Kierkegaard's distinction between the religious and the ethical, a contention that Levinas himself had raised against Kierkegaard. Yet Derrida also hints at the multiple ramifications of this statement. He continues, "It implies that God as wholly other, is to be found everywhere there is something of the wholly other. And since each of us, everyone else, each other is infinitely other in its absolute singularity, inaccessible, solitary, transcendent, nonmanifest, originarily nonpresent to my ego"—here is the crucial implication—"then what can be said about Abraham's relation to God can be said about my relation to every other (one). . . ."[34]

Derrida moves on to deconstruct Kierkegaard's depiction of Abraham's relation to God. I stayed there, however, pondering, with different intent, the theological significance of the question: what if every Other, "my neighbor or my loved ones [were] as inaccessible to me, as secret and transcendent as Jahweh"[35]? Asking why, or in what sense, we might say that our neighbor is transcendent to us, I engage a range of thinkers who have in different ways challenged the modern assumptions of the full accessibility of the other human person to the self. Many of them, like Derrida, have been influenced by Levinas. This exploration thus follows Levinas—even as I intensely write over his text with the help of his feminist and postcolonial readers.

The concrete historical implications and ethical significance of the theoretical moves of deconstruction, however, come into focus for me not in Derrida's texts, but in postcolonial deployments of deconstruction. For postcolonial theory, the import of the "post" of postmodernism does not derive from any presumed sequentiality. Its beyond is explicitly linked to the irreducibly material realities suppressed in Western representations of modernity, civilizing mission, and universal progress. "The wider significance of the postmodern condition lies in the awareness that the epistemological 'limits'" uncovered by postmodern critiques also represent the "enunciative boundaries of a range of other dissonant, even dissident histories and voices—women, the colonized, minority groups, the bearers of policed sexualities."[36] These epistemological limits have long been visible to those on modernity's "underside": such as the heirs of the former colonies. For colonial encounters "have anticipated, *avant la lettre,* many of the problematics of signification and judgment that have become current in contemporary theory. . . ."[37] The early history of postmodern criticism was written beyond the geographical borders of the metropolis.

In postcolonial criticism the beyond (and therefore transcendence, I will argue) becomes inextricable from the witness of oppressed communities. The imaginary spatial distance that "beyond" alludes to is given concrete significance in the geographical space beyond the metropolis. But it should not be reduced to simple spatial distance or separation. "Beyond" also calls attention to the limits of colonial knowledge—an epistemological excess that Walter Mignolo calls "border thinking."[38] The metropolitan centers encounter this epistemological excess—this wisdom that cannot be contained within authoritative systems—in the people on its borders, inside/outsiders of postcolonial societies.

In this postcolonial vision, transformation emerges from the encounters with the otherness beyond. Thus, the realm of beyond is not a static place of separation, but a dynamic space of encounters and transformation. Indeed, encounters with others open the space of transcendence: "our intimation of exceeding the barrier or boundary—the very act of going *beyond*."[39] Going beyond is, of course, not escaping to a space/time unaffected by histories of exclusion. This movement is not toward a suprahistorical transcendence, nor does it follow the linear progression of modern interpretations of history. Quite to the contrary, Bhabha asserts that these acts of going beyond "are unknowable, unrepresentable, without a return to the 'present,'" to reinscribe in it "our human, historic commonality."[40] Exceeding a boundary and returning: is transformation ever possible without these movements?

"Beyond" thus signals both an "intervening space" and a "revisionary time" that open the possibility for transforming "the present into an expanded and ex-centric site of experience and empowerment."[41] Never stepping outside or above the sphere of human relations, it hopes to "*touch the future on its hither side.*"[42]

* * *

This book begins with a reading of explicitly theological texts, which represent recent, influential, and yet starkly different attempts to reclaim the notion of divine transcendence for the sake of promoting social transformation: "radical orthodoxy" and liberation theology. Chapter 2 introduces key concepts related to transcendence—participation, causality, and teleology, among others—while it explores the proposals of radical orthodoxy theologians John Milbank and Catherine Pickstock, noting how their model of divine transcendence depicts God's otherness, the constitution of human beings, and the relation between God and human beings. The engagement with radical orthodoxy eventually leads us to its particular challenge of liberation theology as lacking a viable concept of transcendence. We examine this challenge in chapter 3 by focusing on the countervoices of liberation theologians, particularly of Ignacio Ellacuría; it investigates the not yet fully realized promise within liberation theology of a concept of "transcendence within" creation and history—a concept that, as I hope to show, destabilizes the transcendence/immanence binary stubbornly reinscribed by radical orthodoxy.

Pursuing a model of intracosmic transcendence entails attending to the created realm, as it is precisely there that transcendence emerges. Concentrating particularly on the relations between human beings, the subsequent chapters evaluate a range of critical discourses that deploy the notion of transcendence as a key element in their depictions of—and prescriptions for—ethical human relations. The discourses engaged in chapters 4, 5, and 6—which treat philosophical ethics, feminist philosophy, and postcolonial theory, respectively—consider transcendence in conjunction with "the Other," an elusive term that these chapters investigate.

The works of Jewish philosopher Emmanuel Levinas and Argentinean liberation philosopher Enrique Dussel will guide us through the first stage of this exploration, turning our search for transcendence to the human being facing us—particularly the oppressed person. Levinas builds his influential redefinition of transcendence as a relation of metaphysical desire on two types of metaphors: infinity and exteriority. Chapter 4 expounds the implications of each of these for intersubjective relations. Dussel's deployment of Levinas's conceptual framework to develop an ethics of liberation from the Latin American contexts puts Levinas's philosophy to the test, challenging it to respond to the faces and voices of Latin American "others." Identifying transcendence exclusively with Levinas's metaphor of exteriority, and thus associating transcendence with exclusion and marginalization, Dussel finds it difficult to assert both liberation and transcendence. This difficulty is symptomatic of fundamental problems with the conceptualization of transcendence as exteriority for envisioning social transformation, not least for its tendency to reinstate insider/outsider dualism and images of self-contained subjectivities. Also committed to the liberation paradigm, the theological anthropologies developed by U.S. Hispanic theologians Fernando Segovia and Roberto Goizueta offer alternative visions.

In chapter 5 we return to Levinas's notion of transcendence, this time raising feminist questions. If Dussel finds Latin American "others" too uncomfortable in the "exteriority" in which Levinas places them, Luce

Irigaray's woman bluntly refuses her role as "immanent," "beloved" Other. As she resists the separation on which Levinas establishes inter-human transcendence, Irigaray seeks a more intimate encounter with the transcendence of the sexual Other. Chapter 5 relies upon Irigaray's depiction of transcendence in the sexual encounter to move us from Levinas's and Dussel's images of transcendence in the face of the Other to a more complex vision of the space between self and Other. This space of interhuman transcendence is congruent with the sinuous contours of whole bodies, and its movements of transformation are attuned to the patterns of repetition and advancement that characterize cosmic life.

In our engagement with the work of postcolonial critic Gayatri Chakravorty Spivak, the space of transcendence unfolds into a broad interhumanity and eventually even a radically inclusive "planetarity" that opens toward a possible theological cosmology. Chapter 6 takes a look at the geopolitical scene to investigate the relation between images of otherness formed within systems of political and symbolic representation, on the one hand, and transcendence, on the other. This will allow us to further develop our model of relational transcendence such that we might see the multiplicity that, by virtue of her/his historicity, each human being incarnates in her/his irreducible singularity. As subjects branch out in their links to other persons and other times, they also appear to join in the common space of their shared planet.

The threads of a relational transcendence encountered in the human Other, within and through a living cosmic space, join in the final chapter, which embraces theological language to proclaim the divine glory enfolding all.

CHAPTER 2

Radical Transcendence?

A theology of divine transcendence tries to express what cannot be represented: the ineffability of God. This paradox is inescapable. Augustine's words whisper softly in the theologian's ears, like a soft breeze that blows over words written in the sand: "If you have understood, then it is not God. If you were able to understand, then you understood something else instead of God. If you were able to understand partially, then you have deceived yourself with your own thoughts."[1] Ignoring Augustine's voice, theology often keeps writing, trading soft sands for solid stone—forgetting that Moses smashed the tablets when confronted with idolatry. When theology remembers its own limits, however, it composes images that reveal the traces of the passing wind and the imminence of their erasure, in faithful response to the unsettling caress of an indescribable God.

Transcendence cannot be exposed, as such, without that which it transcends. Images and language reify, yet no theology can do without names, images, symbols, logos. Only through images can we speak or even think about the ineffable. Thus there cannot be a pure theology of transcendence. Even "apophatic" theologies write, and they inscribe the very negation of the divine attributes that they affirm, thus rebelling against the idolatry of names or images. The temptation of treating the name as if it had the power to fully capture the One whom it names must be fenced off—for "easy reference" can be as dangerous as "cheap grace."[2]

Not all theologies of transcendence belong to the apophatic tradition. "Kataphatic" theologies immerse themselves in language and do not always thematize their representational struggles. However, as long as they remain committed to respect the ineffability of God, kataphatic theologies write under the influence of the apophatic spirit and in resistance to idolatrous temptations. They rely on affirmations about God in the hopes of finding language and images that keep them and their readers aware of divine inexhaustibility and the unavoidable inadequacy of all human language and representations; they search for images that express openness to that which transcends them.

Images of transcendence thus convey ideas about human knowledge in its relation to God and the rest of creation.[3] Indeed, in Christian theology, in addition to invoking divine ineffability, the word "transcendence" is closely associated with views of divine providence. Christianity affirms that God brought forth the cosmos and that God sustains the creation's being and becoming. Only because the world is a divine creation that "participates" in the divine can human beings know and speak about God at all. In Christian thought, transcendence is inseparable from cosmological visions of the divine-creature relation.

Classical statements that we now associate with the concept of divine transcendence—such as immateriality, omnipresence, infinity, and so on—functioned within the cosmologies of their time to assert God's otherness in ways that were also deemed compatible with divine providence. When they adopted the attributes listed above, early Christian theologians asserted that God is the ever-present life force of the cosmos that provides coherence and unity to the multiplicity of the world. That is, because God transcends the limits of the world, God can relate all the elements of creation to one another. Furthermore, God is proclaimed to be the source of novelty for the transformation of the world: God makes possible the creation's self-transcendence. However, how these relationships are represented varies widely, because the particular form that a depiction of transcendence takes in each theology reflects assumptions about the characteristics of the cosmos and its relationship with the divine. What is the nature of creation and of each creature? How does the world change? Do creatures develop toward a predetermined end ("telos")? How much freedom do creatures have to change their destiny? What types of bonds link creatures to one another and to God?

The theologies that I engage in this and the next chapter—radical orthodoxy and Latin American liberation theologies, respectively—set out to offer images of the divine that uphold transcendence. These theologies are thus subject to the tensions arising from the aporia of transcendence: to speak of that which is ultimately inexpressible. They follow their theological predecessors in seeing transcendence in close relation to cosmology, and there is also a clear ethical concern in their theological projects, as they hope to put forth visions of the world that promote the development of just societies.

"Radical orthodoxy" seeks to prove that certain traditional images that have the stability of centuries of Christian tradition capture the significance of a notion of transcendence—one that is both firmly orthodox and radically ethical: a radical transcendence. This chapter engages the works of two influential radical orthodoxy theologians: John Milbank's *Being Reconciled* as well as Catherine Pickstock's *After Writing,* on which Milbank relies. Their theologies address the unique challenges of the contemporary world using the language of classical theology as well as that of postmodern philosophy, and will help us identify ethical questions that are crucial for this book's engagement with transcendence. Beginning with a theology committed to "orthodoxy," we will be exposed to well-established Christian and platonic depictions of divine transcendence.

THE PROBLEM OF THE DEMISE OF TRANSCENDENCE

Radical orthodoxy understands itself as a theological response to the crisis of the contemporary ("postmodern") world. The roots of the perceived problems are located in the cultural transformations that began during the modern period, where the Western world drifted away from the vision of a divinely ordered reality that characterized premodern worldviews. In contrast with the idea that "everything had its appointed and relative value in relation to a *distant, transcendent* source," modernity placed its trust in the human person as the source of the world's meaning and values, and questioned the idea of an external goal toward which individuals and societies moved.[4] Human beings took the center stage, effecting a cultural shift commonly called "the turn to the subject." Descartes's memorable "ego cogito" captures the confidence in the possibility of firmly establishing all knowledge, even the recognition of the existence of God, in the inquisitive capacity of the human mind. Human rationality becomes the tool for opening up the world to the eyes of scientists, finally revealing its underlying mysteries. Emboldened by the assumed power of the mind, modern man sees himself as the sovereign of his own future. The order of nature and societies, as well as the goals toward which they move, are seen as directed by the powers of rationality.

That this rationality was not the universal power it purported to be, but a limited reflection of the values and interests of the elite males of Western societies, is now a common postmodern observation.

For John Milbank, the modern loss of teleology and hierarchy had another unwanted effect: "the world was . . . accorded full reality, meaning and value in itself," resulting in the emergence of a "spatial plane of immanence."[5] Rather than having a "distant and transcendent" source as its organizing principle, in modernity "fixed natures, especially human natures" were assumed to be distributed and ranked across a "fixed spatial grid."[6] The ordering of the world no longer referred to anything outside the cosmos, resulting in the birth of humanism and secularism, which Milbank associates, as we will see through this discussion, with "immanence." What Milbank describes as the transcendence which modernity lost is an external source of value associated with vertical dimensionality itself. A loss of height, it is assumed, is a loss of transcendence. In modernity, "[h]eight was lost, but there was still depth."[7]

While modern worldviews tended to limit appeals to an otherworldly source of value, intraworldly hierarchies have always been in place, making their own appeals to height. What Milbank describes as a "fixed spatial grid," which entailed the ordering of human beings in discrete types ("races") distributed geographically, was never devoid of a symbolic vertical dimension. Appeals to nature to define, for instance, the superiority of the Aryan race or the innate domesticity of women anchored hierarchies in the dependable foundation of "nature" conceived as stable and fully knowable. The categorization of human beings was simultaneously hierarchical and temporal; each geographical area/race was thought to represent a different stage in the evolution of the human species. North was high and contemporary; South was low and primitive.[8] Indeed, the North/South division looms large in the mental cartographies of postmodern subjects, immersed as we are in the force fields of a globalized capitalist economy where that division coincides with the division of labor that organizes contemporary hierarchies. Many people living under this economic structure experience it as all-encompassing and inescapable, as if it were indeed imposed by an invisible, external force from above.

In radical orthodoxy's account, the fall from modernity to postmodernity is a further loss of spatial dimensions. Today the technological advances in travel and communication have made spatial distance less constraining because information can now move instantly throughout the world. Theorists of postmodernity describe this phenomenon as the obliteration of space by time.[9] For Milbank, a "shifting surface flux" replaces the fixed grid that anchored modern social structures. As a consequence, not only height, but also "depth is lost as 'immanence' comes to be conceived in terms of time, not space."[10] The main structure that orders life on earth has become temporal rather than spatial and, as a consequence, dynamic rather than fixed. What the term "immanence" signifies in the radical orthodox corpus is a crucial question to be addressed later in this chapter.

In Milbank's view, this privilege of time gives way to the "dissolution of limits"—his main contention against postmodern culture.[11] Because postmodern culture emphasizes rapid change and impermanence, differences become less significant, even as they are proclaimed more loudly. "In the postmodern times, there is no longer any easy distinction to be made between nature and culture, private interior and public exterior, hierarchical summit and material depth; nor between idea and thing, message and means, production and exchange, product and delivery, the State and the market, humans and animals, image and reality—nor beginning, middle and end."[12] As a consequence, Milbank protests, humans no longer perceive their development as limited by nature, nor moving toward a teleological goal. Based on this perceived loss of a stable foundation for identity—either in nature or telos—radical orthodoxy identifies postmodernity with nihilism (an identification that most postmodern theorists reject).

The examples that Milbank offers are indicative of the social realities that he finds problematic. He argues, for instance, that the distinction between men and women is blurred, and thus heterosexuality is being replaced by multiple relations in a matrix of homosexual sameness.[13] Human intervention in nature—an invasion of nature by culture—has produced undesirable effects, from AIDS to global warming. Home has been invaded by public media, while the public spaces have almost vanished.[14] The obliteration of political boundaries has supported the economic devastation of globalization.

These concerns with the increased commodification of all aspects of life and the destabilization of former institutions of communal and individual identity in postmodern culture have been voiced by many theorists, both secular and religious, some of whom identify themselves as postmodern thinkers. But radical orthodoxy's theological claim is that immanence is the cultural presupposition that underlies the blurring of boundaries described above. Thus, the root of these problems is held to be the fall from a premodern life based on the prevailing medieval conception of divine transcendence. This historical development is described as a fall from a past society structured on the basis of an external realm of the transcendent in two clearly defined historical steps: modernity and postmodernity.[15]

Radical orthodoxy's account of the problems of contemporary culture as a fall from a past when social structures referred to external and hierarchical transcendence shapes Milbank's proposed solution. To overcome the modern (heightless), spatially fixed categorizations or the postmodern (depthless) dissolution of limits, radical orthodoxy seeks to reassert the stability of essences by a return to premodern thought. There are, of course, different responses to this assessment of the dangers of postmodern culture, some of which, as we will see, interpret them as opening new possibilities for more democratic and pluralistic models of collectivity, truth, and value than modernity allowed, shaking the restrictive foundations of traditional social structures.[16] In fact, radical orthodoxy's retrieval of the premodern is indelibly marked by postmodern sensibilities, as evidenced, for instance, by its deployment of temporal deferral as a key concept for describing divine transcendence. But the gaze of radical orthodoxy is turned to the past, as it calls for the reappropriation of "*our* Western legacy" expressed in "the creeds of transcendence in Judaism, Christianity and Islam."[17]

PARTICIPATION

The idea of divine transcendence is inextricable from radical orthodoxy's definition of its own theological identity. The model of "super-hierarchical transcendence" that it espouses rejects "universal accounts of *immanent human value* (humanism)" as well as postmodern models, which are described simply as nihilism disguised as misconceived negative theology.[18] Instead they propose a "return to patristic and medieval roots," to articulate the theological claim that "only *transcendence*, which suspends [embodied life, self-expression, sexuality, aesthetic experience, human political community] in the sense of interrupting them, 'suspends' them also in the other sense of upholding their relative worth *over-against the void*."[19]

This formula captures a basic pattern in radical orthodoxy's cosmology, the intricacies of which this chapter analyzes. The main elements of the structure can already be identified: transcendence, the void, and a humanity whose worth dangles between the two. Like all cosmologies, this one has epistemological implications that need to be foregrounded. Its "over-against" will prove to be as determinant of radical orthodoxy's theological enterprise as of its model of transcendence. From its moment of self-definition, radical orthodoxy sets itself off against liberal theology, modernity, humanism, and secularism—a gesture sustained and mirrored by a divine transcendence set off against the void.

Radical orthodoxy's cosmology draws significantly from a platonic vision of a reality divided in two distinct realms: the sphere of the intelligible forms that are eternal and immutable, on the one hand, and the worldly region of becoming, on the other. The worldly realm derives its reality from its "participation" (*methexis*) in the immutable forms. This view was woven into Christian theology, not least through the Middle Platonism that flourished during theology's formative years. The idea of a divine realm that is preeminently real, immutable, and immaterial has continued to shape Christian theology and predominant Western worldviews.

Reasserting this basic cosmological structure, radical orthodoxy seeks to recover the notion of participation to describe the relationship between the divine and worldly realms, which also structures the relationships between other contrasting traits that characterize the created realm: flux and permanence, eternity and transience, old and new meanings, particularity and universality, respectively.[20] The divine is imagined as inhabiting, indeed constituting, an external space of ontological elevation which is also the eternal *telos* of all creatures. The cosmos is seen as the region of "indeterminacy" and of "infinite interpersonal relations," where access to the divine is "mediated throughout by an elusive participation."[21] This vision of distributed rather than centralized power is claimed to have characterized Christian and Jewish descriptions of God until the end of the Middle Ages, and to have developed as a "revolt against *either* particularism *or* the cult of universalizable power" of its time.[22] Through the concept of participation, Christians and Jews imagined a God who is always beyond and always multiply, if elusively, present, and thus is "only available as diversely mediated by local pathways," Milbank argues.[23]

However, in Milbank's account the relationship between the worldly and "transcendent" poles is not a mutual intertwining of two distinct realities, one human, the other divine. The divine is not only spatially distant and high, but also eminently real. "*[R]eality itself* is regarded as 'given' from some *beyond*."[24] The inherent reality of creation is thus called into question.

What then is that which receives reality from beyond? Is it something, or nothing? Creation is in this cosmology closely associated with "the void." Against humanism, which "denies the inherent nothingness of things," this model of transcendence "interprets the *intrinsic nothingness of things* in time as their existing by participation."[25] "This vision . . . regards all temporalities as *nothing* and yet," because of their participation in the divine, they are "the way to everything."[26] As said before, for radical orthodoxy only divine transcendence upholds the creatures' "relative worth over-against the void."[27] In this model, even the bodies' "solidity," as Milbank puts it, is derivative from their participation in God.[28]

This assertion that the reality of the creation is not intrinsic to it but derived from God can be read as following in a long tradition that goes back to the platonic cosmology mentioned above, not least in Thomas Aquinas's influential appropriation of it. The medieval theologian submitted: "The being of every creature depends on God, so that not for a moment could it subsist, but would fall into nothingness were it not kept in being by the operation of the Divine power."[29] At best, this statement emphasizes the inextricable relation between all creation and God's life-sustaining presence: nothing that lives is devoid of the divine. Such reading rests on the Christian conviction of God's presence in all creation. To exist is to participate in the divine. But Aquinas's assertion can have very different connotations. If the basic assumption were rather that God is preeminently external to the cosmos, rather than affirming divine sustenance this model instead intensifies the ontological gap—not only delimiting God to a space outside the world, but also placing creatures perilously close to nonbeing. This was clearly an aspect of Aquinas's teaching: being was not essential to creatures. Creatures' worth is thus placed in something other than the creatures—in a realm external to and independent of all cosmic life.

The ethical consequences of this split between the creature and its value shall not be ignored. Discourses where, as Jacques Derrida describes them, "life has absolute value only if it is worth *more than* life"[30] extract the worth of creatures from their very existence. This logic has supported great atrocities in human history: the colonization and extermination of the Native Peoples of the Americas and enslaved Africans judged as lacking in rationality or Christian virtue, and the numerous attacks against "infidels" and "heretics" are two notable examples. This is not to say that we can or should fully avoid the abstractions through which we define and debate human values. However, these ethical considerations should call us to assess the implications of the assumption of the inherent nothingness of things for its tendency to subordinate the value of the very existence of creatures to other "more real" principles—an argument developed by liberation theologies, as we will see in the next chapter.

BEYOND

Radical orthodoxy claims that what upholds the "relative worth" of creatures is the superhierarchical transcendence *beyond*. But where or what is it? Allusions to the beyond are implicit in any discourse of transcendence. To transcend is by definition to move—physically or metaphorically—beyond. In common parlance, we speak of a society that transcends the boundaries of current political regimes, for instance, by moving beyond the status quo in the direction of what has never existed. At an individual level, a person's self-transcendence implies a profound transformation, a rebirth beyond the limits of what that person had ever been. Those transformations might be conceived as driven by or moving toward a person who is metaphorically "outside"—outside the self or excluded from particular social structures.

The idea that transformation emerges in relation to the realm of the beyond—beyond the self, the community, the present moment—is of special import for the notion of relational transcendence developed in this work. In contrast with modern conceptions of subjectivity, where self-development is envisioned as a process of becoming detached and independent from others, transformation is here affirmed as rooted in relationships to others beyond the self, family, nation, and so on. Transcendence is always in relation to something that the self can never fully contain within itself, something that is always beyond its full grasp.

From this perspective, Milbank's statement that beyond—an "elsewhere" (so to speak) that invades our passing reality—is the "precondition of justice" seems consonant with a key affirmation of this book.[31] Indeed, images of an elsewhere that irrupts in our daily life—of a something beyond our individual selves, whose coming we experience as the irruption of the alien, or the encounter with the Other—have helped liberation thinkers reclaim and reformulate transcendence as an ethical opening of the self to the Other. Indeed, liberation theologians affirm that welcoming what comes from elsewhere, from beyond the self, is indeed a precondition of justice. In these liberationist descriptions of the driving force of transformation, "beyond" is not merely spatial externality, even as the limits that it pushes against are not necessarily physical boundaries.[32]

Radical orthodoxy rejects such liberation moves, however. The superhierarchical transcendence of radical orthodoxy is not merely beyond the self or beyond the present (although at times it is certainly that); it is also outside the cosmos. Thus, although the emphasis on participation evokes the internal connections between creation and the divine, radical orthodoxy's "beyond" is set apart from the cosmos. It is simply "*other-worldly*."[33] For radical orthodoxy, spatial externality is also the foundation of temporal discontinuity.

In its temporal sense, "beyond" marks the imaginary space of a time on the far side of the present—either what has already passed or what is "not yet." I have already touched on the significance of this beyond for postcolonial critics—where "beyond" signifies both the "intervening space" of excluded others and a "revisionary time" that open the possibility for transforming the present.[34] For postcolonial thinkers, this imaginary space is never envisioned as a realm outside or above the sphere of human relations, but instead a boundary that may only be touched and displaced from the (in)side of the present.[35]

In contrast with these relational images of time and transformation—where space and time, as well as past, present, and future are inextricably linked—the model of superhierarchical transcendence asserts an absolute future that comes directly from outside history. The future arises "from another space, or from a space forever constituted by externalities," as opposed to emerging through time and history.[36] The spatial externality of radical orthodoxy's transcendence assures the absolute independence of God from human history and thus "guarantee[s] that the future contingency is super-added to the present."[37] External transcendence works through external causality. Milbank stresses his objection to models that envision the future as emerging from the present, which he argues amounts to proposing that it unfolds "by mere instrumental causality," that is, produced by a cause that is subordinated to another cause. Milbank's example of "mere instrumental causality" is "a flower issuing forth from a shoot."[38] The "absolute sway" of such process, he submits, implies that "everything was given from the very first instance of time."[39] To say that God intervenes from the outside, he argues, avoids the implication that the future is simply the disclosure of what was already contained in creation, as potentialities that would spontaneously develop over time.

CAUSALITY

Western philosophy and Christian theology have developed both organic and external accounts of causality and thus of the ways in which God affects creatures. Divine transcendence is most frequently associated with external causality, while "immanence" gets identified with internal causality. Early Christian theologies proposed that God directed creation toward its goal and fulfillment ("final causation") through the actualization of the innate potential of creatures. Second-century theologian Justin Martyr described the divine seeds ("*logos spermaticus*") in creatures as that part or image of the divine Logos which allows humans to be in accordance with the Logos. Similarly, Origen of Alexandria, the third-century theologian (possibly the first systematic theologian), portrayed the "image of God" in humans as the "seed" that allows humans to participate in divine nature. Even if humans fall away from God, he argued, they contain within themselves "certain *seeds of restoration and renewal* to a better understanding, seeing the 'inner,' which is also called the 'rational' man, is renewed after 'the image and likeness of God, who created him.'"[40] We need not assent to the classical allusions to "the rational man"—or the deterministic connotations of later teleological anthropologies—to appreciate the inner-relationality of this model, where creatures develop through the connection between the inner seeds of divinity and the divine—an innate and internal relation between divine and creaturely being.[41]

The most distinctively modern models of causation are external rather than organic. This is due in part to the advances in the physical sciences. In a world defined by newly emerging physics, God was imagined as a physical force, which would logically move objects from without.[42] Mechanistic views of the universe were privileged over vitalistic cosmologies. Isaac Newton explicitly rejected the idea of a God that worked organically in nature. After all, nothing but predictable laws and testable principles had room in the inner workings of this increasingly mechanistic world. Thus Newton's God worked not as the world-soul, but like the force of gravity. These cultural transformations also affected views about matter. There were philosophical antecedents for the idea of matter as a passive principle upon which a divine active principle operated: the idea of God as mover, indeed, as an "unmoved mover" (as Aristotle had described it long before) had had great influence in Western thought. Correspondingly, Aquinas's well-known claim that "whatever is moved is moved by another" suggests a view of the world that operates through extrinsic forces. With Newton this mechanistic model acquired greater scientific standing in a worldview that clearly extricated divine action from matter. Newton distinguished between innate and impressed forces on matter, and defined the former as "nothing but inertia." Devoid of external intervention, matter would simply remain unchanged.[43]

The contrast between external and "mere instrumental causality" described above seems to reinstate this modern paradigm. Milbank offers us only two alternatives: either the future emerges from "mere" instrumental causality, totally given from the beginning, or it comes from an absolute exteriority. A "flower issuing forth from a shoot" might indeed be seen as an instance of the many cycles that characterize the natural world. As a mere repetition of what was always already there, a blooming rose would seem antithetical to the newness of the absolute future that Milbank describes. But this contrast between a repetitive nature and an absolute future is based on the reductive visions of the world that we need to question; it relies on the identification between matter and inertia and thus imagines that the future will arrive independently of the rhythms and needs of the cosmos. Like Newtonian (nonrational) matter, creatures are in this view condemned to inertia, unless an external force acts upon them. Such an idea undermines the power of participation in the divine, implying that something else must be *externally superadded* to, or is lacking in, a cosmos-participating-in-the-divine—something that must be unilaterally given from above. A cosmos minus the externally constituted future would be "mere instrumental causality"—driven by whatever was given from the very first instance of time.

Milbank argues that transcendence establishes the continuity between the old and the new. He also claims that transcendence guarantees (from the outside) the outcome: "We can, one day, be liberated."[44] This is a powerful statement of faith. But how would external intervention maintain the continuity between the new and the old? The externality of this transcendence may (indeed, must be able to) overwhelm the delicate relational processes of natural evolution as well as the complex interdependence of historical transformation, by proposing a more real transformative power that bypasses these worldly processes. Its unrestrained power may render ultimately inconsequential the creatures' movement toward God.

THE ONE AND THE MANY

Radical orthodoxy's notion of participation asserts the presence of God diversely mediated through a multiplicity of passages, as indicated before. Affirming divine transcendence thus entails the legitimization of "infinitely many regional perspectives," each of them "particular and ineffable."[45] Milbank asserts, however, that this multiplicity must be complemented by the "constantly renewed attempt to characterize the one human 'region' in the cosmos."[46] In other words, theology must relentlessly describe the human reality while recognizing the multiplicity and ineffability of the contexts in which God is diversely present. The balance between the need for descriptions and the recognition of the ultimate irreducibility of the divine is crucial for theology. Admitting the difficulty of this task, Milbank offers a disquieting proposal: "to *erect*, as it were, the *universal totem*."[47] This totem is "tangible, and yet non-fetishistic." That is, it is the product of the collective agreement, rather than individual construction.[48]

The use of a phallic image precisely at this point, where the discussion moves to the question of universals, is hard to ignore—especially for those concerned about the effects of the symbolic links between "phallo-centrism" and Western rationality. As Luce Irigaray has shown, the models that have traditionally defined Western universals are phallic ones, and the characterizations that they produced are thus founded on the privilege of the male organ. These models bear the marks of masculine morphology and share "the values promulgated by patriarchal society and culture, values inscribed in the philosophical corpus: property, production, order, form, unity, visibility . . . and erection."[49] This phallic economy subtends the Western culture's privilege of sameness over difference, sight over sensation, and of course man over woman, where woman is defined by lack.[50] The proposal of a universal totem should alert us to the subtle ways in which the privilege of masculinity is inscribed in discourses that are not explicitly about gender. I discuss later the gender structure that Milbank explicitly delineates. Before that we consider in greater detail the contours of the totemic structure being proposed.

According to Milbank, Catherine Pickstock provides an "exemplary account of how one *'universal totem'* . . . supremely operates in a fashion that is at once entirely tangible, and yet non-fetishistic and non-socially divisive."[51] That universal totem is the Catholic Eucharist. The rite represents and enacts the relationship between the Christian community and transcendence. This relationship is depicted as structurally parallel to the relationship between linguistic signs and their referents, and is enacted through the use of liturgical signs. Language, and signs in general, are the focus of this description of the divine-human interaction.

Like Milbank, Pickstock associates transcendence with spatial distance, "always *vertically beyond*."[52] However, her account of the rite gives special attention to the dynamic aspect of the relationship with transcendence. Pickstock highlights the repetitive movement of the worshiper toward an ever-receding divine reality as an enactment of the constant deferral of the fulfillment of the liturgy—and thus of communal identity—grounded in the deferral of God's full presence. Signs always point beyond themselves, without ever making fully present what they name. Liturgical language must thus be ceaselessly repeated, striving for that which will always exceed it.[53] The continuous repetitions and recommencements in the liturgy perform the deferral of the completion of liturgy until the eschatological time. Although Pickstock's emphasis here falls not on spatial distance, but on temporal deferral, for her they are intrinsically linked. The "apophatic reserve" of language "betokens our constitutive, positive, and analogical distance from God."[54]

The liturgical deferral of fulfillment and the fact that the "symbolic power is not, primarily, mediated by a human hierarchy" but "by the general ingestion of these symbols through time" have important social implications.[55] The "ruling principle" that this reading of liturgy expresses "is a deferral to a plenitudinous unknown Good which is always still awaited," Milbank explains. "Liturgical rule is able to await on further capacities of the self as yet undisclosed or ungranted."[56] From this "rule," Milbank derives a principle for sociopolitical analysis: "Rule itself is (at least in principle) understood as the possibility of a self-critique through attention to what lies *beyond the self* (individual or collective)" and the "avoidance of absolutization of the self making this critique."[57] It is a relation to that which is beyond the self that prevents persons and collectivities from closing around themselves. Although Milbank is quick to add the spatial otherworldly dimension of this beyond and the assurance of a definitive completion, the openness to what lies beyond the self that this statement depicts is sustained by what Milbank suggestively calls a "culturally imbued sense of transcendence."[58]

A culturally imbued sense of transcendence is consonant with a participative and relational ontology, if it is understood as a structure of being in which access to the divine is always mediated through multiple contexts and relations. But other aspects of this model suggest contrasting images of direct, unconditioned contact between God and creature, undermining the irreducibility of the historical and collective dimensions of mediating cultures. This tension is exemplified in the descriptions of liturgical language.

The possibility of the encounter between the transcendent God and the community is founded on a strong, even essential, link between the sign and the referent. The names Father, Son, and Holy Spirit are described as "one name," which is "not a static name affixed outside being, but is an *essential* name *commensurate* with the existential space of the Trinitarian journey."[59] Similarly, the "Amen" pronounced in the liturgy "is the language *in common* between God and worshipper, for it is at once the incarnational bodying forth of God and the true human response to God."[60] Through the words of the liturgy, God approaches the person as the person approaches God: as meeting "places" for the human/divine encounter. But how complete can we claim that encounter to be? Is this a moment of full presence and thus of epistemic closure? Set as commensurate with God, these signs seem to exceed their finitude. If the allusions to constant deferral, incompletion, and apophatic reserve emphasize the beyondness of the transcendent God, and highlight the inadequacy of our representations of God, these descriptions of liturgical language as commensurate with God seem to undermine such precautions by claiming instead the power of liturgical language to overcome linguistic limitations.

A similar claim is made about the eucharistic bread and wine: they are "a *literal* participation in and *essential* symbolization of the Body, including not only the sacramental Body, but also the historical body of Jesus and the ecclesial body." They are "the coincidence of sign and body."[61] Instead of a separation of the referent from the sign, Pickstock proposes a fusion between them—an interpretation that allows for "*leaping over* the stage of indication or reference."[62] This leap requires the liberation of the signs, as it were, so that their "character as *bounded things* become dislodged."[63] At the same time, God is said to be moving as well—not *leaping over* but folding *into* language: God, "the indicated," "is no longer that 'other' of language which anchors all signs, but instead is that which folds back into language."[64]

We are thus offered an enticing image: a God who folds into language. We could restate this idea in Christian metaphors: the transcendent God is Word that becomes flesh and abides in the world—thus evoking the (radical) experience of an incarnational faith. Yet, the incarnation of the Word—or God folding into language—does not imply that words, or any other thing, are dislodged from their character as bounded things, if being "dislodged" means that they acquire the ability to leap over the limitations of finitude or their embeddedness in culture and history. Signs leaping over—rather than enmeshing in—the material realities of language: does this not suggest a direct path toward divine transcendence that sidesteps the ties of our incarnate existence, even if temporarily?[65]

In these theologies language and the eucharistic elements take on a role akin to the mystical experience, transgressing the logic of common experience and conventions in order to claim union of the finite with the ineffable God. But the moment of mystical union entails giving up images, not making divine claims about them. And to avoid turning that experience into a self-authorizing claim, the mystic must soon grapple with the boundedness of language and resist the temptation to reification.

Any suggestion that a sign may leap over the stage of reference has important epistemological implications: it undermines the dependence of all signs on systems of meanings that are marked by history and social context. Where it emphasizes the coincidence of sign and referent, Pickstock's proposal may be at risk of suggesting that we possess the ability, even if for a moment, to leap over and become dislodged from our character as finite beings constrained by histories of interpretation. Such an assumption may lead us to imagine that certain discourses, values, and so on, are in fact untainted by our shortcomings and thus lie beyond critique. Would this not count as a form of idolatry? Theologies of transcendence have often failed to avoid this problem, especially when it comes to their own privileged discourses. Claiming access to that which is transcendent quickly turns into claiming transcendent knowledge—the very deception against which the notion of transcendence should warn us.

A culturally imbued sense of transcendence should consistently insist on the embeddedness of all language—and all theo-logos—in its contexts, with all their limitations and ineffable potentialities. This sense of transcendence shall also foreground the complexity of the God-human relation, which is mediated not only by language but also by concrete ties with other people. Although Pickstock describes the Eucharist as a collective event, the depiction offered suggests the image of a priestly God dispensing the elements to a congregation of individuals with no sense of each other. In this model, we find a collection of selves turned toward the overwhelming subjectivity of a God that gives them from without whatever reality they have. This relation reconstitutes the community entirely from without, without the mediation of human hierarchy. Apart from the difficulties and dangers entailed in any claims to dislodge human activity from its entanglement in its context, this scene of the human/divine encounter as a model for the constitution of a collectivity seems to occlude an essential element: other human beings.[66] Human relations recede in the background. The selves in this scene never look at or talk to each other. They do not seem to give or receive from each other anything worthy of consideration for the constitution of the collectivity.

AFFINITY AND DIFFERENCE

As the Father has loved me, so I have loved you; abide in my love. If you keep my commandments, you will abide in my love, just as I have kept my Father's commandments and abide in his love. . . . This is my commandment, that you love one another as I have loved you.
—*John 15:9–10, 12*

These are Jesus' words to his disciples, words that tie a potentially infinite web of loving repetitions—from the Father to the Son, from the Son to disciples who were there with him, and also to those who would later come. As Origen describes it, the bond of affection between the Father and the Son that made possible the incarnation also weaves together all creatures, for the Son "granted invisibly to all rational creatures . . . a participation in himself." Through this gift, each creature "obtained a degree of participation proportionate to the loving affection with which he had clung to him."[67] Thus the bond between Jesus and the Father brings forth networks of affinity.

"Affinity" is the term that Milbank uses to describe the dynamics of identity formation grounded in the idea of deferral of completion of the constitution of collectivities, but also to the development of individual identities. As Milbank defines it, affinity is "the arriving *gift* of something that we must partially discover in patient quest, active shaping and faithful pursuing."[68] Identity is thus not something already given, as implied in the modern ideas of fixed "nature" or essence, but something yet to come.

His prime example of identity formed by affinity is Jesus. In agreement with (shall I say "in affinity with"?) Origen, Milbank explains that "Jesus was God because his affinity with God was so extreme as to constitute identity . . . not of substantial nature, but of character. . . ."[69] This bond of affinity has the traits of a relationship with the dynamic transformations implied by the idea of transcendence. It is "non-theorizable and almost *ineffable*," and cannot be contained by what has already been.[70]

In contrast to the modern notions of fixed and categorizable identities, Milbank proposes to think of identities as becoming. However, this openness toward transformation, expressed by the concept of affinity, is limited by his assertion of teleological ends. Identities are not known here and now, but they "may eventually be disclosed . . . with and through time."[71] The two poles of this definition of identity—dynamically evolving and externally predetermined—mirror the two poles we have identified in Milbank's descriptions of transcendence: one emphasizes the inexhaustibility of the divine in which all participate, while the other highlights its distance, autonomy, and power.

The tension between the two poles of identity becomes most visible in Milbank's treatment of gender difference. An idea of gender identity as disclosed through time rather than already given seems congruent with the feminist tradition, from Simone de Beauvoir to Judith Butler, that "one is not born, but rather *becomes* a woman. . . . [*W*]*oman* itself is a term in process, a becoming."[72] But Milbank is not assenting to such "gender trouble." The becoming of identity is for him not open-ended, but guided toward a preset teleological end. We may thus gain "true knowledge" about bodies only "when *we* share something of God's insight into how he wished them to be."[73] One can only hope not to be excluded from that "we"!

While Milbank begins by describing affinity as a "non-theorizable and almost ineffable identity," never fully present, he surprisingly proceeds to equate it to ontology.[74] "Affinity or ontological kinship," he says in passing, and moves on to describe sexual difference as "ontologically more *resistant* than people would suppose."[75] When the ontological nature of sexual difference is rejected, as was the case of Aristotle's philosophy, femininity is deemed a mere deficiency. Milbank's feminine-affirmative gesture is nonetheless not followed by his welcoming of the unpredictable challenges of women's views—that is, by openness to the Other as she might reveal herself, beyond masculinist prerogatives. Instead he attempts to categorize his sexual Others. Despite disclaimers and even an encouraging nod to Luce Irigaray, the results are hardly "*radical*": "men are more nomadic, direct, *abstractive* and forceful, women are more settled, subtle, particular and beautiful."[76] This restatement of "inherited generalizations" cannot but lend a patronizing tone to the following: "both sexes are innovative, legislative, commanding and conservative *within* these different modes."[77] Asserting the "equality of difference" supposedly implied in the gender depictions he has just offered, Milbank explains, "Without the feminine settled, male *abstraction* is not an abstraction but only another . . . settled view."[78] Indeed! Male abstractions require the feminine settled—and, for this reason, patriarchal societies are so intent on maintaining the structures of domesticity on which they secretly depend. This argument pertains to the protection of a male ideal through the projection of its opposite onto woman: a male ideal imposed on women by men.[79] This mechanism has been deployed repeatedly to protect not only gender hierarchies, but also racial and ethnic ones. To inscribe them in a narrative of divinely given identities occludes their historicity and, more dangerously, masks human hierarchies as divine telos. Rather than affirming a culturally imbued sense of transcendence, is this not after all transcendentalizing select cultural values?

Tellingly, we find the gendered abstractive/settled dichotomy replayed in the very characterization of Christian identity. This time it is "Jewish specificity" that occupies the feminine space of the "settled" to which "Christian *abstraction* is necessarily *betrothed*."[80] In another (related) statement of "inherited generalizations," Milbank characterizes Christianity as "the religion of the obliteration of boundaries"—"forceful," indeed!—and Judaism as "perhaps the very opposite."[81] Predictably, Christianity's Other, Judaism, occupies the space of the feminine, an association only confirmed by describing their relation as a betrothal—after all, for Milbank, marriage is strictly heterosexual.

Milbank's invocation of Irigaray in this discussion may at first glance seem appropriate. Irigaray, like Milbank, observes that "masculine culture has generally ignored the objectivity which exists in the pre-given: the body, bodies, the cosmic universe."[82] (The "culture" she refers to is a masculinist, rather than postmodern culture.[83]) Irigaray further argues that ignoring the objectivity of the body has led to the loss of the transcendent potentials of the encounters across sexual difference. I would welcome a theological encounter between Irigaray's transcendence in the relation across sexual difference and Milbank's transcendence as affinity in the ineffable bond between creatures. But this is an unlikely betrothal. Milbank asserts the need to affirm a "supra-human power beyond" in order to provide society with a principle by which "it might be *measured* and *limited* . . ."[84] Irigaray, by contrast, sees the construction of a transcendental subjectivity not as a correction, but a symptom of the erasure of the objectivity of bodies, or, to use Milbank's language, their depiction as inherently nothing. The need to pose a supranatural limit to our subjectivity derives from the "erasure of the other as other," as a contiguous transcendent other always beyond the self.[85] The fact that such a gesture of setting up one transcendental against the multiplicity takes the phallic form of the totem is hardly incidental. I return to this matter later (chap. 4).

Just as Milbank's male and Christian abstractions depend on a settled woman and a settled Judaism, respectively, his depiction of transcendence seems to depend on a settled Other: immanence. But the distance between the two poles of the transcendence/immanence dyad tends to infinity. Although the contraposition of transcendence to immanence is almost common sense in theology, notice its distinctive overtones for

Milbank and Pickstock. Whereas many contemporary theologians attempt to hold together the "immanent" with the "transcendent" as aspects of God, evoking images of God's presence both inside and outside of creation, in the writings of radical orthodoxy we have considered, "immanent," "immanentist," and "immanence" are frequently used to evoke the rejection or absence of God. That which denies the beyond is said to be immanentist. In general, one finds it associated with the terms "secular," "modern," "*nihil.*"[86] Indeed, Milbank is willing to attribute to "secular immanence" the horrors that contemporary criticism—he refers to Hannah Arendt—has credited to "totalitarianism."[87] "Secular immanence," Milbank writes, is "totalizing and terroristic because it acknowledges no supra-human power beyond itself by which it might be *measured* and *limited.* . . ."[88] This identification of immanence with God-less totality is also apparent in Pickstock's *After Writing.* Platonic myths of transcendence, she argues, represent a radical challenge to "the immanentist city," "the beginnings of a technocratic, manipulative, dogmatically rationalist, anti-corporeal and homogenizing society undergirded by *secularity* and *pure immanence.*"[89]

This tendency to set off a "purely immanent" realm is most evident in radical orthodox engagements, with other theologies. Milbank identifies two versions of "postmodern modes of religiosity." On the one hand, he identifies "new age religions," characterized by their assertion of "the sanctity of an empty mystical self able to transcend, identify with, and promote or else refuse the totality of process in the name of a truer 'life' which is invisible." More relevant for my discussion here is Milbank's critique of the second group, which he describes as the addition of a "Spinozistic twist" to "postmodern Marxist atheism," of which philosopher Gilles Deleuze and political theorists Antonio Negri and Michael Hardt are given as examples. These he denounces for seeing "*the plane of immanence* . . . as the sphere of active, productive forces, which manifest themselves in human terms as love and desire . . ."[90] But why is posing a sphere of forces that manifest in human love, where, "once oppression is surpassed, liberated nature-going-beyond-nature fully appears," problematic for Milbank?[91] An assumption at work in Milbank's rebuttal is that divine transcendence is external to the cosmos and thus to talk about the plane of immanence is to deny divine transcendence; Milbank shares this assumption with Deleuze, Negri, and Hardt. Indeed, Deleuze and Guatari contrast the philosophers' plane of immanence with the religious "transcendent order imposed from the outside by a great despot or by one god higher than the others."[92] However, there is a second assumption in which Milbank differs from these thinkers: that the goals of the flourishing of creation and the liberation of human beings are subordinated to other higher principles, from which ethical standards certainly derive, but only secondarily. The implications of these assumptions become clearer in radical orthodoxy's critique of liberation theology, discussed in the next chapter.

THE APOPHATIC RESERVE OF LANGUAGE—AND CREATURES

An important concern drives radical orthodoxy's allusions to transcendence: "if the immanent world is all there is, then it tends to reduce to our abstract grasp of it."[93] Radical orthodoxy thus proclaims that creation is more than it seems to be, as it is suspended by God against nothingness. Sustained by divine providence, human development is not arbitrary: it is limited by nature and moving toward a goal that is not fully knowable to creatures, but securely founded in God. Similarly, words are not mere floating signs that only refer to other signs and have no intrinsic meaning; there is an excess to language—an apophatic reserve—that escapes our manipulations.

I share radical orthodoxy's consternation with worldviews that tend to reduce creation to something that can be fully grasped by human constructs or reduced to categories within social systems. I further concur with radical orthodoxy's claim that the notion of divine transcendence can help us overcome these reductionist views. Radical orthodox images of a world that participates in God and thus is always open to that which is beyond itself, and of humans whose development is not determined by some fixed nature but by potentially infinite and ineffable bonds of affinity, infuse our predominantly modernist depictions of the world with much-needed complexity and dynamism. The importance of this proposed change in our views of transcendence is related to its sociopolitical implications: the orientation of a creature's development comes from what lies beyond the self, and thus the openness of societies to others should become a principle of communal rule that promotes self-critique and avoids self-absolutization.

But radical orthodox depictions of a world that is always beyond our grasp are limited by the insistence that the beyond is also outside the world. The vision of God and the world as two extrinsic realities is, to be sure, an assumption deeply ingrained in Christian theology and Western philosophy, but it is an (unnecessary) assumption with problematic implications, which we have traced in this chapter. These implications can be grouped in two broad and related categories. First, the world's value is imagined as extrinsic to it, and creatures are frequently depicted as inherently nothing. This view also affects the way in which transformation is imagined: The complexity of the relational transformations that occur in the world tends to be overwhelmed by appeals to another type of transcendence—absolute, independent, unconstrained—that renders the worldly processes ultimately insignificant. Worldly realities are depicted as "merely" immanent—not transcending.

The externality of transcendence also directs our attention to a realm imagined as unconditioned by the world, which is the source of other-worldly principles and absolute novelty. The imaginary space of exteriority that is thus opened is meant to protect the mystery of God, but it also leads us to desire that space. Longing for the pure transcendence of God that such space represents, we dream of gaining unmediated access to the purely transcendent or to expect a future that does not depend on the arduous and endless work entailed by all worldly relational transformations. This is, of course, not encouraged by radical orthodoxy. However, as we have seen, ideas such as having a language that is "commensurate" with God or that can "leap over the stages of reference" are symptoms of a dangerous temptation to ignore the inescapable embeddedness of all our language and all our endeavors in their worldly contexts. The relationship with divine transcendence can thus harden into self-authorizing claims. To claim to have unmediated access to a transcendent realm, no matter how limited or temporary, is dangerously close to claiming to have overcome finitude.

The image of transcendence that this book strives for affirms the excess of all creatures as grounded in God. However, it envisions the theological promise of transcendence not in proposing a reality other than the world, but rather in its potential to help us overcome the habit of reducing the "immanent" to the graspable, or more precisely, to regard the created world as "purely immanent." The ineffable affinity that links all creatures in open relations of mutual transformation may help us envision the beyond *in* the world, without losing sight of the transcending character of all creation. This world is indeed more than it appears, calling us to apophatic alertness: God, other creatures, and even we exceed all our representations. The claim that "the human being, the individual, is a subject that transcends all his or her objectifications in language and institutions"[94] draws Latin American liberation theologies to the idea of divine transcendence. We now turn to their vision of transcendence.

CHAPTER 3

Intracosmic Transcendence

Liberation Theology

Every blade of grass has an angel that bends over it and whispers,
"Grow! grow!"

—The Talmud

The pro-fane . . . no longer exists.

—Gustavo Gutiérrez[1]

Explicit references to divine transcendence have not been nearly as common in liberation theology as they are in radical orthodoxy. However, the liberationist interpretation of divine transcendence is implicit in its reconfiguration of the boundary between the sacred and profane, as well as in its central theme of the reign of God. Not surprisingly, then, some of the main critiques of liberation theology focus on its interpretation of divine transcendence. These critiques come from the opposing perspectives of radical orthodoxy and feminist theology. As we have already seen, radical orthodoxy suspects liberation theology of compromising the very idea of transcendence. In a recent volume dedicated to Enrique Dussel's work, U.S. Hispanic theologian Roberto Goizueta observes that one of the most persistent accusations against Dussel and liberation theology in general has been that "of reducing faith to political action, thereby *eliminating the transcendence of God.*"[2] Goizueta points out that these accusations fail to recognize the concern of liberation theologians to "*safeguard* the transcendence of God over against those theologies which . . . would identify God with the status quo . . ."[3] As we have seen, liberation theology is concerned with the appropriation of transcendence as a foundation for claiming to possess unquestionable knowledge. However, liberation theology offers more than a rebuttal of epistemological claims using the notion of transcendence. The notion itself is reimagined. Indeed, Manuel Mejido argues that it is precisely its reinterpretation of transcendence that constitutes the core of liberation theology's contribution to theology—a fact that, in his view, U.S. Hispanic theologians have not yet fully realized.[4]

However, it must be admitted that liberation theologies' depictions of transcendence have often relied on images of spatial separation and total independence similar to those that we have found in radical orthodoxy. As we will see, this tendency has been challenged from within—notably by Latin American feminist liberation theologians.

MODERNITY AND POSTMODERNITY IN LIBERATION THEOLOGY

A small circle is quite as infinite as a large circle; but, though it is quite as infinite, it is not so large. . . . There is such a thing as a narrow universality; there is such a thing as a small and cramped eternity.
—*G. K. Chesterton*

Latin American liberation theology shares radical orthodoxy's interest in challenging the false and imperialistic universals of modernity. Yet liberation theology complicates its portrayals of the modern and the postmodern, not by placing postmodern paradigms against those of premodernity, but by bringing other histories to bear in modern representations of "modernity." Latin American liberation theology looks at modernity from its underside.[5] From that perspective, the "project of modernity" is "rendered contradictory and unresolved," as Homi Bhabha observes. For "what is modernity in those colonial conditions where its imposition is itself the denial of historical freedom, civic autonomy and the 'ethical' choice of refashioning?"[6] Where modernity was not the triumph of human autonomy, but of the values of a particular (then foreign) culture, its failures are not simply seen as the rejection of external (divine) authority. From the perspective of the colonized people, the triumph of modern man is their own subjection to an external authority. Having been for centuries the receptors of externally imposed "Western" universals, having seen their own human value and needs subordinated to its principles, Latin Americans are keenly aware of the dangers involved in raising one set of values as predefined "universals"—modern or premodern.

Exposing the myths of modernity, however, does not lead Latin American liberation theology to mourn the loss of the medieval Western tradition, which after all supported the persecution of the Jews, the expulsion of the Moors, and witch hunts. Their view, indeed their experience, of history reveals complexities that challenge Milbank's appraisal. Philosopher Eduardo Mendieta explicitly questions Milbank's portrayal of modernity and postmodernity as well as their relation to transcendence. Like many postmodern critics, Mendieta observes that modernity mir-

rored certain notions of transcendence and sovereignty. Rather than relying on "pure immanence," Mendieta argues, modernity depended on the
"assimilation, consumption, and usurpation of divine transcendence." Yet
it also relied on the teleological mind-set that was intrinsic to the notion
of transcendence. Modernity depended "on the surplus of transcendence
that remained beyond its own grasp" and toward which it moved asymp-
totically.[7] Postmodernity, in turn, is only postsecular in the sense that it
calls into question the dichotomy between the sacred and the profane.

Rather than turning to the premodern past, Latin American liberation theology expresses a cautious affinity with postmodernity. Thus,
liberation philosopher Enrique Dussel—whose ideas we engage in the
next chapter—argues that the philosophy of liberation is "postmodern,"
although more recently he has opted for the term "trans-modern."[8]

Modern notions of transcendence, however, have driven not only secular economic and political projects, they have also been an important
part of Christianity. Postmodern challenges to modern thought are thus
implicit challenges to modern Christianity. Although liberation theology has from its inception concurred with, indeed anticipated, many of
the critiques against modernity, some of liberation theology's main
themes and assumptions have also been found in need of postmodern
(or transmodern) challenges. We return to those challenges after dis-
cussing the indispensable contributions of liberation theology to rethinking divine transcendence.

TRANSCENDENCE IN HISTORY: IGNACIO ELLACURÍA

Ignacio Ellacuría offers one of the most explicit descriptions of the
liberationist interpretation of divine transcendence with respect to the
cosmological vision that grounds it. The Jesuit theologian and philosopher—one of six priests murdered in 1989 at the Central American University in San Salvador—uses biblical, theological, and philosophical
sources to expound what he calls "transcendence in history."

Ellacuría attributes to "pernicious philosophical influences" the fact
that transcendence has been identified with *separateness*.[9] The root of
this misleading identification of transcendence with separation is a
worldview that opposes rationality to the senses, and spirituality to physicality, leading to depictions of the cosmos and God as realities extrinsic
to each other and closed around themselves.[10] As long as we continue to
think of God as extrinsic to creation, Ellacuría argues, we will not be able
to realize the profound implications of what many theologies of his time

were asserting: that salvation is historical. It is thus necessary to rethink our models of intracosmic existence as much as our notions of divine transcendence.

In order to overcome reductionist views of creation, Ellacuría draws from the work of the Basque philosopher Xavier Zubiri to develop a model of history that takes physicality as its unavoidable ground.[11] Ellacuría's cosmology takes as its starting point the unity and the intrinsically dynamic character of reality. Reality is a "single physical unity that is complex and differentiated, in such a way that the unity does not nullify differences and the differences do not nullify the unity."[12] The insights of sciences—especially evolutionary theory, but also quantum theory and even sociohistorical theory—depict a reality in which everything evolves through relational processes. The evolution of new species driven by ecological transformations or changes in the populations of the other species in the area, the development of a child's subjectivity in relation to parents and other community members, the effects of the observer in the behavior of subatomic particles: all have increased our awareness of the complex ways in which we affect and are affected by others. Rather than being isolated entities, we are all open to one another. It is not simply that things necessarily relate to one another, but that they only are what they are, or better, they only *become* in relation to others. In other words, relationality is not constituted by (and thus after) the things related, but the things are constituted by relationality.[13] The unity of the universe is more than a conceptual abstraction; it is a principle of reality: everything is "intrinsically and constitutively" connected to all other things.

The unity of reality is intrinsic to it, for it is the result of relationality; this unity does not imply that reality is self-enclosed or united by an external force that imposes coherence or overcomes the internal differences of the universe.[14] The idea that unity must be provided by an external force is based on the assumptions that things are not otherwise interrelated. As I said before, the unity that Ellacuría describes is always complex and differentiated. Furthermore, being the unity of dynamic things, reality is also intrinsically dynamic. The dynamism of reality, like its unity, is not something added to reality which is neither the subject-of, nor subjected-to dynamism. Reality is inherently dynamic. The emphasis on its intrinsic dynamism is crucial for Ellacuría, because to overcome the images of the world and God as extrinsic realities entails moving away from the notion of matter as a passive substance (trapped in inertia) which can only be acted upon by external forces. Matter itself is not seen as an object, but as the conjunction of mass and energy, which is a principle of reality and history. The dynamism of reality expressed in processes is a crucial aspect of Ellacuría's model. History is a process springing from a basis of materiality and biological vitality.

History presupposes the potentialities and faculties that emerge through evolutionary processes and contributes to evolutionary processes, but history is differentiated from evolution in that purely evolutionary processes depend on random mutation, while history entails options. History is the actualization of possibilities, not simply the actualization of potentialities that are transmitted genetically. In the actualization of possibilities, new things are created and new possibilities come into being that may never have existed. Newness is not just discovered as being always already present in nature, nor is it externally imposed upon reality. Genuinely new things come into existence from the actualization of possibilities through collective choices, which, though not necessarily conscious, imply the "realization of a project or setting to work a system of possibilities."[15]

The distinction between history and nature does not imply that historical development is ever detached from or unconstrained by the organic processes of nature. Only those things that have been made possible through the natural/historical actualization of potentialities can be called real possibilities. Not all that is conceivable is possible. For instance, the emergence of the human species entailed the emergence of new possibilities that had not previously been available. The biological structures of our bodies are like that of our first human ancestors. However, the possibilities of our lives are starkly different from their possibilities. Through history, humanity has chosen among different possible paths, and through those decisions, new possibilities have emerged, while other possibilities have been closed off. The paths chosen affect not only what human beings are and what they can accomplish, but also the material characteristics of the nonhuman world.

History is inseparable from nature. While many idealist notions of history tend to view history as proceeding in a linear fashion, Ellacuría contends that the "time of history" is "a biological time." Time cannot be detached from things, just like possibilities cannot be conceived in isolation from their material ground. History "will have all the modulations which a biological process carries with it."[16]

The relationship between nature and history is always intrinsic and mutually determining. Just as nature flows into history, history flows into nature. The mutual interdeterminations of nature and history are dramatically evident in the possibility that history has developed in such a way as to be able to destroy its own natural ground—a fact that Ellacuría had already called attention to in the early 1970s.

RELATING IN GOD

The complex and dynamic model of reality just sketched, which Ellacuría calls an "open historical realism," is the basis for the notion of transcendence in history. As we have seen, the processes of transformation in the world are based on the unity and dynamism that are intrinsic aspects of reality. New things do emerge in the cosmos—but not by breaking from materiality or rising independently from history. The emergence of new things from within the cosmos and the dynamic unity of reality are signs that divine transcendence subtends all reality. Transcendence is thus not imagined in terms of distance, exteriority, or otherworldliness. Instead, transcendence "calls attention to a contextual structural difference without implying a duality."[17] In a cosmological vision that affirms "the dual unity of God in humanity and humanity in God," transcendence "enables us to speak of an intrinsic unity without implying a strict identity."[18]

Rather than the static images of spatial gap between God and creation, Ellacuría's notion of transcendence is a dynamic one that alludes to the transformative power which infuses creation. Because transformation always presupposes the historical, material, and biological developments that make new things possible, transcendence is seen in its relation to all these aspects of reality. It is possible "to see transcendence as something that transcends *in* and not as something that transcends *away* from; as something that physically impels to more but not by taking out of; as something that *pushes* forward, but at the same time *retains*," Ellacuría submits.[19] In this model of intracosmic transcendence—where transcendence pushes forward and retains—the future emerges from within the matrices of relations that characterize created life, which include sociopolitical relations as well as the organic energies that sustain life and evolution in the cosmos. The old does not predetermine the new, but supports it. As in radical orthodoxy's model, the future is said to emerge not simply by unfolding spontaneously from genetically inherited potentiality: as a flower from its shoot. But in contrast with radical orthodoxy's model, the future is never independent from, or external to, the organic processes. The future entails the addition of new things, but history is inextricable from nature and a flower rarely blooms unaffected by historical conditions. Transcendence in history implies that new things emerge that are not predetermined by biological legacies, but they come in and through the physical, vital reality that we call nature: a reality that is grounded in the divine.

This description of intracosmic transcendence is never a denial of divine involvement, as implied in Milbank's description of the "plane of immanence" discussed in the previous chapter. Transcendence within creation implies not the expulsion of God from creation, but quite to the contrary, the affirmation of the internal relations between God and creation. Divine causality is internal rather than external to creatures. Within creation, God sustains and directs creation. Even the end (*telos*) toward which creation moves, which is represented by the vision of the reign of God, emerges and is constantly reconstituted within history. In contrast with the classical ideas that place teleological ends in the realm of the unchanging, intracosmic transcendence and the concept of the reign of God suggest an interpretation of final causes that are neither eternal, external, or predetermined, but rather spring from the complex and dynamic fabric of reality.[20]

Because in this model divine causality is seen as internal to creation, Ellacuría does not contrast transcendence with immanence. In fact, the term "immanence" does not play a significant role in Ellacuría's argument. The absence of this transcendence/immanence opposition results in an account of the Christ event quite different from that offered by radical orthodox theologians. For radical orthodox theology, as James K. A. Smith explains, the incarnation of Jesus requires God's "condescension," without which "there would be no revelation, only silence or ignorance . . . only incommensurability without contact."[21] This applies, Smith argues, not only to Jesus' incarnation, but to every instance of contact between God and creatures. "God's incarnational appearance is . . . a *condescension* to the conditions of finite, created perceivers."[22] Incarnation is portrayed as a downward movement, from the heights of transcendence to the lowliness of creation. The imperial overtones of this depiction are hard to miss.[23] In contrast, Ellacuría interprets Jesus not as the radical example of God's condescension toward immanence, but rather as "the supreme form of historical transcendence."[24]

An intracosmic model of transcendence has important implications for theological anthropology. While radical orthodoxy's descriptions of creatures emphasize that their value derives from their dependence on a transcendent (external) source, Ellacuría insists upon a certain innate worth, even divinity, in their finitude.[25] All creation is grounded in and linked to God who is its source. However, that relation is not something external or superadded to reality, but something inherent to reality. Thus, the value of human life does not reside outside of it, in something to which one may or may not relate or respond; this vision places the value of human life *in* human life. Ellacuría asserts that God's creation is the "grafting *ad extra* of Trinitarian life itself," and thus "each thing, within its own limits, is a limited way of being God. This limited way is precisely the *nature* of each thing."[26] It is not "simply that God is in all things, as essence, presence, and potential"—following Aquinas's description of God's relation to creation—but that the Trinitarian life is "*intrinsic* to all things."[27] Things are inherently linked to the divine—not to nothingness.

In this model human beings are essentially open to other things and to one another; human beings become in relation to others. That openness may lead to the actualization of possibilities that result in greater creative possibilities as well as to the foreclosure of those possibilities. In the very openness to other things and to others, human beings are indeed in contact with the divine fountain. Everyone "moves in God," even if they don't know it, Zubiri argues.[28] However, God and reality are not the same thing: God transcends in reality. To open oneself to God's more entails an awareness of divine transcendence in all beings. An awareness of intracosmic transcendence leads humans toward the rest of creation, not away from it, and to a praxis guided by that awareness of divinity in reality. Opening to God's more not only prevents each human person from closing around him or herself, from absolutizing her or his own particularity, but also calls that person to turn toward creation and toward the human Other—dynamics that are examined throughout this book. Conversely, when the dynamic openness is limited, a negation of Trinitarian life occurs, which is sin. There is thus historical sin, but there is also historical goodness—historical grace.[29]

To live with an awareness of intracosmic transcendence requires a constant renewal of the received experience of God, a reception of "more than the God of the fathers" and the "historical repetition of what the scripture expresses as *theopraxy*."[30] This praxis is understood in light of the model of history described herein, where human beings receive and actualize possibilities that contribute to the flow of history. As with the case of radical orthodoxy's vision, the reception of the divine excess is not considered a completed event, but one that compels the faithful to continually move toward God. As we saw in the previous chapter, for radical orthodoxy the constant deferral of the consummation of God's full presence is exemplified in liturgy, which becomes a site of contact between a transcendent God and humanity, between "Word and word."[31] In contrast, for liberation theology the "place of transcendence" is history understood in the wider sense that Ellacuría gives to the term.[32] The human response is theopraxis.

What is received from God, revelation, is not limited to the acquisition of knowledge about God, but a "difference that makes a difference," as Juan Luis Segundo describes it.[33] Divine-human communication succeeds only inasmuch as the recipient succeeds in "transforming it into a humanizing difference within history."[34] In history, "God and humanity collaborate," so that the future depends, "although in a different way, on God's faithfulness and human response."[35] Human-divine relationship leads to transcendence (in its sense of transformation), that is, to the emergence of new possibilities, for individual persons and in turn for collectivities. According to Ellacuría, the historical repetition of theopraxy brings about a future "which invalidates negativity and recovers old experience in a new way," maintaining the continuity between the old and the new.[36] In other words, the interconnectedness of past, present, and future is not externally imposed by God, but preserved through transformative practice in the world—a practice based on the recognition of reality as life in God.

KNOWING IN HISTORY

Contrary to what is generally believed, meaning and sense were never the same thing, meaning shows itself at once, direct, literal, explicit, enclosed in itself, univocal, if you like, while sense cannot stay still, it seethes with second, third and fourth senses, radiating out in different directions that divide and subdivide into branches and branchlets, until they disappear from view, the sense of every word is like a star hurling spring tides out into space, cosmic winds, magnetic perturbations, afflictions.

—*José Saramago*, All the Names

A theology that affirms transcendence in history also asserts the historicity of all concepts, including theological ones. Not only are human concepts historical and marked by the realities that ground all human productions, but concepts, as language in general, shape human thought. Furthermore, because reality is always in process, the meaning and the impact of concepts in reality change through time and space. "Concepts themselves only exist in process."[37] This demands a constant analysis of how a concept functions within its concrete contexts.

Similarly, theology is influenced by the ideological and material grounds of the historical reality from which it emerges. Theology is produced by humans who are conditioned by history. "It takes a more or less biased naïveté to believe that theology . . . enjoys a special status which makes it immune from every disfiguring conditioning factor."[38] Furthermore, what theology addresses and witnesses to is the experience of God in history. Not only the language and the concepts, but the very transcendence that liberation theology (and indeed all theology) speaks about is enmeshed in the complex and multiple reality of history.

This is a critical point for a theology that reacts against appropriations of the idea of divine transcendence to assert an all-too-human authority. As Marcella Althaus-Reid puts it, theology "as the representation of an absolute essence is a Hegelian idea which has been disputed by the liberationist Marxist approach." Liberation theology asserts that the alleged "absolute essence is nothing more than a political ideology *homologizing itself with a God-like discourse* of sacred authority." Such endowments of religious thought with divine authority are frequently based on the idea that certain concepts, symbols, or words work independently and thus remain unaffected by history. They tend to deny the historicity of theological concepts, both in terms of the past social realities inscribed in them and of their relationship with, and dependence upon, contemporary systems of meaning. Detached from the uncertainties inherent in our complex world, Althaus-Reid adds, revelation is imagined "as the almost mediumistic art of pulling down a Platonic idea of an abstract absolute idea of God."[39]

Liberation theologies emphasize that revelation is *enmeshed in* human language and in all aspects of human bodiliness. "In any case, revelation reveals (unveils, undresses) God in our historical circumstances, and assumes a materialist twist in our understanding." God is encountered *within*, never outside the complexities of our finite existence. "That is the point of doing theology from people's experiences, *and*"—adding her own zesty challenge to established liberation theology—"from their *sexual* stories, because they reveal the *falsity of the border limits* between the material and divine dimensions of our lives."[40] Rather than assuming it has leaped over boundaries of signification, this theology questions the assumption that there are loci of unconditioned access to the divine. Thus, instead of dreaming of escaping historical influence, theology must reestablish the relationship between dogmatic themes and history. This entails not simply tracing the historical development of theology, but also uncovering its interests and the possibilities that it wants to actualize in history.

THE DEBATE WITH RADICAL ORTHODOXY

In the previous chapter I summarized Milbank's critique of Deleuze, Negri, and Hardt, which focuses on their view of "the plane of immanence" as the "sphere of active, productive forces" with the assumption of the possibility of a "liberated nature-going-beyond-nature."[41] A similar critique is raised against liberation theology, which is fundamentally a challenge to their depiction of the relationship between transcendence and human flourishing.

In his essay "Founding the Supernatural: Political and Liberation Theology in the Context of Modern Catholic Thought," Milbank contends that liberation theology replaces transcendence with social processes.[42] He claims that the root of the problem is that liberation theology has "embraced" the "*immanent* principles of secularization and politics," as evidenced in their use of Marxism.[43] Rather than subordinating social sciences to theology, Milbank argues that liberation theology has assumed that the world can be explained using social sciences.[44] He further contends that as a result of the alleged adoption of immanent principles, liberation theology has posited an autonomous "profane sphere" which it has assumed can be understood outside of theology while, at the same time, claiming this space to be the site of God's grace.

In liberation theology, "the social process is identified as the site of transcendence," which means that liberation theology has mistaken "immanence" for transcendence. As we explained earlier, radical orthodoxy's assumption is that transcendence is exterior to the cosmos; therefore, the sphere of natural and social processes is not considered the site of transcendence. In Milbank's opinion, liberation theology's praxis is nothing but "political practice" "*outside* Christian tradition."[45] Liberation theology's description of human beings is also problematic for radical orthodoxy, as it subscribes to the idea of "immanent human value" that radical orthodoxy rejects.[46] Although the process of liberation "is a purely human one, and although there are no human needs which cannot be immanently met, liberation can still be identified by theology as the anonymous site of all divine action," Milbank complains.[47] As a consequence of its emphasis on human processes, Milbank continues, liberation theology's concept of salvation has to do with an "empty, formless epistemological *transcendence*"—which he considers to be no transcendence at all.

The contrast between "purely human processes" and divine action in this analysis is grounded in radical orthodoxy's cosmological structure which draws a sharp distinction between the realm of creation and an external transcendence conceived as preeminently real. In that view where God is imagined as extrinsic to creation, immanence and transcendence are in tension, if not in sheer opposition. This is still the case in radical orthodoxy, as it is in classical and predominant Christian theologies today, although, as we saw in the previous chapter, Milbank's use of the term "immanence" tends to have connotations of nihilism and secularism that are absent in most contemporary theologies. The opposition between immanence and transcendence, and the resulting implicit (albeit denied) division between the profane and the sacred are the basis for radical orthodoxy's contentions against liberation theology.

In his argument, Milbank takes for granted the existence of "purely human" processes (devoid of transcendence), where human needs are met "immanently." Within this worldview, the energies that operate within the world (organically, or by human action) are dissociated from transcendence. But liberation theologies do not subscribe to this cosmology. Conversely, Milbank seems also to assume the existence of a purely Christian realm, clearly divided from the purely human one and thus somehow immune to conscious or unconscious, past or present, sociopolitical assumptions and interests. In short, the discussion seems to imply the presence of a realm detached of historical contingency from which Christian principles derive that can judge society as if from the outside. We have seen this tendency to set up spaces claimed to be above the rules that apply to common reality, for instance, in Pickstock's treatment of liturgical language, where she claimed that the words "Father," "Son," and "Holy Spirit" are essential and "commensurate with the existential space" of the Trinity, and that some signs could become dislodged from their "character as bounded things." While crucially resisting the reduction of language to mere play of signifiers unrelated to the concrete world, Pickstock's assertions could create the illusion of having identified words that are exempt from critique by failing to attend not only to the historical development of that language, but also the inextricable relation between words and the symbolic systems in place where those words are used. The risk of the latter is to unwittingly cross the line between protecting God from appropriation and claiming a transcendent authority for one's own discourse.

Liberation theologies may be reluctant to subsume all ethics under the Christian understanding of the Christ event. This circumspection, however, does not spring from an assumption of the autonomy of social ethics from the divine, as Milbank supposes. Instead, liberation theologies harbor a desire, indeed a commitment, to uphold all spheres of society—Christian or not—as potential sites of divine action. This is based on a strong affirmation that all existence is *existence in God*. There is no region of "pure immanence," if that means the possibility of existing outside the divine. There is no *purely* human, if that means devoid of participation in the divine: "The very being of the human is constitutively a being in God."[48] As Michael Lee explains, "Christian praxis, as the historicization of faith . . . which might employ social sciences in analysis of intramundane reality, still perceives reality's deeper *theologal* dimension"—that is, the rootedness of all creation in God.[49]

GOD-TALK IN HISTORY

Prophetism and utopia, history and transcendence, nourish each other. Both are historical and both are transcendent, but neither becomes what it is meant to become except in relation to the other.

—*Ignacio Ellacuría*

Despite the emphasis on the intracosmic character of transcendence, liberation theology's transcendence retains its independence from the created realm. "In history," Ellacuría explains, "transcendence must be seen more in the relationship between necessity and freedom than between absence and presence. God is transcendent, among other reasons, not by being absent, but by being freely present. . . ."[50] As we have seen, when describing human freedom, Ellacuría emphasizes that freedom is always conditioned by matrices of historical, material, and biological factors. It is from this perspective that I read Ellacuría's descriptions of the radical novelty God introduces in history as something "breaking into" the ongoing historical processes so that "something *more* than history becomes present *in* history."[51] In other words, unexpected events may interrupt what had seemed the "natural" course of history. In Walter Benjamin's famous formulation: "Every second of time is the strait gate through which the Messiah might enter."[52]

The depiction of intracosmic transcendence as that which retains as it impels forward—an image of development that evokes the organic rhythms of nature or the subtle modulations of history—is frequently overshadowed by the (more phallic) imagery of something "breaking in" from the outside. In spite of the emphasis of the theology discussed in this chapter on the continuous transformation brought about in the divine/human interaction in history, liberation theologies do in general assert the freedom of God to break in from "outside" history, both in present history, and at the end of history. This reassertion of the idea of God's intervention from outside may undermine human participation—even the notion of transcendence within creation. It risks reinscribing the subordination of the concern for the needs of creatures to some absolute principle outside of the cosmos, and transformations that arise from complex relations are surpassed by changes imposed independently of them.

Latin American liberation theologians nevertheless seek to propose a close link between the historical and the eschatological aspects of their account of transcendence. Jon Sobrino explains that "the utopian element of the Reign is understood in the theology of liberation as a guide along the path already traversed."[53] Unlike other theologies, liberation theology "does not emphasize, although of course it accepts, the relativizing character of the utopian Reign where anything historical is concerned."[54] Given the social reality of Latin America, Sobrino objects that a warning against mistaking its reality with the reign of God "sounds like sarcasm."[55] More significantly, liberation theology wants to affirm that "eschatology does not relativize historical configurations on an equal basis; it ranks them."[56] Thus, the utopian understanding of the reign of God provides the principles of prophetic challenge against current injustices.

The possibility of social critique is crucial for liberation theology. But we must here remember Ellacuría's epistemological warnings, discussed above: "there is no escape from the historicity of place and time."[57] The principles that guide liberation theology's prophetic voice are always enmeshed in the complexities of personal and social realities. To forget this puts the theologian in danger of claiming unmediated access to absolute authority—one of the most common traps into which theologies of transcendence have fallen. Feminist liberation theologians have been mindful of this risk and have tried to keep theology aware of its own limits. Arguing from within the force field of Latin American liberation movements, these feminist theologians do not heed Milbank's call to "replace theology mediated by social science" with "theology as 'metanarrative realism,'"[58] but quite to the contrary argue that liberation theology's questioning of the metanarratives—secular *and* Christian—has not gone far enough. These intimate *Others* of liberation theology have urged liberation theologians to a "permanent exercise of serious doubting,"[59] or, as Milbank would say, of constant self-critique and avoidance of absolutization of the self (or one's theology, I would add). This requires letting go of any illusion of "leaping over" contextual mediation. "Theological discourse about God gives God a historical substance, an image, and a role. But who are the people who give God a role?" asks Ivone Gebara—thus turning the critical gaze to the theologians themselves.[60]

"The point is," explains Althaus-Reid, "that Liberation Theology is not a self-contained entity or peculiar category of analysis related to God and a particular theological subject as the poor."[61] Even when liberation theology proclaims its intention to ground its experience of God in the encounter with the human Other, it may dangerously retain its claim (perhaps unavoidably, though not necessarily innocently) to discern which aspects of the Other reflected God's image and God's calling. Althaus-Reid specifically observes that, in its relation to both secular and theological discourses, liberation theology has had problems accepting that "the simplistic confrontation between oppressive and liberative aspects of our lives" is "a farce." "In the end," she explains, "Liberation Theology and structures of oppression both share a common epistemological field."[62] And so does all theology.

The goal of maintaining a close relation between the reign of God and each and every moment of history is better served when the ranking of historical configurations is envisioned as part of the movement of transcendence-within rather than as something superadded to it. As we recognize the always *beyond* of the reign of God, rather than "homologizing [our theologies] with a God-like discourse," we affirm that all theological principles are part of reality: historically conditioned and transcending. Theology cannot trespass the limits of finitude, but it can open itself to reality and strive to actualize possibilities of more life.

INTRACOSMIC TRANSCENDENCE

A theological model of divine transcendence within creation and history calls us to seek divine transcendence within the folds of a divinely created reality. Creation's unity, value, and the ends toward which it moves emerge from within reality and flow through bonds of relationality that are inherent to all reality. In the previous chapter, we explored radical orthodoxy's depiction of transcendence as an external realm in which all reality participates and which safeguards the divine ends for creation. By contrast, in this chapter we have explored a cosmology in which transcendence flows through reality as the sap through the branches of a tree. Transcendence moves in the world, with its material and vital forces in their relation to human freedom, producing transformations that follow the nonlinear patterns of biological time.

Connecting branches delinate the structure of reality's unity; unity is not imposed as a container from outside, but is implicit in the very structure of the world. Because all reality is interrelated, the actual outcome of the creative processes that characterize reality depends not only on the nurturing gift of its divine ground, but also on the human input in actualizing possibilities. Human freedom to actualize the possibilities that make possible new and greater creative capacities also entails great risks. Humanity might destroy the very world upon which its own life depends —in and through which it touches the divine.

Intracosmic transcendence implies a need to deepen our awareness of the reality that surrounds us and to open ourselves to Others as divine creatures. Things are indeed "more than they appear" (Pickstock) and exceed our most radical expectations. Thus, a theology of intracosmic transcendence entails a reinterpretation of creation, of Others, and of our relationship with them, for creatures are not inherently nothing. Instead, this theology recognizes the irreducibility of other human beings, and sees them as "ineffable likenesses of God."[63] In this vision, interhuman relations are regarded as "non-identical repetitions" (Milbank) of our relations to the intimate but ineffable God. This "culturally imbued sense of transcendence" would not think of human needs as only "immanent needs" subordinated to some other (higher?) need. Instead, the processes by which human needs are met—people are fed, sheltered, and loved, and societies become mediators of such nurturing processes—are manifestations of a transcendence that is always already taking place in creation.

To further develop the notion of intracosmic transcendence, we now move from the broad visions of the relationship between God and creation to consider the realm of human relations. We have said that a model of intracosmic transcendence entails opening oneself to encounter reality as the site of transcendence. We now need to ask: How do we encounter transcendence? What does transcendence imply for interhuman relations? To address these questions, we turn to insights of philosophy, feminism, and postcolonial thought. In so doing we never abandon the realm of divine transcendence, but look deeper into its folds.

CHAPTER 4

Transcendence in the Face of the Other

The three victims mounted together onto chairs.
The three necks were placed at the same moment within the nooses.
"Long live liberty!" cried the two adults.
But the child was silent.
"Where is God? Where is He?" someone behind me asked.
At a sign from the head of the camp, the three chairs tipped over.
. . .

[The child] was still alive when I passed in front of him. . . .
Behind me, I heard the same man asking:
"Where is God now?"
And I heard a voice within me answer him:
"Where is He? Here He is—He is hanging here on this gallows."

—*Elie Wiesel,* Night

Thus the Hungarian author and Noble Prize winner describes his experience at a Nazi concentration camp. In the memoir that relates the utter helplessness of those imprisoned, Wiesel redirects the gaze of the God-seeker. "Where is God?" the man asked, and we also wonder as we imagine the horrific scene. In response, we are compelled to look not at the heights of heaven or even to the wonders of creation, but rather at the face of a single victim right in front of us. Wiesel's "Here he is—He is hanging here" is not simply an answer, but also a demand to consider the ethical implications of the question: where is God? "Here He is" is a call to responsibility that echoes in the writings of the thinkers engaged in this chapter.

The works of Emmanuel Levinas who, like Wiesel, suffered the violence of the Holocaust, and of the Argentinian philosopher Enrique Dussel, some of it written in the midst of extreme state violence, approach the question of transcendence with their eyes turned to the ethical demands met in the face of a singular human being. Although both write from outside the field of theology, Dussel and Levinas work in close proximity with the language, histories, and political concerns of their respective religious communities. They are philosophers who turn to the notion of transcendence as a response to what they perceive as the failures of the dominant groups to respect the human other as Other. They seek to interrupt the complacencies of modern and postmodern geopolitical systems concerning the plight of the oppressed, exposing our tendencies to objectify and appropriate the human Other. In the face of the Other, they argue, we are encountered by transcendence.

With Levinas and Dussel our discussion of transcendence moves from the broad cosmological questions that have concerned us for most of the previous chapters to their implications for interhuman relations. We proceed from intracosmic to interhuman transcendence. We have seen that conceiving divine transcendence as intracosmic transcendence compels us to turn toward the complexities of our own finite existence, rather than away from them, and that to seek divine transcendence implies opening ourselves to transcendence *in* things, and *between* creatures. In this chapter, we turn to consider transcendence in and between human beings, linking the imperative defense of the irreducibility of the human person to divine transcendence. Focusing on human relations will add new elements to our model of transcendence pertaining to the effects of particular images of transcendence on the ways we understand and act in relation to other people, especially those who are excluded from full participation in our society. As we begin to seek metaphors that allow us to imagine transcendence encountered in other human beings, we will explore the connotations of the concepts of exteriority and infinity in connection to ideas about otherness and relation.

The long-term relationship between Dussel's liberation philosophy and Levinas's thought has greatly influenced the language and images with which Latin American liberation theologies imagine the human Other.[1] Attending to Latin America, Dussel's work enriches the theoretical categories that he adopts from Levinas: giving the "face of the Other" a context and linking Levinas's philosophy to concrete hopes of liberation. Yet it is precisely the aim of liberation that ultimately bursts Levinas's imagery of transcendence as exteriority or absolute separation. Hopes for historical liberation, I will argue, may be impeded by the static, impermeable walls of absolute separation. Liberation requires a dynamic transcendence, and an anthropology in which otherness is not conceived as fixed or absolute. U.S. Hispanic theological anthropology leads us in that direction.

FROM TOTALITY TO TRANSCENDENCE: EMMANUEL LEVINAS[2]

Emmanuel Levinas dedicates *Otherwise Than Being* "To the memory of those who were closest among the six million assassinated by the National Socialists, and of the millions upon millions of all confessions and all nations, victims of the same hatred of the *other* man, the same anti-semitism."[3] It is the context of totalitarism and its hatred of the Other that leads Levinas to a philosophical engagement with the idea of transcendence. For the Jewish philosopher, who has been called "the philosopher of otherness,"[4] transcendence is inextricable from an absolute otherness that shows itself in human relations.

Confronted by the horrors of Nazism, Levinas sensed the alluring and annihilating force of totalitarism in the very structures of the Western philosophical tradition. The philosophical privilege of sameness over difference, of the One over multiplicity, of the universal over the particular, Levinas observed, collude with political and religious ideologies that subsume multiplicity under an all-encompassing "system." In such systems there is no place for real otherness. Totalities reduce persons to categories within a self-enclosed system, defining them as instances of the same, to functions within a state, a philosophical model, or an ontological and/or theological structure. Persons are thus stripped of their irreducible otherness.

This tendency to reduce and objectify others is also common in personal relations. A subject shaped by the logic of oneness and universality tends to conceive himself or herself as the center of a world that is apprehended and assimiliated into the self. Such a subject is thus likely to approach other human beings as objects to be accommodated within the subject's schemes and purposes instead of seeing other people as truly Others. The Other becomes objectified, while the subject remains the same, Levinas argues.

The objectification of persons is pervasive in most societies, but its effects are not merely conceptual aberrations; it is a powerful dehumanizing tool often leading to death. *A Thread of Grace*, a novel by Mary Doria Russell, proffers a shockingly clear example of the Nazis' deployment of objectification as ideological strategy: a requirement to wear the distinctive mark. A sign of identity helped erase the singularity of each human being so identified. "Eyes skimmed past the star on your armband." Even those who had been friends "were embarrassed for you—by you." The complexity of human relations was thus effectively subsumed under a clearly defined category, with chilling effects: "Stop seeing real Jews, and it's easy for people to believe lies. Jews are lazy. Jews are ugly. Jews are evil. Day after day."[5]

Transcendence

In view of the loss of human lives in the name of One totalitarian system, Levinas's work sought to "liberate itself from the Greek domination of the Same and the One . . . as if from oppression itself."[6] Derrida explains that for Levinas the tyranny of the supremacy of sameness was "comparable to none other in the world"; its rule amounted to "an ontological or transcendental oppression, but also the origin or alibi of all oppression in the world."[7] In *Totality and Infinity*, Levinas calls for a radical philosophical departure—an exodus, as it were—a turn "from the experience of totality back to a situation where totality breaks up": from the sameness of totality, to "the gleam of exteriority or of transcendence in the face of the Other."[8]

Using the term "transcendence" to denote the "situation where totality breaks up," Levinas reclaims a term frequently associated with totality itself. Transcendence has often denoted, and still does denote, a transcendental totality. Indeed, philosophy and religion have repeatedly laid claims on "transcendence"—they have even proclaimed its "presence," its immediate fulfillment here and now—as a source of an unquestionable authority. Levinas is concerned about these moves and asserts the distinction between his definition of transcendence and self-authorizing uses of that term. On the one hand, he warns against philosophies of transcendence that situate "elsewhere the true life to which man, escaping from here, would gain access in the privileged moments of liturgical, mystical elevation, or in dying." These otherworldly transcendences not only turn their backs to "the unfolding of terrestrial existence, of economic existence," but also, by claiming to have access to a realm beyond creation, they place themselves beyond the challenges to which all human claims are subject.[9] In Levinas's opinion, theologies of participation fall prey to this self-authorizing temptation.

Levinas is also worried about the demise of transcendence, which he characterizes as the thought of "immanence." Such demise comprises philosophies that put forward a goal of total fusion, "in which we would truly come into possession of being when every 'other' . . . encompassed by the same, would vanish at the end of history."[10] These are ideologies with no other, no beyond; in these philosophies there is only the same.

In this depiction of "philosophies of immanence," Levinas restates the common opposition between transcendence and immanence to which I alluded in the previous chapters. But the terms of Levinas's opposition are different from those found in the discussion of radical orthodoxy. As we saw, for radical orthodoxy, "immanence" denotes a world without "height," that is, without reference to the "otherworldly." Immanence is opposed to a transcendent God outside the created world. For Levinas, on the other hand, the distinction between immanence and transcendence is defined specifically in terms of relation to otherness. "Immanence" is contrasted not to the heavenly realm, but to difference. What Levinas calls "immanent" is that which is self-sufficient, self-same, solipsistic; it tolerates no Other. The attempts to appropriate the Other, to reduce it to a self or the same, to contain it within a totality—human or divine—or to eliminate differences, are for Levinas moves toward immanence. Immanence means sameness.

Transcendence as Levinas describes it is the opening of sameness to its Other. Transcendence breaks the totality of any system—conceptual or political, earthly or heavenly—appearing concretely "in the face of the Other."[11] The face of the Other is not an abstraction, but the very singularity of the Other. Marilynne Robinson describes this sense of uniqueness in her novel *Gilead:* "I realized there is nothing more astonishing than a human face. . . . Any human face is a claim on you, because you can't help but understand the singularity of it, the courage and loneliness of it."[12] The singularity of the Other reveals to us our own responsibility, indeed "calling into question" the self.[13] Although Levinas's depictions of transcendence do include references to heights, indeed to the "Most High," transcendence is not outside the realm of human relations. Transcendence is there in the encounter of one person facing another, when the self is met by the face of the Other.

God *and* the Other
"The gleam of transcendence in the face of the Other" is Levinas's distinctive image of transcendence within the world. Its biblical undertones are hard to miss. Thus described, transcendence brings to mind images of divine glory in the Hebrew Scripture—the glory of God fills all creation and manifests itself in the ordinary, as a burning bush or the cloud that accompanied the Israelites, even shining in Moses' face after his encounter with God—and yet that very glory appeared also as radiance that humans could not behold directly, which reminded Israelites of their own limits in relation to God's otherness. These images of radiance, pervasive and yet awesome, attractive for its beauty and yet marking out limits that shall not be transgressed, are reflected in Levinas's depictions of transcendence. And yet Levinas specifically refers to transcendence in the face of other human beings. Is transcendence then an implicit allusion to God? Is the Other a manifestation of God?

Although Levinas's *Totality and Infinity* is not presented as a dogmatic discussion of divine transcendence, it is not a simple "secular" departure from God-talk. For Levinas, references to alterity are probably always also indirect references to divinity. Alterity might refer always both to the Other and to the "Most High," to the Other and the Holy Other. The explicit "and" in Levinas's statement, "the alterity of the Other *and* the Most-High," appears to be implicit in most of his allusions to alterity.[14] "In welcoming the Other," Levinas clearly explains, "I welcome the On High to which my freedom is subordinated."[15] Yet we must still ask: is the human "Other" intrinsically transcendent to us, or is it God's transcendence which manifests itself in the Other? Levinas seems to leave the door open to both readings, perhaps because the question is ultimately undecidable. As Edith Wyschogrod puts it, "God-talk in Levinas can be thought of as prefaced by an unstated '*perhaps*' in the Derridean sense, a perhaps that points to an irresolvable uncertainty."[16] This uncertainty is a necessary condition for Levinas.

A story from the Gospel of Matthew illustrates the ethical implications of the uncertainty that marks our relationships with others and with God: the scene of the "great judgment." Christ welcomes the righteous ones to the kingdom saying, "I was hungry and you gave me food, I was thirsty and you gave me something to drink, I was a stranger and you welcomed me."[17] The righteous ones are startled, and that is the key to the story. Their response accentuates their puzzlement: "When was it that we saw you hungry and gave you food, or thirsty and gave you something to drink?" (Matt. 25:37). The point of the story is not that the righteous ones showed Christ generosity, which would be the logical action for those seeking eternal rewards, but that they did not know. The fact that the Gospel tells the story is thus profoundly ironic, because once it is told the secret is revealed: we already know what the righteous ones could not have known. This narrative too might need to be prefaced by a "perhaps."

To erase Levinas's unstated "perhaps" would indeed undermine the radical ethical implications of transcendence in the face of the Other: the refusal to open a hatch for a relation to God that bypasses the relation with the created Other.[18] Levinas implicitly gives this prohibition to circumvent ethical responsibility the authority of the biblical injunction: "You shall not make wrongful use of the name of the LORD your God" (Exod. 20:7), which he interprets as a commandment to respond to the human Other. "The heteronomy of ethical obedience . . . submission to the order issued in the face of the other man" is for Levinas the condition implicit in the commandment: "*not naming God* except on the basis of this obedience."[19] *Totality and Infinity* does not name God except through the language of a philosophy turned toward the Other. Furthermore, this zeal against idolatry extends also to his view of the relation to the human

Other. Ethical obedience implies *not naming the Other* except on the basis of an ethical relation—what we may call an apophatic anthropology.

The Other and the Self

What then can be said of the Other? The Other in whom we are to find the gleam of transcendence is a human person in his radical singularity, as Other. To face the other as Other is *not* to contrast him to me or to some universal standard. To conceive the Other only as "the simple reverse of identity"[20] is still to define him in terms of the self, as relative to the self. The same is true when we define the other as the limits of the self, for then the Other is still a function of the self. To meet a person face-to-face is to encounter the singularity of the Other, not his opposition to the self. The Other in whose face transcendence shines "is not formed out of resistance to the same," which would still be a function of the same. The Other does not derive from the self or from our own categories of analysis, but is "prior to every initiative, to all imperialism of the same."[21] His alterity is not "a quality that would distinguish him from me," as if we were examples of two different categories within a common system. "A distinction of this nature would precisely imply between us that community of genus which already nullifies alterity." The alterity of the Other is absolute: the other is absolutely Other.[22]

In contrast to modern notions of subjectivity that construe the self as the center and origin of knowledge, as well as in distinction to theological models in which an otherworldly divinity becomes the origin and source of value (to which we referred in chapter 2), Levinas argues that it is the sheer existence of the Other that calls the priority of the self into question and opens the way to ethics. Yet in order to encounter the other as Other, we must resist the tendency to reduce the Other to an object to be grasped, comprehended, and assimilated. This implies a transformation in prevalent notions of subjectivity. Claiming a theory of subjectivity per se would be, to be sure, a decidedly un-Levinasian project. Levinas consistently refuses to provide a system that would explain others in general, insisting instead that the Other is singular and thus cannot be objectified in theory. However, as we have seen, his analysis directly refutes dominant ideas about other human beings. To take Levinas's challenges into account is, first and foremost, to privilege the Other's claim over any system—sociopolitical or philosophical. However, we must also strive to transform those systems, even as we insist that they never take precedence over the encounter with the Other. Attempting to overcome the imperialism of the self entails moving away from models that tend to objectify the Other, but also those that construe humans as intrinsically nothing, such as the one that Pickstock and Milbank espouse. In the modern models, the system or the self takes priority over the Other. In some theistic models it is in reference to a God and "his" rules that others are catalogued and valued. By contrast, in Levinas's ethics the Other resists the appropriating impulse of the self. She or he is inherently beyond my grasp.

Transcendence, Infinity, and Exteriority

> Transcendence designates a relation with a reality infinitely distant from my own reality, yet without this distance destroying this relation and without the relation destroying this distance.
> —*Emmanuel Levinas*[23]

Levinas describes transcendence using the concepts of infinity and exteriority. Levinas frequently uses these terms interchangeably; he states, for instance: "Such a situation is the gleam of *exteriority* or of *transcendence* in the face of the Other. The rigorously developed concept of this transcendence is expressed by the term *infinity*."[24] Each of these terms, however, has particular connotations that we shall carefully explore.

Infinity, as Levinas defines it, denotes the inexhaustibility of transcendence. Significantly, Levinas's descriptions of infinity emerge from a depiction of transcendence as relation. "Transcendence designates a relation," Levinas proposes.[25] This relation—which he calls the "metaphysical relation"—is characterized by nonviolence, by the respect of the other as Other. The metaphysical relation established between the self and the Other is based neither on knowledge nor on a dynamics of revelation (or dis-covery). It is a relationship of desire. Metaphysical desire is distinguished from the needs of the body, which, like hunger, are satisfied by the incorporation of the desired object into the self. Metaphysical desire does not aim at appropriation or consumption; it "desires beyond everything that can simply complete it."[26]

This desire for the infinite is inseparable from the relation to the human Other. For infinity is not an otherworldly reservoir of meaning or authority. It is not something given or static, but rather "produced"— both brought about and revealed—"in the relationship of the same with the other."[27] This ambiguity about the provenance of infinity, the impossibility of fixing its origin—the fact that it is "produced" in being revealed—evokes a temporal dimension that is not apparent in accounts of transcendence as exteriority. Indeed, Levinas describes the relation with infinity—which, following Descartes, he calls "the idea of infinity"—as "the infinition" of infinity. For "[i]nfinity does not first exist, and *then* reveal itself. Its infinition is produced as revelation, as positing of its idea in *me*."[28] As openness at the heart of relation, Levinas's distinctive description of infinity inspires this theology of relational transcendence, which resists the opposition between difference and relation.

Levinas's infinity, however, is always associated with "exteriority." The term "exteriority"—as well as other metaphors such as "separation" and "distance"—depicts transcendence in clearly spatial terms. The Other is met as an exteriority, Levinas insists. This exteriority is not otherworldly; it does not imply there is a reality beyond the world that would become revealed in the coming of the Other. Instead, for Levinas the term "exteriority" refers to "that by which the alterity of the Other escapes" the totality.[29] In other words, while totalities attempt to fully define individuals according to their systems of classification, human beings always exceed categories. Being "exterior" to the totality means that the Other cannot be defined in terms of the system, and that his values might be foreign to the values of the totality. The coming of the Other breaks the logic of the system; the Other is an absolute with regard to the system. The claims of a poor person, for instance, cannot be justified within the rules of distribution of goods that our society has established. Indeed, according to the rules of our society, those claims might be absurd. Yet Levinas's contention is that we remain responsible for the Other, even when we cannot understand him.

This responsibility to the Other, undeterred by the rules that govern the communities in which we live, is captured in Ellacuría's description of every creature as a "relative absolute," as we saw in the previous chapter. Ellacuría's model asserts the constitutive relationality of all creatures, hence the term "relative" in his phrase: human beings are absolutes in regard to the totality, but are relative because they are related to all other creatures. Contrastingly, Levinas's starting point is the "self" constituted as free and independent from others—"at home with himself." This is a self who does not need others, who only after encountering the Other realizes his debt to the Other. The self remains radically separated from the Other: "The relation with the Other does not nullify separation," he clearly states.[30] For Levinas, the transcendence of the Other is that separation, a distance between the self and the Other.

The reliance on spatial metaphors of separation and exteriority has important consequences for Levinas's model of transcendence. Spatial metaphors tend to reinstate the common association between transcendence and a particular location, losing the dynamic element that the notion of infinity conveys. Exteriority also conveys the idea that there is a need for a rigid boundary between self and Other. In *Totality and Infinity,* for instance, Levinas envisions relationships in terms of discourse, precisely because discourse maintains the physical separation between the subjects.[31] This severely limits the kinds of relationships he considers as relations of transcendence.

Irreversibility and Asymmetry in Relation to the Other

For Levinas, the separation between the self and the Other is needed in order to resist the tendency to deny the otherness of the Other by assimilating him into our own categories, and thus to our system/sameness. Self and Other do not belong to the same system; they do not constitute a totality. The relation between the self and the Other is thus irreversible. This implies not only "that the same goes unto the Other differently than the other unto the same," but that it is impossible "to place oneself outside of the correlation between the same and other" in order to evaluate the correspondence (or lack thereof) between self and Other.[32] To maintain that the Other cannot be encompassed by the self precludes our posing any equivalence or reversibility between self and Other, because such a move would entail reestablishing a new totality to contain us both. The fact is, Levinas explains, that only as an "I" can I think of my relationship to another person, never as the Other. In the ethical relation, it is the Other who presents himself; I can never take his place, assume his perspective, or challenge myself in the way the Other does. I must *face* the Other.

However, Levinas asserts not only the irreversibility of the relation but also the asymmetry. In addition to claiming the impossibility of evaluating the correspondence between the self and the Other, Levinas insists that the Other must be approached as an other "in need." The implicit hierarchy of this statement is then reversed by considering the Other-in-need as "master." "The transcendence of the Other, which is his eminence, his height, his lordship, in its concrete meaning includes his destitution, his exile, and his rights as a stranger."[33] The Other *demands me, requires me, summons me.* The Other is the one "toward whom I have obligations."[34]

The relationship to transcendence is thus tightly linked to specific social realities: the Other is not any other person, but one that has been excluded from the spheres of social power. Levinas proposes, for instance, that "The transcendence of the face is at the same time its absence from this world, the exiling of a being, his condition of *being* a stranger, destitute, or proletarian."[35] But what does it imply to affirm that, by definition, transcendence manifests itself in the destitute person? Is this not to predefine transcendence, to limit it to certain relations obtaining within existing social structures?

Exclusion is a way in which society denies certain individuals or groups their transcendence, seeing them as expendable objects rather than as "relative absolutes." To see transcendence in the faces of the excluded ones is perhaps the most radical affirmation of transcendence in human relations. Yet there are also significant ethical risks in simply identifying transcendence and exclusion, as this may lead to the reduction of transcendence to a location in regard to, or within, a system. Identifying the condition of *being* a stranger, destitute, or proletarian with transcendence may further lead us to ignore the concrete social conditions that account for a person's exclusion. The ethical implications of these questions are immense.

Sarah Ahmed argues that Levinas himself fails to thematize the relationship between the categories of exclusion that he associates with transcendence and the social system from which they emerge.[36] Levinas's allusions to the Stranger are informed by Jewish Scriptures' advocacy for the foreigner, the widow, the orphan. Ahmed observes that while "Levinas writes the other, *as* the other, by employing various figures of the other, including the widow, the poor and the orphan (all of which appear in the Bible, as figures of the needy whom one should welcome)," his work erases the specificity of these figures.[37] Levinas fails to address the intricate relation between these figures and the communities that name them—as foreigner, widow, orphan—or, for that matter, as stranger, destitute, or proletarian, Ahmed argues. "[C]utting off 'the other' from the modes of encounter in which one meets an-other," that is, from their contexts and histories, "allows 'the other' to appear in Levinas's texts as an *alien being,* whom one might then encounter, in the *entirety* of that very form."[38] The image evoked is that of two self-contained entities at opposite sides of a border. Ahmed adds that, as far as Levinas describes otherness as a characteristic of the Other, he is implicitly posing the existence of two types of beings: beings and "alien beings."[39] Alien beings, one would have to conclude, are transcendent.

These critiques pertain to the concrete social implications of a notion of interhuman transcendence. Would a notion of transcendence in the face of the destitute help promote the development of just sociopolitical systems? Or would the reliance on the figure of the Other as stranger, destitute, or proletarian result in naturalizing the other person in the position that the system has tried to reduce her/him to—a stranger, destitute, proletarian—even if they are given priority over the self?[40] Does it not risk giving a transcendental aura to existing social structures? These questions concerning the relationship between transcendence and social structures are crucial ones that we continue to explore in the following chapters, beginning with Dussel's rereading of Levinas, to which we now return.

FROM MODERNITY TO TRANSMODERNITY: ENRIQUE DUSSEL

The men of the vineyards were
somber and downcast,
their skin, clouded
and their hearts imploring;
they were men from a foreign land.

Mejicanos, gathering grapes
in borrowed frontiers.
. . .
[My gaze] met them,
and identified their solitude with ours.
It recognized them as men
accused,
men punished for their dark skin.

I approached
them
and offered them my heart
. . .
I spoke in Spanish
and for a second
they were not statues
just men.

—*Marjorie Agosín, "Napa"*

Enrique Dussel was part of an intellectual movement known as the philosophy of liberation that emerged in Argentina in the 1970s. The group began to work before President Juan Peron's death in 1974 and continued their joint project until their diverging positions in relation to the 1976 military coup created divisions among the philosophers, even forcing some of them, including Dussel, into exile. To the present, Dussel continues to identify his work as a philosophy, or ethics, of liberation, which applies liberation principles to contemporary issues such as globalization.

Dussel uses Levinas's phenomenological categories to analyze concrete sociopolitical situations and to contribute to their transformation. Since the publication of *Para una ética de la liberación latinoamericana* (*Toward an Ethics of Latin American Liberation*) in 1973, Dussel's work has been in dialogue with Levinas's philosophy. Indeed, Dussel, who had been a Heideggerian, described his encounter with Levinas in terms that evoke the shock produced by the encounter with the Other. "When I first read Levinas' book *Totality and Infinity*," he writes, "a sort of subversive disruption (*desquiciamiento*) of everything hitherto learned took place in my soul."[41] This philosophical *desquiciamiento* sent Dussel in a search for ways to set Levinas's philosophy to work.[42] How can Levinas's philosophical discourse be continued from Latin America? Dussel ponders.

This "from Latin America" is determinative for Dussel. The social context from which an ethical proposal emerges is as important for him as that of the situation being analyzed. Indeed his depictions of Levinas's contribution, as well as his view of his own project and of Western thought in general, are framed by discussions of social location.[43] For instance, more than two decades after *Liberación latinoamericana y Emmanuel Levinas*, Dussel introduces Levinas with a detailed account of the context of his work. Levinas is, Dussel explains, a "Lithuanian Jew—whose maternal languages were Russian and Lithuanian, student in the French Strasbourg and the German Freiburg—[who] lived the 'experience', in his concrete vulnerable body, of five traumatic years in the Nazi concentration camp (Stammlager)."[44] Levinas, the Jew facing Nazism, provides Dussel with the key concepts of alterity and totality with which he interprets the experience of a Latin America facing an Eurocentric totality "ever since colonial Christianity," indeed, since its very "invention" at the dawn of Modernity.[45]

Europe and the Other

Dussel's strategy anticipates that of postcolonial thinkers who read philosophical concepts from the perspectives of dissident histories and voices. Levinas's call to turn from the totality back to the situation where totality breaks up, receives not only philosophical, but also political and historical interpretations. Dussel turns from modern Latin America back to the historical space/time where the narrative of the totality comes into its own: to the "originary" encounter of modernity, the colonial encounter. The colonial encounter becomes the focal point for an analysis of the categories of identity and otherness that emerge from the contests for political power.

Modernity, Dussel argues, can only be understood in relation to the encounter between Europe and its Other. "Whereas modernity gestated in the free, creative medieval European cities, it came to birth in Europe's confrontation with the Other," he contends.[46] "Europe" and "America" did not preexist the colonial confrontation, but emerged from it, both as essential elements of modernity. "By controlling, conquering, and violating the Other, Europe defined itself as discoverer, conquistador, and colonizer of an alterity likewise constitutive of modernity."[47] This need of Europe for its Other is nonetheless denied. Dussel's work, as Spivak's later, attempts to make visible the foreclosure of Europe's colonized Others—those who made possible the very identity of Europe.

Dussel's analysis of the colonial encounter follows the structure of Levinas's analysis of totality. The otherness of the others against whom Europe defined itself was erased from the colonizer's view as their presence was scratched out of the history of modernity. The encounter with América, Dussel argues, was dominated by previous conceptions and appropriating gestures, and thus it never became revelation. The Other was never encountered in its alterity. "Europe never discovered (*descubierto*) this Other as Other but covered over (*encubierto*) the Other as part of the Same: i.e., Europe." Dussel uses the term "Other" to refer not only to the alterity of América, but also to the product of colonial assimilation—América as Europe's inverse image. In the end, Dussel seems to concede the success of modernity as totality. "Modernity dawned in 1492 and with it the myth of a special kind of sacrificial violence which eventually eclipsed whatever was non-European."[48]

The totalizing impulse of modern conquest cannot be disentangled from its concepts of subjectivity. Columbus was "the first modern man," and he epitomized the failure of the modern subject to engage the Other.[49] Against the claim, most recently espoused by Jürgen Habermas, that the "key historical events for the implantation of the principle of subjectivity are the Reformation, the Enlightenment, and the French Revolution," Dussel argues that the emergence of an "ego cogito" was grounded in the conquest of América. European philosophical tradition thus evolves from the "I conquer" to the "I think."[50]

The modern ego thus constitutes itself "not only as a subjectivity . . . that takes itself to be the center or end of history" (Eurocentrism), but also as one that "progresses" without restraints, "developing" by taking in.[51] As Jorge Luis Borges describes it, "Materialism told human beings: 'Become rich in space' . . . and humans dedicated themselves to the conquest . . . of people and territories. Thus was born the fallacy of progressivism. And as its brutal consequence, the shadow of progressivism was born. Imperialism was born."[52] To accumulate space, Borges adds, is also to amass time. Founded upon images of transcendence as linear progress, "Eurocentrism and the developmentalist fallacy are two aspects of the same world-view."[53] Developmentalism, Dussel observes, has nonetheless managed to erase its beginnings as an ontological category to reappear as a sociological one, a model that has come to define the First

World's relation to Latin America.[54] More recently, Dussel has expanded his analysis in response to the new geopolitical reality of globalized capitalism. His critique of this neocolonial situation also relies on the categories of "totality" and "the Other." It is from the totality of the one economic system—both Eurocentric and developmentalist—and its legacies inscribed in the postrevolutionary exclusions that Dussel turns back to where totality (the system) breaks: to the face-to-face.

Dussel seeks to bear witness to the presence of the Other, not only to those subsumed in the originary experience of Latin America (Native Peoples and the African slaves), but also to the subsequent others that the triumph of modernity "covered over." As Roberto Goizueta explains, this concrete starting point "allows Dussel to both preserve the transcendence of God and avoid the tendency in North Atlantic theologies to reduce transcendence to an ahistorical abstraction. The philosophical analogue of this expressly theological tendency has been the empty, ahistorical notion of Otherness and difference evident in postmodern philosophies."[55] By contextualizing Levinasian categories, Dussel offers not only a richer ground from which to ponder the complexities of promoting just relationships with human Others, but also resources for developing an ethically sound notion of divine transcendence: a matter of utmost importance for our contemporary world. For as Goizueta states it: "In an era dominated ... by capitalist economic monopolies ... the defense of human and divine transcendence is no longer a mere option; it is the principal and most urgent imperative. And that global defense can be articulated theologically only in the form of analogically-related liberation theologies which proclaim the irreducibility of both God and the person to any system. . . ."[56] Divine *and* human transcendence, the irreducibility of both God *and* the person—respect for God's otherness becomes inextricable from our respect of other creatures.

Transcendence and Liberation

Like Levinas, Dussel asserts that the Other not only signals the limits of present systems, but also opens the way beyond it. The "conversion to the Other" is the beginning of the process of liberation.[57] Dussel expands the theological import of the ethical discussion by recasting the basic narrative of liberation theology in Levinasian terms. He identifies four elements for an analysis of an ethics of liberation: totality, the Other, alienation/sin/oppression, and liberation/salvation/"going out" of the totality.[58] The ethics of liberation, he argues, begins with recognition of the dominant system as a totality. The totality is metaphorically related to the biblical allusions to Egypt, "this world" or "the flesh."[59] "The 'sin of the flesh' or the 'sin of Adam,'" he argues, is "idolatry, fetishism; it is treating the 'totality' as the ultimate, absolute totality and by so doing denying the existence of the other (Abel) and so of God (the absolute Other)."[60] To sin is to be complacent with the totality. An ethics of liberation, indeed salvation, then requires "going out" of the totality in response to the "demands of 'responsibility'" for the Other.[61]

The Other is beyond the limits of the totality. The Other is not of "this world," Dussel says. The Other, the poor person "confronting the system is the metaphysical *reality* beyond the ontological *being* of the system. As a result he or she is 'exteriority,' what is most alien to the system as a totality. . . ."[62] The Other is not "a mode of comprehension; but a mode of incomprehension," a "nothing in my world," for if it could be comprehended "it would no longer be 'the Other.'"[63] Although "the poor" is "exteriority," she appears *in* the system. Politically, Dussel explains, victims are the effect of "the system." Every system produces victims, either intentionally or by the sheer fact of the limited capacity of any finite system. Given that the system claims to comprehend all, the recognition that there are victims—people whose needs the system does not satisfy—reveals the limits of the system. The victim's existence is a "negation" of the system's representation of itself as an all-encompassing structure. Thus the victim's exclusion *is* his/her "exteriority" or transcendence, Dussel argues.

Interpreting "the Other" in terms of Levinas's concept of exteriority, Dussel asserts that "the exteriority of the person is grounded in the exteriority, or transcendence, of God as its condition of possibility."[64] The transcendence of the excluded person is grounded in divine transcendence. This link is described in terms of the exteriority of both God and the excluded person. The poor are not intrinsically Other, to be sure, but in relation to the system, which denies their whole human existence and admits them only as the objects that the system intends them to be. Those who are excluded from the system are, like God, "exteriority."

The special relationship between God and the excluded implies that God's revelation in the system takes place in that which is "other than the system, the poor."[65] "He or she is the 'locus' of God's epiphany in those who are non-system. . . ."[66] This is the significance of the image of Moses facing a burning bush in the midst of the desert: it epitomizes for Dussel the face-to-face.[67] The Other beyond sight interpolates the self, like God in the burning bush. The Other calls the self to see (and thus move) beyond the boundaries of the system, which requires openness to a surplus of meaning in common reality, like that represented by the burning bush. Only thus can there be a possibility for welcoming what is beyond in the finite existence of the human Other.

An ethics of liberation is thus turned toward the "*exteriority* of the other (the creator, Christ, the poor person)." It affirms "as its first premise the absolute priority of the poor person ... in whom we encounter, as an absolute challenge and responsibility, Christ, a poor person who is God himself."[68] The encounters with these *others*—the creator, Christ, the poor—are interwoven; responsibility toward the poor is not a secondary response to the encounter with God, but its primary moment. The ethical response to the Other cannot be disjoined from the faithful response to God.

The inextricability of the divine and the human characterizes also all theological language and ritual. In contrast to radical orthodoxy's descriptions of liturgy, where liturgical symbols were said to "leap over the stage of signification," Dussell describes the liturgy as an example of entanglement of all human encounters with God in the complex matrix of creaturely life. Eucharistic liturgy is "always at the same time a religious act and an *economic* act," Dussel asserts, following the notable conversion narrative of Bartolomé de las Casas. "The Eucharistic bread is *at the same time* the 'substance of the Eucharistic offering' and the 'fruit of common labor, exchanged among those who produce it.'" Since the bread is "'the objectivized life of the worker,'" the eucharistic liturgical act "is always at the same time a religious act and an economic act." The ritual is directly related to the practices of economic exchange with those whose work makes possible the celebration of the Eucharist through the production of the bread and wine as well as with the earth from which those fruits derive. Thus, the reverent participation in the Eucharist presupposes a concern for justice.[69]

Exteriority

The metaphor of exteriority helps both Levinas and Dussel name the link between divine transcendence and ethical responsibility—a connection that Dussel makes more explicit by elaborating on the founding of the metaphorical exteriority of the Other on the (assumed) exteriority of God.[70] In the previous chapters we discussed the problems entailed in the identification of divine transcendence with God's separation from the world. Dussel's connection is thus based on a theological premise that we have already called into question. We shall take note of that difficulty. However, here I focus on the implications of the metaphor of exteriority for interhuman difference.

In the discussion of Levinas's model I observed that for him the exteriority of the Other is linked to the sociopolitical exclusion of the stranger, the destitute, or the proletarian. Although foregrounding the relationship between transcendence and exclusion is crucial for examining the ethical implications of this notion, I noted that the spatial connotations of the term "exteriority" may lead us to imagine transcendence simply as a function of fixed spatial location. This static view occludes the dynamism of transcendence implicit in the idea of infinity or infinition, and may mask its transformative aim. Exteriority places the emphasis on separation rather than relation. In addition to evoking a static transcendence, the identification may cast a transcendental aura on social location. There is a risk in equating categories of otherness with transcendence, instead of attending to the ways in which those categories are produced by the system.

Because of his attention to historical context, Dussel is attentive to links between "the system" and the exclusion of the Other. Although he follows Levinas's strategy of identifying exteriority (and thus transcendence) with exclusion—indeed making that connection more explicit—Dussel's liberationist perspective uncovers additional limitations that result from defining transcendence in terms of exteriority. The image of external transcendence works only within a structure defined by the system/victim dyad. As Dussel moves on to imagine liberation, as we shall see, the metaphor of exteriority becomes less helpful for asserting the transcendence of the human Other.

Dussel is troubled by the seemingly abstract nature of Levinas's Other and about the possible naturalization of the Other as victim. Defining the Other as victim can easily become part of the system's objectification of the Other.[71] In his absolute otherness, Levinas's Other produces an undeniable shock in the totality, but there seems to be no other role for him. Time seems to freeze in the primal scene of the face-to-face encounter. In light of this danger, "in liberation theology the Other of the discourse of Levinas was given a face, a name and a surname, together with a refusal to accept its own destiny," as Marcella Althaus-Reid puts it.[72] To give a name, a surname, and a place to Levinas's Other, Dussel looks at the conquest of America as the paradigmatic moment of modernity and a crucial example of the failure to face the other as Other. Yet, an ethics of liberation cannot be content with focusing exclusively on the moment a person or system encounters the Other as victim. It would also pursue the hope of transformation. Dussel finds Levinas's work limiting in this respect. He complains that for Levinas, the Other who "presents himself as absolutely

Other, is in the end equivocal, absolutely incomprehensible, incommunicable, irretrievable, cannot be liberated (saved). The poor provokes, but in the end is always poor, miserable."[73] The subject of liberation refuses this position as destiny.

In order to overcome the passivity of Levinas's Other, Dussel modifies his depiction of the Other through a Thomist move. Elaborating on the possibilities of human speech about the ineffable God, Thomas Aquinas suggested that discourse about God can only be analogical. That is, because God's infinity cannot possibly be contained in finite human concepts, what we say about God shall not be assumed to correspond "univocally" to God: the appropriateness of our concepts to different worldly realities cannot be directly applied to God. My friend can be said to be good in the same sense as my sister is, but when we apply that term to God, its meaning exceeds all that we can possibly imagine. This does not mean that there is no relation between my sister's goodness and God's: that the meaning of the attribute is "equivocal" when applied to God. The Christian affirmation of God as creator and sustainer of the world entails a relationship between God and creatures. However, that relationship cannot be expressed directly, but only "analogically."

Dussel borrows from Aquinas's work for his proposal of a discourse about the relationship with the human Other that is infused by apophatic principles. "It is necessary to understand the other as other (and not absolutely other), not equivocal but analogical," Dussel proposes. The Other should be imagined neither as "univocal as a thing in the Totality of my world," nor as "equivocal as the absolutely exterior either." Interhuman difference is thus described as inexhaustible, rather than absolute, in a promising move that opens the possibility for conceiving the relationship with the Other in ways that avoid the illusion that one can grasp fully the Other in univocal representations and the fatalism of denying the possibility of relating to the Other.

Totality, the Other, and the Critic

The possibility of a consistent apophatic anthropology is undermined in Dussel's formulation when he represents it as a condition that shall be surpassed. "'The Other' possesses the exteriority proper of the *persona* (in Greek, *face*)," Dussel explains, and therefore, "when it reveals itself it is *still* not adequately comprehensible." Rather than an inherent characteristic of human beings, this statement suggests that the inadequacy of the system or its categories to comprehend the Other is something that will change "in time, by living together in commitment to solidarity."[74]

To be sure, all that Dussel wants to assert is that communication becomes possible, just as Aquinas insists that we can and must talk about God. However, an anthropological vision that expounds interhuman transcendence must avoid the implication that any person can ever be fully represented by concepts or categories, that the Other will ever be "adequately comprehensible." Communicating with the Other, like speaking about God, does not entail overcoming an initial inadequacy. Quite to the contrary, the illusion of overcoming the limits of our language and concepts can obstruct ethical relationships by leading a subject to impose her own constructs on the Other, lapsing into the tendency to construe the Other as an object of knowledge and representation, and repeating the imperialist tendencies to appropriate the Other for the constitution of the self.

The dangers of unwittingly appropriating the Other that arise from overconfidence in our own representations affect even those people who are genuinely committed to emancipation. Dussel's account of his own position as an ethical subject is exemplary of the difficulties that liberationist discourses must grapple with—difficulties that Levinas's thought helps us recognize. The perspective of Dussel's representations slips ambivalently from that of a *subject* faced by the Other to the voice of *the Other* in the totality. Dussel argues that philosophers may perform the role of the prophet: "the unequivocal man," "he who announces the new revealed in alterity."[75] But Dussel also imagines the subject taking the position of the Other. "When I discover myself as Other of every Other . . . ,"[76] he remarks. This generalization is perhaps unavoidable, but it may lead to change the focus from my own responsibility to the Other to my entitlement. The direction of Dussel's critique turns from exhorting us to open ourselves to Other to proclaiming himself as Other, which leads him to startling conclusions. "When that moment comes, at the limit, in which one *wants* to abandon totality, to *constitute oneself* as an Other, and does not collaborate with totality, war begins."[77] The problem with this statement is that encountering transcendence in the face of the Other is not the same as attempting to liberate *oneself*, initiating a movement out of the totality, rescuing oneself from the constraints of the totality by one's own will. By claiming that an "I" can discover her/himself as "Other," Dussel treats "self" and "Other" as reversible positions, accessible for the self to occupy them or not. The singularity of the Other is here compromised.

Dussel's description of a liberation ethics reveals yet another instance of this difficulty. He argues that liberation ethics "subsumes" the assessments of the great critics of modernity, because whereas the latter challenge the elements of domination within modernity, liberation ethics can also defend "the universality of reason as such, and especially ethical-critical reason, to which nothing is immune. But it can also defend the universality of life, of corporeality, etc., in a greater complexity."[78] This is possible, Dussel argues, because, in contrast with the ethics of discourse (Apel, Habermas) and the "postmodern irrationalisms," liberation ethics "can situate itself *outside, against or transcendentally* [in the Levinasian sense] in relation to the current system." Paralleling the account of the movement of the "subject" in "abandoning" the totality to constitute itself as Other, Dussel claims that liberation ethics "adopts *as its own* the alterity of the victims, of the subjugated ones." It adopts "the exteriority of the excluded as its critical position, deconstructing the 'hegemonic validity' of the system, now discovered as dominating: capitalism, sexism, racism, etc."[79] If liberation ethics can "situate itself in the *alterity* of the system," it is because it "know[s] how to adopt the perspective of the victims."[80]

To learn from the Other, to welcome the challenge to transcend the limits of one's previous position by facing another person as the Other is indeed the aspiration of the ethical subject. However, the language of "*adopting* the other's alterity" suggests a logic of appropriation that we must guard against. If anyone could adopt as one's *own* the alterity of the Other, would she or he not erase said alterity? In her critique of Dussel's work, Ofelia Schutte argues that in it "'alterity' ceases to refer to an otherness or a difference" which lies "behond absolute knowledge."[81] Rather than accomplishing the critical goal of keeping "the circle of knowledge from closing itself off . . . in the form of an absolute knowing," the Other becomes a source of authority. In Dussel's depiction, "alterity" "comes to designate the ground of a new absolute, but one constructed in the name of the poor, the exploited, and the oppressed," Schutte contends.[82]

Rather than comprising an exceptional mistake, the slippages in Dussel's work—between calling for openness to the irreducible alterity of the Other and assuming the Other's identity—exemplify intrinsic risks with which liberation thought must grapple. The complexity of these slippages into (a transcendent) self-authorization is made poignant when they threaten even a discourse that adopts otherness as its point of departure. The temptation of self-authorization found in ethical discourses of otherness is not unlike the draw that threatens so many theologies of divine transcendence: to construe divine transcendence as a foundation for absolute certainty rather than as the very negation of the possibility of ever attaining total knowledge of the divine.

The philosophies of Levinas and Dussel offer invaluable resources to ward off the common temptations that would undermine the ethical goals that they set forth. Liberation thought must question Levinas's assumption of the need for asserting the asymmetry in the self-Other relation, as Dussel convincingly argues. However, that does not imply that we may ignore the irreversibility of the relation. Quite to the contrary, Levinas's insistence on the irreversibility of our relation to the Other may help us avoid losing sight of our own limits. The principle of the irreversibility of the self-Other relation, we have said, is a way of asserting that one cannot give to oneself the transcendence that is made possible in relation to the Other. Transcendence is produced in the relation with the Other. Through the transformations of the self, it will always be the self—it will not be her/his Other. I face the Other as an "I." This subject is best conceived as a subject in process, more congruent with Ellacuría's model of constitutive relationality than with Levinas's self-sufficient I/same. And yet, no matter how welcoming of the Other, I cannot possibly accomplish a clean departure from the totality, erase my own complicity within "the system," fully understanding and conquering my own determinations. As Spivak articulates the problem, "We too run the risk of effacing the 'native' and stepping forth as 'the real Caliban'": the monstrous slave in William Shakespeare's *The Tempest*, frequently used as a literary metaphor for the Other.[83] Indeed, "claiming to *be* Caliban legitimizes the very individualism that we must persistently attempt to undermine from within."[84] As critics we find ourselves standing ambivalently between a totality we denounce and an Other whom we may represent—as if attempting to call attention to a boundary that seems, at times, to disappear within our own selves. At these moments, a notion of the irreducibility of the human Other becomes crucial.

This is not to say that one cannot profess allegiance to another person or groups, or that there should never be attempts made to understand or represent the perspectives and demands of other persons or groups. As I argue in chapter 5, such strategies are not only unavoidable, they are politically important. The images of otherness thus produced are part of our own systems of analysis, however. The transcendence of the Other is never fully present to me, even in the best of representations. Modernity/colonialism can be seen as a moment in the history of the effacement of the transcendence of the human person. But if the conquest of America opened the way to modernity by appropriating the bodies and cultures of América's peoples, postmodernity brings its own postcolonial modes of appropriation—its own "*postcolonial reason*."[85]

The difficulties in Dussel's model of a liberative encounter with the Other disclose serious deficiencies intrinsic to the use of the metaphors of exteriority for models of transcendence. Dussel follows Levinas's identification of transcendence with exteriority and thus its association with sociopolitical exclusion—the otherness of the Other is his/her subordination. However, liberation thought must look beyond assertions of an absolute separation between the self and the excluded Other in order to envision liberation. Evidently, a struggle for liberation entails working against exclusion. Having identified exclusion with transcendence, eliminating sociopolitical exclusion ends up implying the need to eliminate interhuman transcendence as well. Who would want to protect transcendence if it depended on exclusion? Dussel's reliance on the metaphor of exteriority, which evokes images of fixed spatial locations, is perhaps at the root of this dilemma. For spatial metaphors lead to a notion of transcendence imagined as a function of location, physical or social, and clear boundaries, bringing back the very ideas of extrinsic transcendence that these models of interhuman transcendence are attempting to overcome.[86]

A model of interhuman transcendence shall avoid the images of clear and fixed boundaries between self and Other as well as the illusions of fully assimilating the Other into any conceptual category or social role. Dussel's assessment of the need to move beyond Levinas's model in understanding the other as Other and not as absolutely Other is thus indispensable. The apophatic insights of Aquinas with respect to analogy adopted by Dussel shall be allowed to infuse this model of human otherness as thoroughly as all God-talk. This model must emphasize the need to thematize the concrete realities by which the Other is excluded—the "modes of encounter" between self and Other, as Sarah Ahmed puts it. And from the exploration of encounters, constantly return to apophasis. A model of transcendence that affirms the rootedness of all creation in the ineffable God, the analogical nature of its images, and the infinition of the relationship to the Other, moves beyond the notion of exteriority.

TRANSCENDENCE IN-BETWEEN: U.S. HISPANIC THEOLOGY

In an attempt to chart a postcolonial pathway for theology, it is crucial to keep in mind the subtle but consequential difference between defining transcendence as a characteristic or location, and as a 0product of relations between irreducibly different beings. The in-finity of human beings springs from the intrinsic relationship between God and all creation. Creatures are thus always already in relation to transcendence: the infinite in the finite, the more in the less. But why associate this infinity with any-thing absolute, whether absolutely Other or absolutely exterior? Is this tendency not a side effect of the very notion of otherworldly transcen-dence that both Levinas and Dussel are attempting to subvert?

Although Levinas's Other is prior to the self, and puts the self into question, his account of the face-to-face encounter tends to allow us to forget the constitution of the other as Other and the implication of the self in that very constitution. By relying exclusively on a dyadic construal of self and Other, Levinas's exposition allows us to lose sight of the com-plex (and potentially infinite) relations that make possible, mediate, and emerge out of each and every encounter. Dussel's account, on the other hand, brings to the fore the implication of the self in the constitution of the Other as stranger. However, because he relies on an interpretation of transcendence as exteriority, he has difficulties providing us with a model for asserting the irreducibility of the Other that is not based on his/her exclusion.

U.S. Hispanic theology is inherently linked to Latin American libera-tion movements and to their fundamental attempt to develop a theology where God-talk is inseparable from the encounter with the human Other, especially the oppressed. Like Dussel, U.S. Hispanic theologies understand themselves as speaking from the place of the Other. Rather than speaking as an I/same seeking to articulate how it can possibly encounter its Other, U.S. Hispanic theology understands itself as the speaking Other. For this reason, U.S. Hispanic theology is particularly susceptible to some of the dangers I identified in the discussion of Dus-sel's construction of the Other.

There are, however, important differences between the U.S. Hispanics' self-understanding and that of Latin American liberation philosophy and theology. The main focus of U.S. Hispanic theology is not the peoples physically outside the geopolitical centers of power, but the marginalized subjects within it. The totality it is mainly concerned with is the United States, but it is from within the United States that they engage the question of the Other. Their complex position in relation to both the United States and Latin America, to the present U.S. sociopolitical realities as well as to the past colonial experiences, lead U.S. Hispanics to thoroughly relational, complex, and open constructions of identity and subjectivity. These con-structions of subjectivity fruitfully problematize the model of face-to-face encounter. They suggest possibilities for developing alternate models that maintain the attention to the concrete, particular Other, while accounting for the complexities and ambiguities of those encounters.

U.S. Hispanic theology is, by definition, a theology of the Others *within* the territory of hegemonic power, of the Others *within* the same. It is not surprising, then, that in U.S. Hispanic theology otherness is not described through metaphors of spatial exteriority. I am not suggesting that Dussel literalizes exteriority, but only calling attention to the significant differences in imagery that emerge from a different context. U.S. Hispanic theology's theorization of the encounter between a dominant system and its Other relies on an understanding of the other as Other, not absolutely Other.

Boldly identifying the challenges that the position of U.S. Hispanics as others within the center of power entails, Fernando Segovia has advocated the development of a theology of "otherness and mixture," a hermeneutics of "otherness and engagement."[87] Segovia distinguishes between two uses of "the Other:" a pejorative one that refers to the image imposed on others, and a positive one that arises "when the other is allowed to surface and describe itself as the other."[88] The first one—which he keeps in quotation marks—alludes to a function within the system, where U.S. Hispanics are strangers or aliens, "the undesirable 'others,' the ones who do not fit."[89] The second use of Other attempts to account for the challenge that comes from beyond the system's epistemological limits. This distinction is crucial. Segovia proposes a development of a theology "ultimately and radically grounded in our profound sense of otherness," one that does not "eschew otherness and alienation,"[90] while simultaneously taking measure of its own history of mixture and the ethical implications of that history. The conjunction of otherness and mixture is based on an acknowledgment and embrace of U.S. Hispanic otherness as irreducibly mixed, "mestiza." Such self-understanding, along with a commitment to freedom, life, dignity, and the struggle to "make a home under the democratic principles of the nation," Segovia argues, "provide us with an identity that recognizes the others but *refuses to define them*."[91] Segovia is thus attentive to the fact that otherness is generated within the "system," while also highlighting the heterogeneity and ineffability of those who bear the marks of otherness. He conceives differences as irreducible, not absolute.

U.S. Hispanic theology thus takes as its point of departure a complex and ambiguous concept: *mestizaje/mulatez*. This leads to an intrinsically multiple and relational understanding of identity.[92] Originally coined to describe (and categorize) the genetic mixture of Spanish colonizers with the indigenous peoples and with African slaves, respectively, the terms have been redeployed catachrestically to embrace the constant intermixing from which "Hispanics" emerged as a principle that defines their identity. That is, mestizaje/mulatez in contemporary Latina/o discourses not only embraces the complex and ambiguous product of a colonial past but attempts to redeploy it as a critical tool for rethinking identity in/as mixture. Choosing mestizaje/mulatez as privileged metaphors for the articulation of identity implies that the singularity of an individual person becomes unthinkable outside a network of relations—socio-political as much as familial—that extends spatially through continents and temporarily through generations.[93] In Latina/o theology's use of mestizaje/mulatez, scholars propose a subjectivity formed by an affinity (to invoke John Milbank's term) that is nevertheless marked by the ambiguities of human history.

A model of identity that takes mestizaje/mulatez as its main metaphor links the subject, and thus the self-Other encounter, to the history of encounters from which it emerges. As I mentioned before, Levinas's failure to elucidate the sociopolitical specificities that mark a person as the excluded Other may lead to the interpretation of otherness as a characteristic of that person rather than as the historical product of modes of encounter. Dussel's account, on the other hand, brings to the fore the history of exclusion that has produced the power dynamics that organize today's world, but tends to downplay the effects of the totality in constituting the subjects, especially those who, like himself, profess alliance to the excluded Others. In contrast, an articulation of otherness in relation to mestizaje/mulatez calls for a model where the encounter with the poor, the stranger, the migrant, or the Latina/o is not represented as a self-contained event, but as one that reopens past encounters and future possibilities. In the words of Ahmed, "What is required is a hospitality that *remembers* the encounters that are already implicated in such names (including the name of 'the stranger'), and how they affect the movement and 'arrival' of others, in a way which opens out the possibility of these names being moved *from*."[94] As it opens itself to the multiple ramifications—past, present, and future—this model of encounter recognizes that it is in the particularity of a single encounter that we are called to respond.

In addition to attending to the historical dimension of subjectivity, U.S. Hispanic theologians emphasize the relational nature of subjects, a trait that leads to an anthropology turned to the outside, to Others. Like Ellacuría, Goizueta grounds this assertion of the "more" of human existence in God's intracosmic transcendence. "The assertion that personal identity is intrinsically relational," Goizueta explains, is "the corollary of a sacramental worldview which asserts that the identity of every concrete, particular entity is relational."[95] In this worldview, the cosmos is "an intrinsically relational reality" where "each member is necessarily related to every other member."[96]

Each subject mirrors the cosmos by being also an "intrinsically relational reality": the human person is a subject-in-community. Community preexists and is constitutive of the individual, regardless of choice.[97] Therefore, Goizueta explains, a relational anthropology implies that "[t]he option for the poor"—the paradigmatic encounter with the Other for liberation theologians—is not simply an act of will. It is "*an active recognition of that which we already are through no choice of our own.*"[98] As for Levinas, the encounter of the Other reveals to the subject the priority of the Other. In opting for the poor, the subject realizes itself as always already in relation to others. Through these complex relations with otherness the otherness of God is mediated to humans. Because the ethical response to the Other is conceived as a welcome into one's community, Goizueta adds, it is place-specific and entails the development of affective bonds.[99]

The intensely relational anthropologies developed by U.S. Hispanic theologians highlight the irreducibility of a person to the apparent contours of her/his body and thus problematize the image of the face-to-face as an encounter between self-contained entities. It affirms that persons are "more than they appear" (Pickstock). Indeed, when subjects are envisioned as always already in relation to multiple others, the scene of an encounter between two persons begins to reveal previously hidden complexities.[100]

OPENINGS FOR TRANSCENDENCE AS INFINITION

The notion of intracosmic transcendence conceived as the outcome of the creation's rootedness in the divine as its inexhaustible source of life and novelty serves as the basis for the theological notion of interhuman transcendence that this chapter begins to set forth. Interhuman transcendence implies interhuman difference. Yet a model where otherness is not equated with separation, but may be found in mixture, where the common is what surprises, where encounters extend far beyond present, and where the finite transcends without breaking off, I suggest, is best described using the metaphor of infinity. Thus defined, transcendence may evoke a sense of incompleteness and excess, rather than exteriority. Others are conceived as irreducibly Other, instead of absolutely Other.

Such interpretation may help deter any claim to complete comprehension of God or the human Other. An apophatic anthropology is indeed needed. However, the need of such anthropology is not the result of the absolute exteriority of the Other, but of the complex and infinite relationality of creatures—who are intrinsically divine. The notion of infinity, we have indicated, is neither abstract nor otherworldly, but openness at the heart of relation, *infinition* rather than exteriority, relation rather than separation. Modifying Levinas's definition, I want to propose the following axiom: *Transcendence designates a relation with a reality irreducibly different from my own reality, without this difference destroying this relation and without the relation destroying this difference.*

A model of transcendence based on infinity rather than just exteriority entails a model of subjectivity different than the one Levinas assumes. This is a subjectivity turned outward, always already called to respond beyond the boundaries of the self—a subjectivity responsible to that which is "non-encompassable within the totality and as primordial as the totality."[101] A theology of interhuman transcendence incorporates Levinas's insight to define subjectivity in terms of "welcoming the other, as hospitality,"[102] but does not follow him in defining a subject as "a *separated being* fixed in its identity, the same, the I." Instead subjectivity is described as constituted in relation, always unfinished: produced in relation to the transcendence of the Other.

Following Dussel, we will seek a model of transcendence that is attentive to the concrete sociopolitical significance of otherness. Taking infinity as our main metaphor of transcendence, however, we attempt to offer a model that emphasizes the in-finite openness and singularity of the other person, within the particularity and complexity of her/his context. Our aim to open ourselves to transcendence in the face of the Other leads us to give special attention to our relationships with those who are marginalized in our communities or simply excluded from them, not because we define transcendence as sociopolitical exclusion, but because we recognize exclusion as an effect of having ignored the transcendence of the Other. This notion of relational transcendence should not extract transcendence from the finitude of the person (imagining it as something outside or disguised behind "mere presences"). Instead it will seek to affirm the "presence" of the "infinite in the finite, the more in the less."

CHAPTER 5

Transcendence in the Flesh of the Other[1]

They were held in peace, one inside the other, one in the shelter of the
    other, by means of a moment of immortality.
This was their marriage before the lions and the clouds. And before the
    car. . . .
This quarter of an hour lasted an entire lifetime. They returned, sliding
    softly into the car. A birth occurred.
The stable was in the car. And time around them was held still and
    silent like the Singular night.
At that moment they were each the other's newborn. . . . And both
    thought it right that for ox and for ass they had a lion and a
    lioness. . . .
The car was a stable.
                 Hélène Cixous, Manna: For the Mandelstams for the Mandelas[2]

T he setting of this nativity scene is South Africa. One inside the other,
one in the shelter of the other, on a *Singular night,* the characters
mediate each other's new birth. A man and a woman become mediators
of divine incarnation, agents of a carnal transcendence bringing forth
rebirth. "By passing through the face, they entered smoothly into the
warm breast of the inner future."[3] This "space" where they both enter—
"the warm breast of the inner future"—may we think of it as the space of
transcendence? As in the Christian narratives of Jesus' birth, nativity
takes *place:* in a welcoming stable, before the lions and the clouds. The
place was a South Africa crisscrossed by the ethical demands of ethnic
conflict. The place of the encounter is the site of its complication: where
singularity opens up to multiplicity. The peacefulness of this encounter
is soon interrupted. "That day, two hundred and thirty people were
arrested. . . . And those arrested were waiting for Nelson Mandela to
come and *wed them all.* . . ."[4]

Nativity, rebirth, and transformation are for Luce Irigaray, not unlike
Hélène Cixous, the fruits of transcendence: transcendence in the flesh
and in the cosmos. An incarnate transcendence is encountered not just
in the *face,* but in the *flesh* of the Other. Lured not only by the demands
of responsibility toward the Other, but also by desire for the (sexual)
Other, these encounters are touched by wonder. From the face-to-face
we move toward body-to-body encounters. A transcendence imagined
in terms of a relation to heights, exteriority, and straightforwardness is

here challenged by a different spatio-temporality traced by the sinuous contours of bodies and by the rhythms of embodied existence.

Considering the body in the ethical relation entails much more than the addition of a special case to Levinas's interhuman encounter; it unsettles boundaries and twists the organizing hierarchy on which the spatiality of the face-to-face rests. Levinas sets apart the sexual encounter and ultimately opposes ethics to eroticism. This is a common dichotomy that threatens Levinas's critical reformulation of transcendence. Luce Irigaray's interrogation of the role that Levinas assigns to the feminine in the production of transcendence will help us uncover the implicit gendering of Levinas's transcendence. Her reading of Levinas's *Totality and Infinity* not only exposes the problem but also opens his proposal toward the possibility of an "ethics of sexual difference."

After a brief synopsis of Irigaray's assessment of classic philosophical notions of transcendence, this chapter traces the move from Levinas's face-to-face to Irigaray's body-to-body encounter and its effect on the spatio-temporal imaginary of transcendence. It explores the interpenetration of transcendence in the flesh and between persons as well as its broader cosmic dimensions. This broadness requires, paradoxically, greater singularity. The work of Chicana scholars Gloria Anzaldúa and Cherríe Moraga allow us to move beyond Irigaray's images of the body, to see the body in the singularity of its multiple differences and limitations.

DISEMBODIED TRANSCENDENCES

Philosophers have rightly recognized their need for transcendence as a basis for the becoming of subjectivity, both as an external limit to their subjectivity, and as a telos for their intentionality.[5] These philosophers, Irigaray reminds us, "were men and they were debating between men. Their solution was, of course, a masculine one."[6] As we know, they conceived the journey toward transcendence as entailing the overcoming of their own bodies—indeed, of material nature as such—which they viewed as constraints to freedom. They projected these constraints onto women, and posited a God as the "opposite pole of their instincts and natural inclinations." God would be their external limit and the objective toward which their intentions could be guided.[7] They proposed: "The subject develops between . . . two extremes: nature and God, nature and spirit, mother-nature and father-Logos, irreducible birth and absolute creation."[8] An imaginary rift is thus opened between nature and God, which in turn divides nature from spirit, and birth from creation.

God was their Other, perhaps their only transcendent Other, for the masculinist culture ignored the transcendence of the body, of bodies, of the cosmos. Thus, Irigaray calls us to turn back to the relation between the sexes for a carnal ethics—an ethics of the passions.[9] "Transcendence is no longer ecstasy, going out of the self toward the inaccessible, extra-sensible, extra-earthly entirely-other."[10] But this does not entail expounding a plane of "pure immanence." Rather than choosing one side of the cosmological divide opened by the philosophers' transcendence, an ethics of the passions interrogates its assumptions. What is needed is a model for the relations between nature and God, nature and spirit, flesh and transcendence, which allows spirit to touch the most intimate spaces of life.

LEVINAS'S EROS

Irigaray's most sustained discussion of her notion of relational transcendence unfolds in the context of her response to Levinas's *Totality and Infinity*, and so we shall return to his depiction of interhuman transcendence in order to encounter Irigaray's difference.[11] As we have seen, in *Totality and Infinity*, Levinas takes us back to the singular encounter of the self with the Other (whom I will never be) to reinscribe responsibility at the core of subjectivity. On the basis of such an understanding of responsible subjectivity he poses the question of transcendence—one that does not bypass the human Other, but is encountered in "his" face. Levinas thinks of transcendence as the "welcoming of the other by the same, of the Other by me," "a relation with a reality infinitely distant from my own reality, yet without this distance destroying this relation and without this relation destroying this distance."[12] This metaphysical relation established between the self and the Other is based neither on knowledge nor on a dynamics of revelation, but on desire. Indeed, "Transcendence is *desire*."[13] Metaphysical desire is strictly opposed to the needs of the body, which, like hunger, are satisfied by the incorporation of the desired object into the self. Metaphysical desire "desires beyond everything that can simply complete it"; it does not aim at appropriation or consumption, nor even consummation.[14] I have already argued that this interpretation of the relation of transcendence in terms of desire is a promising move toward a relational transcendence, where the irreducibility of difference is not in conflict with desire, and where desire does not seek the elimination of difference.

But before we get too excited by his description of metaphysical desire, we should note that Levinas sets it apart from Eros—in a move that reveals his desire to be less sexy than sexist. Levinas does ponder the ethical import of the sexual relation between man and woman, at least for a moment, but ultimately Eros fails his test of transcendence. Eros, he argues, like physical needs, seeks satisfaction; it *returns to itself.* For Levinas, ethics does not return; transcendence is always an outward movement, without cycles.[15] However, cycles are intrinsic to the temporality of nature, to the life of the body; a purely linear transcendence is famously prone to leave the flesh behind. Admittedly, this abstract, progressive impulse is not the transcendence that Levinas seeks in the face-to-face encounter. Nonetheless, a common patriarchal anxiety about the workings of bodies seems to haunt his encounter with the erotic. He concludes: "The metaphysical event of transcendence—the welcome of the Other, hospitality—Desire and language—is not accomplished as love."[16] So love is relegated to the nether side of transcendence.

Indeed, Levinas's account of the sexual encounter is doomed from the start, for the feminine has already been given a role: the beloved is frailty, tenderness, vulnerability, irresponsible animality, infancy, equivocation.[17] Transcendence is not accomplished as love, except when love engenders the son. It is paternity that saves love, furnishing a transcendence that becomes incarnate among men—made possible by, but foreclosed to women. Woman here is only womb, an immanence from which transcendence has been plucked. In Levinas's work, the promise of a philosophy of transcendence in the finite is thwarted by replicating the immanence/ transcendence divide within the created realm—across sexual difference. The assumed chasm between God and creation of common conceptions of transcendence is displaced, but not its undergirding logic: the gendered structure comprising a transcending man and an immanent woman. In consequence, a rift opens also between justice and passion, between responsibility and love.[18]

Commenting on the Song of Songs, Levinas writes, "Perhaps justice is founded on the *mastery* of passion." Not only does Levinas reinstate the dichotomy between justice and passion—oddly, while reading the Song of Songs—but his description of the logic of this mastery also bears eerie resemblances to a well-known structure of subjection of the Other on which the dominating one nonetheless depends. "The justice through which the world subsists is founded on the most *equivocal* order, but on the *domination* exerted at every moment over this order, or this disorder. This order, equivocal *par excellence,* is precisely the order of the erotic, the realm of the sexual."[19] (Let me say in passing that it seems hardly irrelevant that one could use that same sentence to describe patriarchal or imperial logics: Patriarchy [or colonialism] is founded on women [or the colonized], more specifically on the domination exerted at every moment over them.) The reference to an "equivocal order" is revealing, for Levinas specifies in a different context that "equivocation constitutes the epiphany of the feminine."[20] Levinas adds, "Justice would be possible only if it triumphs over this equivocalness."[21] Mastery and domination over the erotic—what kind of justice could this found?

This advocacy of mastery over the erotic seems to be yet another instance of those discourses, to which Irigaray alludes, that imagine transcendence as a journey from nature to God, from body to spirit, from an irreducible birth to an absolute creation—from Eros to justice. The status of the face becomes uncertain. Is it still possible, as Levinas attempts, to prevent the body from becoming detached from its words? Would word and face-as-flesh not fall on different sides of the chasm thus opened?

In his early works, Dussel identified Levinas's portrayal of the relation between man and woman as one of the problematic aspects of Levinas's work that a liberation ethics would need to challenge.[22] Dussel applied Levinas's categories—"Totality" and "the Other"—to analyze phallocentrism. Dussel states: "The phallic ego establishes a world totality and defines the woman as a passive object, as non-I, nonphallus, or as the castrated one. The masculine Totality assigns her the lot of someone dominated and reduced to nonbeing."[23] He argued that the "liberation of women would need to begin by rethinking the essence of Eros."[24] Referring to the *Song of Songs,* Dussel proposes an Eros that privileges "hearing, justice, tactility, and contact," where sexual encounter is also the "recognition of the justice of the other as other."[25] When it comes to the concrete definition of sexual ethics, however, Dussel aligns himself with patriarchal and heterosexual morality, surprisingly confining (transcendence of?) sexuality to procreation—a position that, according to Schutte, he nonetheless has promised to revise.[26]

For Levinas, on the journey toward transcendence Eros can only give us, or more accurately, can only give *him*, the "son"—along with an ethical relation "primordially enacted in conversation." This discourse, Levinas makes clear, is not love.[27] Is this privilege of the spoken word not a typical—though by no means a necessary—assumption of those called by a biblical tradition that proclaims a beginning by the word? The avowal of the primacy of word has a complex history in Western philosophy, and yet the theological resonances of Levinas's "word" are not accidental. Levinas himself casts his account of the encounter in biblical language. "A turning on the basis of the face of the Other, in which, at the very heart of the phenomenon, in its very light, a surplus of signification is signified that could be designated as *glory*. It demands me, requires me, summons me. Should we not call this demand or this interpellation or this summons to responsibility the *word of God*?"[28] Levinas's phenomenological account is linked to the Jewish tradition, where God's transcendence is referred to as glory and to the law as the word of God. This statement offers valuable resources for the constructive proposal regarding the doctrine of God to be presented in chapter 7. However, both glory and word will need to be rethought in their relation to Eros and flesh, open to the surplus of love. Levinas never takes that step. For him, the face presents itself—it is seen and it is heard, it expresses itself visibly and/or audibly, across an infinite separation. Light and sound travel through the divide between the self and the Other in ethical relation. In Levinas's depiction of the relation, light and sound reach out across the gap and touch the eyes and the eardrums of the subject—an approach of waves-to-skin, but never of skin-to-skin.

IN THE BEGINNING: TOUCH

The dichotomy between ethics and the erotic in Levinas's thought is certainly related to his problematic depictions of the feminine, but is not limited to that issue. The spatio-temporality of transcendence in Levinas's imaginary—its heights, exteriority, and straightforwardness—presupposes the exclusion of eroticism. It cannot quite accommodate encounters between bodies, where one is inside the other, where one embraces the other.

A model of transcendence in the flesh calls for other ways to conceive of the bonds between human beings. Like Levinas, Irigaray locates transcendence in the encounter with the Other. However, for her what protects the otherness of the Other is not separation, as it is for Levinas. "*Approaching* involves an irreducible *distancing*, which lies, insurmountable, in the drawing near to one another." The distance that Irigaray imagines here, in contrast with Levinas's separation, defies common intuition; it is insurmountable in touch. It is a figuration of irreducible difference, rather than absolute separation. This difference is an "elusive mystery"—akin to glory—necessary "in order that desire *unfold* toward a blossoming."[29] This elusive mystery welcomes touch; it envelops bodies, within and without.

"Lovers' faces live not only in the face but in the whole body," Irigaray reminds Levinas.[30] The encounter between lovers does not fit the model of two planes facing each other—two facades, as it were—that the Levinasian account evokes (and Dussel adopts), where the Other's transcendence is always exterior. The erotic encounter demands an imaginary that can accommodate bodily transcendence and its rhythms: bodies in touch and within each other, one inside the other, one in the shelter of the other. Irigaray finds a metaphor for this spatiality in our own beginnings in the womb, in that intimacy of a shared membrane, contact between self and Other, before the word. That place, where we were welcomed before our offerings of any welcome, is the site of identification between mother and child as well as of differentiation between the two. *In the beginning was touch.*

The place of initial welcome, however, is no longer there; it does not call us back to it, to perform a regressive move like the ones that Levinas (like most masculinist thought) fears.[31] Touch draws our attention to our beginning in the womb, awakening us to the memories of its primordial caress inscribed in the flesh. In fidelity to that memory of the flesh, subjectivity can be reconceived as welcome and opening to a "birth that has never taken place"—for both man and woman. "Sensual pleasure can reopen and reverse" the control-and-consumption-oriented approaches to the world and to the Other. Placing welcome, rather than grasp or assimilation, at the heart of becoming, the caress suggests an infinite empathy that abides "by the outlines of the other."[32] The caress retraces the borders of the Other. Neither totemic verticality nor one-dimensional separation describes the space between lovers. That space is traced by the contours of bodies.

Drawing near and unfolding—this movement traces a complex spatio-temporality where Eros "touches upon" transcendence. This space is multidimensional, and the flow through it involves cycles and returns as much as forward movement. The morphology of whole bodies challenges the privilege of the phallic imaginary. The caress of the Other summons us to recall the intimacy of a primordial communion that gives birth to difference. "Caressing me, he bids me neither to disappear nor to forget, but to rememorate the place where, for me, the most secret life holds itself in reserve. . . . Plunging me back into the maternal womb and beyond that conception, awakening me to another birth," again and again.[33] The erotic encounter thus opens the possibility of a new birth, in which transcendence takes place.

Transcendence is not achieved through a linear, straightforward development.[34] Like cosmic life, transcendence takes place through cycles of repetitions that bring forth new births, through remembrances which instantiate new possibilities. Transcendence repeats, and brings about the new. Eros and the transcendence it mediates do take flesh. Transcendence is for Irigaray neither deferral nor consummation, but a new outcome of the encounter mediated by Eros: new conception, rebirth, regeneration. Indeed, Irigaray challenges Levinas's deferrals for always maintaining the separation from "the other in the experience of love."[35] Levinas admits no time for returns and no space for communion. In his Ethics, there is only desire, not love. The lovers never enter the place where "the perception of being two persons become indistinct"; they never access the "energy produced together" to be born again. Levinas turns toward "a future where no day is named for the encounter with the other in an embodied love," Irigaray observes.[36] As the actual encounter is deferred, love evades the responsibility of transcendence. Ethics is excluded from the realm of actual sexual relations. Perhaps, as Spivak asserts, "The hardest lesson is the impossible intimacy of the ethical."[37]

TRANSCENDENCE AS SEXUAL DIFFERENCE

This account of interhuman transcendence privileges the difference between man and woman. All other transformative encounters, distant or intimate, seem to be excluded. The place of new births appears to be open only to sexual couples. Is the energy for transcendence absent from other encounters? "Who or what the other is, I never know," Irigaray admits. "But," she adds, "this unknowable other is that which differs sexually from me. This feeling of wonder, surprise, and astonishment in the face of the unknowable ought to be returned to its proper place: the realm of sexual difference."[38] Can there be, however, a "proper place" for wonder and astonishment; can we set rules for surprise?

The status of the sexual pair in Irigaray's work is the subject of much scholarly debate, for Irigaray frequently appears to be subverting the sexual hierarchy while leaving its heterosexist assumptions in place. Levinas's depiction of the sexual encounter follows the patriarchal gendering: he imagines a male (active) lover in relation to a female (passive, settled) beloved. In contrast, Irigaray introduces other characters to the sexual encounter scene: the female lover and the male beloved. This approach seems to open the possibility for resisting heterosexist assumptions. Troublingly, however, Irigaray does claim that "[p]leasure between the same sex does not result in that im-mediate ecstasy between the other and myself."[39] Why would she want to impose limits to the possibilities of sexual experiences?

A Levinasian move might be at play here. Like Levinas, Irigaray wants to guard ethics from a logic of substitution. The Other and the self are not interchangeable. As we have already seen, Levinas says not only "that the same goes unto the other differently than the other unto the same," but that it is impossible "to place oneself outside of the correlation between the same and other."[40] I cannot take the place of the Other or include her within the boundaries of the self; the Other presents himself. I approach the Other only as myself, with all the constraints that implies. Levinas attempts to assure that directionality through the asymmetry of relation: the Other is the poor whom I cannot approach with empty hands. The relation is irreversible. The Other is the destitute one to whom I must respond. While it subverts the predominant social hierarchy by asserting the priority of the destitute person, it raises other ethical concerns: in his framework, the Other is always in the position of victim. This is, as we saw in the previous chapter, Dussel's contention against Levinas: "The poor provokes, but in the end is always poor, miserable."[41] This logic entails an unsurpassable hierarchical relation, even when its values are reversed. Indeed, Irigaray contends that in Levinas's work there is no "recognition of," or "interaction between, two different subjectivities."[42]

Like Levinas, Irigaray wants to guard against substitution. She does so by asserting not the asymmetry of the relation to the Other, but the irreversibility of sexual difference. She locates the relational boundary not between the propertied and the poor or between the citizen and the stranger, but between man and woman. She says, "I will never be in a man's place, never will a man be in mine. Whatever identifications are possible, one will never exactly occupy the place of the other—they are irreducible one to the other."[43] Although this move avoids the implicit hierarchy of Levinas's asymmetry, it still leads her to similar problems: the boundaries of otherness are structurally set. "The confused and changing multiplicity of the other . . . begins to resolve itself into a system of intelligible relationships," to quote Irigaray's own comments regarding Plato's *Hysteria*.

WOMAN, MAN, AND THE THIRD

Irigaray's strategy reifies and indeed transcendentalizes sexual difference, Amy Hollywood argues.[44] At some points Irigaray does invite this reading—and, as we have seen, John Milbank uses it to reinstate in her name the notion of woman-as-settled, the very image that Irigaray attempts to subvert.[45] But this male-female dualism is, at least potentially, destabilized when Irigaray's sexual pair is grounded in the other relations in which she envisions it. This pair is not one! The man-and-woman is always in relation to "the third"—a concrete reality beyond the sexual pair. This third is not, to be sure, an extramundane or extratemporal reality that would submit both man and woman to its immaterial law. After all, we know that the dominant man ultimately slips into the position of such a god, proclaiming the supposed precepts of eternal and immaterial essences. If the third seems to liberate man and woman from the potential tyranny of the dyadic structure, it is not by escaping materiality, but by signaling the multiple relationalities inherent in men and women. The third relates both man and woman to their potential as well as to their own limits: "to the divine, to death, to the social, to the cosmic," or better, to the cosmic *as* material, social, and divine—a formulation that this work interprets theologically.[46]

To conceive these cosmic relations entails imagining space differently. An ethics of the passions requires a reconception of place, as Irigaray announces in the introduction to *An Ethics of Sexual Difference*.[47] Traditionally, woman has been the place for man—the settled one in relation to nomadic men, as Milbank puts it. "Women are more settled, subtle, particular and beautiful," he claims, as indicated before.[48] She has been his envelope. Without her own place, woman is only his object. His world turns her into a seductive and threatening thing, into a container whose engulfment has been the source of innumerable male fantasies. If there is no third, she or he would become "all-powerful."[49] This myth provokes violent reactions: he attempts to contain her in his places which, unlike the womb, are neither alive nor open. No wonder woman appears to Milbank as the settled one. Man has constructed a world where she has no place of her own; she has no third. At the same time, as a man's thing, without her own place in the world, woman has no access to transcendence. She becomes reduced to the immanent ground of his transcendence. If she is *his* place, how could she offer welcome to the Other? For her to receive the Other, for man and woman to welcome each other, each must have his and her own space.

A COSMIC PLACE

Each woman and each man must have her and his own place to enter a common space of the erotic encounter—to enter and to emerge from it. If the relation between the sexes is to bring forth new births, if it will open the flesh to transcendence, it must, quite literally, take place. Incarnation, Christianity has taught us, needs its stable, the ass and ox or lion and lioness, the clouds or the star. Indeed, the "*work* of the flesh is never unconnected" from the world and the universe;[50] it needs the energies of bodies and cosmos, but it also produces energies that contribute to its transformation, to the cosmos' continuous creation. Furthermore, as irreducibly relational, the work of the flesh—incarnation, transcendence-as-incarnation—is never without limits. It is always transcendence-within, becoming within the constraints and promises of embodied existence—never dislodged from it.

A common place in which the self and the Other would enter is not part of Levinas's depiction of the ethical encounter.[51] Indeed, posing a space that could contain both self and the Other would for him amount to creating a totality. For Irigaray, however, the cosmos is never a closed totality, but a living ground.[52] The cosmos does not lead back to sameness. It is not "pure immanence," but quite to the contrary, the site of transcendence in flesh. Yet masculinist cultures have denied their "debt toward that which gives and renews life," just as they have foreclosed the body and the womb.[53] They have reduced the cosmos to a closed totality, as a once-and-for-all product of creation.[54] Believing that it is "given once and for all, to be exploited endlessly, carelessly, irretrievably," human beings have also ignored the transcendence of the cosmos. In this reduction of creation to the "merely immanent," we have also abandoned our own responsibility as mediators of creation, as agents of its transcendence. We have forgotten our own role in the becoming of the cosmos as well as God's concern for it.[55]

As mediators of the becoming of the cosmos, human beings meet the transcendence, not only of the sexual Other, but also of the whole creation. Indeed, the demise of the transcendence of the natural world is most frequently inextricable from the implicit relegation of ethnic Others to sameness, to "immanence." Irigaray does not explore these connections. The role of providing support for man's flight to the heights of ethics, of transcendence, is not exclusively assigned to women. This mechanism is the guiding principle of contemporary geopolitics and capitalist globalization. For example, the Others of the "South" are increasingly confined to a closed space, to the role of supplying the material resources, indeed being the material resources, for satiating the desires and setting free the First World—not accidentally conceived as spatially higher. The South is conceived as being the place from which the North departs to pursue its own transcendence. In these encounters with the Others of the Third World, the cosmos continues to appear as given, once and forever, for incessant exploitation. How do we think of our encounters with the Third World in light of transcendence of the flesh and of the cosmos? It seems crucial, indeed urgent, to find a model of encountering these Others of the Third World—sexually different, but not only—where each is invited to enter a place and have a place, a cosmic dwelling.

In addition to the place into which man and woman enter, and a place for each one, there must be a space between them. "Desire can eat up place." U.S. desire has been consuming the cosmos, eating up place. Similarly, sexual desires may drive attempts to consume the Other. The subsistence of the couple and the desire that unites them thus depends on the protection of the space between them. This distance, introduced above, is neither static nor abyssal, but a dynamic interval subtended "toward and into infinity" by Godself. "The *irreducible*. Opening up the universe . . ."[56] May we imagine God as the living and dynamic fluid envelope that both links—within and throughout—and protects the space between, the sap that subtends the space of difference and thus opens creatures to a relational infinity that is transformed as a result of the relations across differences?

The relation between sexual difference and cosmological unity–multiplicity opens the space for a theological interpretation of the erotic relation. Rather than extracting the sexual pair from their relations to the cosmos, the social, and the divine, might "the third" link them to the multiple complexities of their existence? As a site of incarnation that participates in and contributes to the continuous creation of the cosmos, the erotic encounter may be imagined as an instance in the infinite web of relations across differences that constitute a living creation.

THE SOCIAL BODY

A model of relational transcendence requires attention to the social relations of each of the persons in the sexual relation. It cannot stay in the interstices of sexual difference, for the space between self and Other is hardly a simple frontier.[57]

Touch between sexually differentiated bodies provides us a key figure for the simultaneity of desire and transcendence, and a much-needed supplement to the Levinasian face-to-face. We have seen that the encounter between bodies opens up a more complex spatio-temporality and a richer ground for this model of relational transcendence. Yet an exclusive reliance on the sexual pair as the site of this bodily transcendence is at risk of exiling man-and-woman from their other relations, from the broader (social) world. Abstracting the sexual pair from the irreducible relationality of life might be another version of the otherworldly tendencies of transcendence.

Otherness is multiple in its singularity. The Other is always already implicated in infinitely complex relations: sexual relations are always also political, ethnic, and economic relations. The transcendence of the Other might thus be imagined as that infinite relationality that appears to us at the present time, in this particular encounter, but that extends beyond it, in time as well as in space. For the differences encountered at any given time—as differences that emerge from relations, from other encounters—also extend beyond this moment and the boundaries of sexual difference. The call of other Others is never merely exterior to the relation between the sexes. Other encounters fold into the sexual relation, and sexual relations unfold into the maze of sociopolitical affairs.

Each singular encounter unfurls to an irreducible multiplicity; a singular night opens up to history, and a stable to a whole country. I have already indicated that for Irigaray the work of the flesh is never unrelated to the universe. I want to underscore that the work of the flesh is never unrelated to other persons. Even inside the maternal womb, before conception and differentiation, the traces of the multiple relations that bring forth mother and child subsist. In *This Sex Which Is Not One*, Irigaray turns to female morphology—"*neither one nor two*"; a nearness that does not long for becoming one—to provide an alternative vision for overcoming the phallic economy of the one: "The *one* form, of the individual, of the (male) sexual organ, of the proper name, of the proper meaning."[58] But she never pursues the potential of this multiplicity for a rearticulation of differences along racial/ethnic/cultural axes.[59]

The multiple relations (and their markers) that constitute the person are of particular interest for feminists of color, as our experiences of racial/ethnic marginalization are inextricable from our experiences of the body. For instance, the work of Chicana scholars Gloria Anzaldúa and Cherríe Moraga may be read as attempting to uncover the transcending potential of the sexual relation and the power of touch to bring about new births. Their conceptualization of the sexual is, however, always already also racial/ethnic.

Anzaldúa's use of the term "mestizaje"—which we considered in the previous chapter—illustrates the intertwining of race/ethnicity and sexuality in a single body, a body which is not one. Literally, "mestizaje" refers to the product of the sexual encounters between persons of different races, particularly between European and indigenous people. Chicana scholars have nonetheless used it to refer to the myriad of relations-across-difference that constitute the self—not only the "racial" mixture associated with Latina "identity," but also other social relations that impinge upon and become inextricable from the self. Thus, in Anzaldúa's work, "mestizaje" refers not only to the relation between the Indian mother and the Spanish father, but also to the relation between the Mexican and the Anglo-American elements of her identity. The multiplicity is, to be sure, riddled with ambiguities. This complexity within the self resembles Irigaray's characterization of female sexuality. In their intimate relationship, the different elements of the mestiza are *"neither one nor two."*[60] Furthermore, mestizaje extends the boundaries of the body toward the social body. The body is inscribed by the multiple relations from which it emerges—at birth and beyond. "Pero es difícil differentiating between lo heredado, lo adquirido, lo impuesto"—Anzaldúa ponders, "just what did she inherit from her ancestors? . . . which is the baggage from the Indian mother, which is the baggage from the Spanish father . . . ?"[61] The sociopolitical becomes flesh; it is incarnate in/as sexed bodies. As we saw, Irigaray reminds Levinas that "Lovers' faces live not only in the face but in the whole body."[62] Anzaldúa and Moraga would add that the lovers' bodies live not only within their individual bodies but in the whole sociopolitical body.

Significantly, Irigaray's phrase "memory of the flesh" evoked for me a myriad of carnal reminders that Irigaray never considers: skin color, the texture of hair, the scars on the skin, one's body type—markers of racial difference. Moraga's explicit thematization of the social production of desire and its inscriptions on bodies leads her to more complex and conflictive descriptions of the erotic than those Irigaray offers. Moraga may, like Irigaray, imagine a sex which is not one. But writing from the conflicted space of racial and sexual wars, Moraga represents the social constitution of bodies through figures of multiple, but also partial or wounded forms of embodiment. For instance, a woman's skin appears as the site of memories of the touch of the maternal dwelling, but also of painful and guilt-ridden separation. Her light skin is a sign of her distancing from her brown mother and thus a reminder of her complicity with a racist society. Her skin is a "scar sealing up a woman," she writes. But, from another perspective, Moraga is brown. Her skin is "darkened" by her desire of women—Moraga's sex, she observes, is "brown."[63] "By incorporating pain, difficulty, and failure in the re-imagining of a sexual and social world, [Moraga] represents a non-redemptive vision that obliges the reader or spectator to account for the conflictive social and cultural contexts providing the arena for sexual experience."[64] She imagines bodies that are not-yet-whole, portrayed in her plays as dismembered bodies. These disjointed bodies dramatize the internal wars that afflict them and their yearning to be reborn as one—or at least as a multiplicity capable of lovingly touching itself. For these bodies, the promise of caressing their own multiplicity (as Irigaray's woman does) is yet to be fulfilled.

The lover's flesh remembers. It bears the marks of histories of wonder and pain—even beyond the womb; its individual histories, in its relation to others' histories, mark the skin touching and being touched. They make possible (or foreclose) erotic desire. An account of transcendence in the flesh would need to acknowledge the transformative power of these wounded bodies, whose memories also open the self toward unforeseeable becomings, toward incarnate transcendence.[65]

I proposed in the previous chapter that transcendence is a relation with a reality irreducibly different from my own reality. Irigaray invites us to imagine this irreducible difference as an elusive mystery in the whole body of the Other. The Other is not merely one who summons and judges, but incites feelings of wonder, that preserves the difference necessary for the unfolding of desire. Erotic pleasure and intimacy are returned to the realm of ethics. Interhuman transcendence takes place in the singularity of each encounter. This interhuman transcendence, we have said, is grounded in God's intracosmic transcendence. In this chapter, this idea is given a concrete interpretation. Interhuman transcendence *takes place* —at singular moments in history. Transcendence requires a stable, in a particular place. Interhuman transcendence takes place in the flesh and in the cosmos—a cosmos that is not closed, but always open toward transcendence. This participation in the cosmic universe liberates the ethical relation from the potential tyranny of the dyadic structure—observable in Levinas's account of responsibility in terms of the mastery of the Other. Both self and Other have their own space from which they may welcome the Other.

Touched by feminists of color, the transcendence in the flesh brings forth more incarnate complexities. As we touch one another, we are in touch with a multitude. To account for this requires yet another step in our reconceptualization of the interhuman encounter and of the body. We need to ponder the links between the individual body and the sociopolitical body, between the single encounter and histories of communal encounters which may lead us toward a more inclusive theological articulation of the cosmic as material, social, and divine. To this we now turn.

CHAPTER 6

Transcendence of Planetary Creatures

I am looking for América
I fear not finding it.
Its traces have gotten lost in the darkness.
. . .
I look for you
and I can't find you.
No one knows where your tortured body can be found.
. . .
I am looking for you, América
I am calling you, América.
                    —*Rubén Blades, "Buscando América"* [1]

I track meticulously the dimension of meaning in my great-great-grandmother as chattel: the meaning of money; the power of consumerist
world views, the deaths of those we label the unassertive and the inefficient. I try to imagine where and who she would be today. I am engaged
in a long-term project of tracking his [Austin Miller's] words—through
his letters and opinions—and those of his sons who were also lawyers
and judges, of finding *the shape described by her absence* in all this.
    I see her shape and his hand in the vast networking of our society,
and in the evils and oversights that plague our lives and laws. The control he had over her body. The force he was in her life, in the shape of
my life today. The power he exercised in the choice to breed her or not.
The choice to breed slaves in his image, to choose her mate and be the
mate. In his attempt to own what no man can own, the habit of his
power and the absence of her choice.
    I look for her shape and his hand.
                    —*Patricia Williams* [2]

Looking for the traces of a lost América, tracking the shape of the
absence of a great-great-grandmother, the writers of these epigraphs
hope to encounter an Other—and be transformed. The Others that they
desire have long disappeared. Neither the lost América nor the dead
great-great-grandmother can any longer be met face-to-face or body-to-
body. And yet both have been there, with Blades and Williams, calling
them even before their births. They are perhaps also among us, calling us
still today. But these are specific calls, felt viscerally by members of particular communities—sensed as the call of the Other beyond the present
time who is nonetheless intimately related to their present lives.

    The relationships with these no-longer-living Others are thus quite dif-
ferent from the body-to-body encounters that we explored in the previous
chapter. And yet, the elusive presence of Others beyond the present opens

for us yet another way into the complexities of interhuman relations. These other Others further complicate our account of transcendence in the flesh of the Other. Their appearance highlights the need to ponder the relations between individual bodies and the social bodies—alluded to in the previous chapter—as well as relations between the past and the present as they affect interhuman encounters. We are challenged to consider, for instance, the relationship between the tortured body of América and the bodies of Latin Americans whom we encounter—as "strangers" or "foreigners"—face-to-face. We are also challenged to grapple with the presence of the ghosts of the past—of enslaved great-grandmothers and their masters, who even today haunt the encounters between dark and light faces in the United States. We are called to take notice of their ghostly presence "in the vast networking of our society." How can we imagine the interhuman encounter if our own selves are, perhaps, never free from the ghostly presences of Others? Can the absent presences of other Others still touch us? Is there still a time and a place for their transcendence?

In this chapter I explore the effects of the presence of other Others in any encounter between self and Other and its significance for the notion of relational transcendence. Our engagement with interhuman transcendence has led us from Levinas's image of a face-to-face encounter, where self and Other come in contact through discourse, to that of a body-to-body encounter across sexual difference where transcendence is mediated by Eros. In this chapter I continue to explore the interhuman encounter as a site of intracosmic transcendence. This time, however, I inquire into the emergence of and the relation of each subject, of each body, to multiple Others. I now focus on the relations of subjects with their past (their historicity) and with other Others. As if looking through wide-angle lenses, I try to see each face and each body in the web of relations in which persons become—a web that extends beyond our range of vision, through the world, and throughout history. Individual bodies appear as part of social bodies.

Reimagining encounters as historical and contextual, a multiply relational model of transcendence-within acknowledges and grapples with the multiplicity within the radical singularity of each person as well as with the multiplicity of relations between subjects. These relations give a concrete meaning to Levinas's proposal that we encounter the infinite in the finite. But this attention to the historical and contextual constitution of our ideas about self and Other implicates us in the analyses. We are no longer abstract ethical agents, but subjects within the very systems we attempt to challenge. That is, this model highlights our own limitations as ethical subjects—the difficulties of encountering the other as Other. It also brings to the fore our implication in the lives of those not-yet-living Others, who will share the social worlds that we help build, and the cosmic place that we co-create. If ethical encounters involve more than what is readily visible here and now, ethical behavior demands a constant work of learning and unlearning as preparation for the coming of the Other.

Engaging the work of Gayatri Chakravorty Spivak, this chapter begins with a consideration of postcolonial theory's analysis of the processes of self-definition of subjects in colonial encounters and their relation to the production of categories of difference. These analyses lead us to consider apparent difficulties in the association of transcendence with otherness. If categories like woman, man, the poor one, the stranger, and so on are products of sociopolitical conflicts and antagonistically defined exclusionary practices, would we want to claim that it is precisely in our relations across differences that transcendence manifests itself? What is the relation between differences produced in sociopolitical contests for power and transcendence? How is our image of the interhuman encounter affected when the historicity of differences is considered?

Spivak's frequent, if elusive, references to "the wholly Other" suggest a reliance of postcolonial ethics on interhuman transcendence, which I trace. However, to get to the heart of these insights for a model of relational transcendence, we need to inquire into metaphysical assumptions implicit in Spivak's work. What notions of subjectivity support the kinds of relations that Spivak is calling for? What are the metaphysical concepts in which those notions are grounded?

ENCOUNTERS IN (POSTCOLONIAL) HISTORY

Patricia Williams, calling attention to the persistent effects of a past history of slavery in present U.S. society, testifies: "I see her shape and his hand in the vast networking of our society," in "our lives and laws." Chicana scholars, I have already indicated, analyze their colonial past as a present reality embodied in their mestiza bodies. Moreover, today's "immigrants"—or illegal "aliens"—to "our" country trace their history back to "our" soil, to our history. Each of their identities—their faces and their bodies—is inseparable from other histories, including those histories that exclude them. However, our accounts of the encounter with the Other frequently occlude the complex historicity of relations that these stories reveal. We tend to represent the encounter with the Other as a pure origin. Yet each encounter between a self and her/his Other is a unique moment in a chain of encounters that constitute subjects, societies, and the world. Subjects and collectivities emerge from, and thus are always already in relation to, their Others.

The interhuman encounters depicted by Luce Irigaray and Emmanuel Levinas, considered in the previous chapters, take place in the here and now. The subject was imagined facing the alterity of the Other, while the complex web of social relations in which each subject participates and to which she or he contributes seemed to recede into the background. Although both Levinas and Irigaray hint at the presence of "a third" in each encounter—either as cosmic (Irigaray), or the third person (Levinas)[3]—their main focus is on the present encounter between two persons, and the transcendence that it opens toward the future.

We recall that Levinas defined his project as a turn "from the experience of totality back to a situation where totality breaks up, a situation that conditions the totality itself."[4] In the totality, Levinas observed, subjects are reduced to instances of preestablished concepts, and Others are approached as objects to be appropriated for the constitution of the self. Totalities fail to encounter the other as Other. Thus, we heard Levinas argue that we must turn from the totality to "the gleam of exteriority or of transcendence" in the face of the Other.[5] But how can we overcome totalizing tendencies to appropriate the Other? How can we liberate our very account of the interhuman encounter, indeed our experiences of it, from the logic of the system and its concepts? Derrida summarizes Levinas's proposition: "Categories must be missing for the other not to be overlooked."[6] But how are we to accomplish this?

When we encounter the Other, the process of representation has already begun. We arrive too late. The Other has already been repeatedly encountered, named, and represented, and so have we. We have indeed emerged from those encounters, namings, and representations. Our first glance at the Other is already tainted by endless denials, appropriations, and erasures. We know, or think we know, who the Other is and what she looks like—even if we realize we shouldn't. We "recognize" her face. We "know" the color of the poor person's face, or the accent of the stranger's voice. We are confident we can identify which sex is not ours. The poor, the stranger, and the woman are no longer alien to us; there is a place in our "world" for them; there is a category and a designated space for "aliens." And yet do we not also feel wonder, surprise, and astonishment? Whether we imagine ourselves as subjects in a position to welcome the Other, or as others calling to be welcomed, our lives are—we intuit, and fear, even while denying it—interrelated with that of the Other. In short, we encounter the Other in this fallen world, the world of the totality. But there is always more than we see or know, deny that we see or know. Something escapes our grasp—the concept, the name, the system— something that transcends us. An elusive mystery glows in the bodies of Others. The Other still calls us, as if from beyond.

How then are we to respond to the other as Other when categories are already in place? How can we welcome her/him when the very term "Other," indeed our systems of recognition and languages, are always already implicated in the appropriation of the Other? Unlearning the tendency to look at the Other as an image of ourselves or as something derived from ourselves: what kind of preparation does this demand?

Certainly we cannot purge ourselves from the markings that history has left in us. Such an attempt would be not only impossible but dangerous, for it would allow us to claim the purity of our concepts and close the door to critique. It would amount to claiming that we have transcended-*out*— that we have liberated ourselves from our world and its influences. To pre-pare ourselves to welcome the Other requires not turning away from our histories. To open ourselves to that which is yet to come demands remem-bering the past—a movement that retains as it moves forward.

Within the folds of history—with all its sociopolitical shortcomings— postcolonial theory seeks to transform "the present into an expanded and ex-centric site of experience and empowerment."[7] Postcolonial theory tries not to forget the complex history of our relations to Others in order to respond to their call. Resisting the illusions of leaping out of the pres-ent or the inherited past, it seeks to "touch the future from its hither side."[8] Postcolonial theory has sought to subvert the legacy of imperialism by bringing to the fore the historical production of those very differences that would then be deemed as the "natural" justifications of colonialisms and their aftermath. Like Levinas, Dussel, and Irigaray, postcolonial critics find that the lives of those Others who have suffered the sentence of his-tory lead them to situations in which totality breaks up. But the works of postcolonial critics seek to uncover the production of such differences and thus to "intervene in those discourses . . . that attempt to give a hegemonic 'normality' to the uneven development and the differential, often disad-vantaged, histories of nations, races, communities, peoples."[9] Postcolonial theory thus calls us to re-link interhuman differences to their history; it encourages us to see today's encounters in their relationships to other encounters, with other people, at other places and times.

This enquiry into the history of the differences that appear to us as normal is part of our ethical responsibility. The critic "must attempt to fully realize, and take responsibility for, the unspoken, unrepresented past that haunts the historical present," Bhabha explains.[10] A broad interrelationality necessarily implies a depth in time. The past haunts the present—our past and the Other's past, pasts that might already link us to one another. We might already be complicit in the exclusion of the Other—in his/her "condition of being a stranger, destitute, or proletarian."[11] Furthermore, attention to the broad interrelationality of differences encourages us to take responsibility for, and to seek to transform, the conditions that allow the Other to appear as a stranger—sociopolitical systems, and their legitimizing myths, images, and concepts that inhabit and inhibit our societies as well as our very selves.

THE SOCIAL PRODUCTION OF OTHERNESS: WORLDING AND FORECLOSURE

Don't conspire with oblivion,
Tear down the silence.
. . .
Call my name

—*Marjorie Agosín, "La desaparecida"*

Subjects, communities, and nations define themselves and evolve through processes of identification with and/or differentiation from other persons, groups, and nations. Through these processes of self-definition, communities establish their boundaries and thus define who is to be considered an insider and who is considered a foreigner, a stranger, the Other. Attending to these processes of self-constitution in contexts of sociopolitical marginalization has led theorists from a wide range of disciplines to uncover the mutual imbrications between the self-definition of dominant subjects and their images of otherness.

For instance, in her foundational challenge of patriarchy, Simone de Beauvoir observed that woman is confined to the category of Other, defined as relative to man, inessential, incidental. Toni Morrison explores the role of the African presence—"decidedly not American, decidedly other"—in the self-definition of the United States.[12] Walter Mignolo has written extensively on the role of América in the definition of Spain as European.[13] Edward Said's groundbreaking work uncovered the intrinsic relation between the Orient and the West in the Western imaginary, policy, and scholarship.[14] For these thinkers, the Other is not independent from, but rather a necessary product of the systems of representation intended to justify the exclusion of some people and the privilege of others by making their differences appear as "normal."

These analyses have profound implications for the model of relational transcendence that we have been developing. The apparently independent terms "self" and "Other" on which we have thus far relied begin to reveal ambiguous complications that we must yet consider, lest our adoption of such language results in misleading, if not downright oppression-legitimizing, representations of interhuman transcendence. Before addressing this issue constructively, we shall examine this problematic in more detail.

As we have already seen, the adoption of the image of "stranger" in contemporary appeals to welcome the Other may lead to the problematic assumption that strangeness is an intrinsic characteristic of some persons. The figure of the stranger "is an *effect* of the processes that imagine 'it' can either be taken in or expelled" from a given community. It is, in other words, intrinsic to a community's self-definition. The strangeness that we "see" in another person is thus a function of our own historicity and that of our communities—a crucial part of our self-identity.[15] Setting up the traits that identify a person as an American, for instance, is dependent on the processes of defining the country's others. Furthermore, "his condition of being a stranger, destitute, or proletarian" may have everything to do with the fact that "I" am not.[16] The exclusion of the Other may be partly related to the fact that "I" am accepted or included. The fact that I may imagine myself as a subject is implicit in the fact that "I" see her/him as "the Other."

This seemingly self-evident interdependency of constructions of self and Other is frequently forgotten. As we have seen, some critics argue that Levinas's proposal colludes with this forgetting. As we continue to use categories to name ourselves and others, these categories tend to appear as natural, as if they were characteristics innate to persons or to the world we live in—as if they were external to ourselves. Thus names, descriptions, and values become inscribed in the world and its inhabitants; they become the way in which we perceive, experience, and react to the world around us. Certain people become strangers; not only do we identify them as such, but we develop social, political, and economic structures in which they are defined as strangers. Similarly, through our repeated use of signifiers like "Third World," for instance, we inscribe categories of difference in the world and then allow ourselves to forget the range of forces that went into their production. Spivak calls these processes "worlding," the practices through which sociopolitical configurations of the world are constructed and inscribed (as if) on the earth.[17] The continuous use of labels of difference allows us to forget their worlding.

Contemporary geopolitical realities are still marked by the worlding produced in and through colonial encounters. That worlding affects our perceptions of ourselves, Others, and the contexts we share. Our recognition of each other and of ourselves is influenced by parameters set by a long and complex process of worlding. Therefore, to unsettle the effects of normalcy produced by a long history of colonialist worlding, we must take a critical look at their historicity.

Spivak, like Dussel, takes us back to the colonial encounter. She invites us to observe how both the European Man and his colonized Other emerge from past colonial encounters—the two terms are inextricable. Colonial power could only legitimize itself through the occlusion of this relationship. Although the colonized Other was needed for the constitution of the European Man, that crucial need was foreclosed. That is, the need of the Other is rejected as an incompatible idea, and our history is told as if that need for the Other had never existed at all.[18]

The "expulsion of others from the definition of 'Man'"—and the deaths of those expelled, those whom we label unassertive and inefficient—repeats itself through (post)modernity.[19] The excluding moves of imperial self-definition, "in various guises, still inhabit and inhibit our attempts to overcome the limitations imposed on us by the newest division of the world."[20] Thus, to produce "a counternarrative that will make visible the foreclosure" of the Other in the past is a step in the preparation to encounter the Other today.

Spivak offers a variety of such counternarratives. She guides us through the British invention of India, but also through the invention of a variety of Others on both sides of the (post)colonial divide. The scenes of foreclosure multiply. Spivak recounts the foreclosure of economic value produced by the Third World from the chronicles of the First World's capitalist growth and development. "To the extent that, as the North continues ostensibly to 'aid' the South—as formerly imperialism 'civilized' the New World—the South's crucial assistance to the North in keeping up its resource-hungry lifestyle is forever *foreclosed*," she argues."[21] Spivak similarly calls attention to the exclusion of native women from nationalist discourses; the "First World" woman's appropriation of the "Third World" woman in the interest of self-constitution; the objectification of the native for the self-constitution of migrant elites (and the postcolonial critic); the humanist critic's appropriation of the colonial subaltern for its own scholarly self-definition. The list goes on.

Attending to these multiple axes of expulsion, appropriation, and foreclosure makes visible complex relations that our worlding tends to occlude. First, it calls attention to the oppressive structures within subaltern communities, systems of exclusion and marginalization disguised under our broad divisions of the world: New and Old World, First and Third World, North and South. While these divisions generally and forcefully define the directionality of the flow of goods and power, the fissures created by other exclusions cut through both sides, forming complex patterns of separation and complicity, visible and invisible currents of goods, power, and desire. Power and relations are more complex than our categories of analysis suggest.

Second, and most significant for our model of the self-Other encounter, uncovering the processes of foreclosure in power relations brings to the fore the dependence of enfranchised subjects on their Others. The processes of identification and othering through which our communities emerge mark the very subjectivity of those of us striving to respond to the call of the Other. Not only are the material effects of our histories of colonial and economic exploitation still present in current societies, but also within our selves—in our language, thoughts, and desires. To "realize and take responsibility for the unrepresented past"[22] that haunts us today implies taking a critical look at our selves.

To make the self part of that which the ethical encounter must analyze demands, however, a modification of modern notions of subjectivity. At the heart of the colonial failures to encounter Others lies an objectifying anthropology. Modernity imagined the *ego cogito* of self-identity as transparent, unaffected, autonomous. This self was assumed to be the master of his agency; he knew himself and was in control of his emotions and desires. Thus, it was supposed, his agency did not require further examination. As we become aware of the effects of communal histories in shaping our selves, we move away from that confidence in the autonomy of the subject. Indeed, our preparation to encounter the Other requires unlearning the self-enclosed *I am*. The Other puts the self in question, says Levinas. I suggest that such questioning entails not only the claim of the priority of our responsibility to welcome the Other today, but also the implication of our subjectivity in the processes of exclusion through which a person becomes a community's Other in the first place. We need to open a space for a more radical questioning of the self and of the conditions that exclude the Other.

This mutual implication of Self and Other complicates the scene of the encounter with the Other as Levinas describes it. One would need to ask, for instance, how is my own subjectivity already determined by and determining the fact that a particular person appears to me as a stranger —to be welcomed or excluded—as Other? What allows me to imagine myself approaching her or him with full hands?[23] What relations does a given account of the encounter with an Other foreclose? One would have to grapple, for example, with the dependence of the First World on the goods produced by the Third World, with the reliance of the U.S. economy on the exploitation of citizens of other countries, peoples then labeled as strangers at our borders, and with the legacy of economic advantages derived from the work of enslaved people. The narrative of approaching the Other with full hands may be simply a repetition of these patterns of appropriation and foreclosure, unless it is supplemented by a careful account of each encounter's historicity, of its worlding. We must be mindful of the fact that we arrive at each scene too late: the processes of appropriation and othering have already begun, and our encounters are not independent from them.

The mechanisms of worlding and foreclosure that we have described reveal the reliance of oppressive structures on suppressing and eventually forgetting certain relations. Imperialism, like other systems of domination, depends for its legitimization on the production of a series of opposites: the metropolitan subject/native, civilized/savage, developed/ undeveloped, and so on.[24] A common logic subtends, indeed produces, these oppositions. There is also a heterogeneity that always escapes these distinctions: subjects, groups, or nations that belong to neither side of these divides, or perhaps to both. Within imperialist discourses, however, these oppositions must appear as natural, stable, and essential. Because these oppositions are neither natural, stable, nor essential, imperial discourses perform long, repetitive attempts to cover over the links between the colonizer and the colonized, which, simultaneously, exceed the boundaries of each of the terms. In other words, colonialism must obliterate the relations between colonizers and colonized and deny heterogeneity and the singularity of subjects, arresting them under fixed categories like those of colonizer and colonized.

A constructive account of the relation between interhuman otherness and transcendence must thus take into account both the persisting effects of colonial othering and the constitutive and necessary failure of its categories to respect the singularity of the other person. Before we explore the constructive implications of these insights for this theology of relational transcendence we must examine the role of the wholly Other in Spivak's work.

THE WHOLLY OTHER AND TRANSCENDENCE

Spivak's main concern is not *divine* transcendence. The philosophical and theological weight that this concept carries probably deters Spivak from welcoming it—or any overtly religious language—into her work. However, her use of terms such as "wholly Other," "absolutely Other," and "radical alterity," to name just the most common, occupy a space that I, as one who does use religious language, associate closely with transcendence.[25]

Spivak, like Irigaray, presupposes a relationship with radical alterity in her account of the ethical encounter with the human Other. While other thinkers are uncomfortable with Irigaray's formulation of sexual difference for its apparent essentializing tendencies, Spivak argues that Irigaray "thinks sexual difference as the separation from the absolutely other"—a distance from an unknowable Other. This separation is not based on a "decisive biological fact," but is posited as "*the undecidable.*" Undecidablity, Ernesto Laclau explains, is the "condition from which no course of action necessarily follows."[26] Deconstructive strategies involve making visible the decisions that underlie a "*sedimented* set of social relations" to open a space for new decisions.[27] In Spivak's deconstructive ethics, the space of the undecidable, where differences cannot be fully known, is where subjects "must risk ethicopolitical decisions," indeed the only space where real decisions can be made.[28]

The sexual encounter takes place in the already compromised space of the political, in the midst of its conceptual assimilations. "We must . . . take the risk," Spivak explains, "of positing two universals, one radically other to the other in one crucial respect." While these two universals open a space for decisions, this shall not lock differences into predefined positions within an intelligible system. Thus, the "real universal" is not to be identified with these differences. It is instead that which must be suppressed in order for self-contained definitions to be posed, but which always solicits them, making them tremble. The "real universal," Spivak proposes, lies "on the other side of *différance.*"[29] With this statement, Spivak distinguishes between two spaces: the ethicopolitical realm where we posit universals and the realm of the "real universal," which lies on "the other side of *différance.*" There, I propose, is the "space" of transcendence in her work.

As a critical strategy Spivak's work frequently deploys "universals" in an attempt to open up existing social differentiations to ethicopolitical work. However, to keep her readers alert to the fact that these universals are not the "real universals"—that they are "on this side" of *différance*— Spivak allows these posed universals to be overtly challenged or interrupted by other universals. This second strategic step shows Spivak's resistance to aligning alterity with any preestablished category of difference—sexual, racial, political, or economic. Irigaray does not take this second step; thus, as we observed, in Irigaray's work sexual difference tends to appear as if unaffected by other differences, producing an illusion of transcendental stability.

Appreciating the challenges posed by multiple sets of universals keeps us alert to the limits of everything that we propose in the realm of sociopolitical discussions ("on this side of *différance*"). But what can we say about the other side of *différance*, which I have associated with transcendence? How does this other realm influence our ever uncertain ethicopolitical decisions? To trace Spivak's subtle and frequently merely implicit moves, I turn to the colonial scene once more, from which we can observe the interplay and distinction between sociopolitical differentiations discussed in the previous section and the figure of the wholly Other. Spivak's postcolonial-feminist analyses of the complexities of power and the difficulties and limitations of our ethical encounters help us expand the notion of interhuman transcendence toward a broader sphere of postcolonial relations.

Colonial discourses, as I have indicated, depend on suppressing the heterogeneity of the colonized Others, resolving irreducible multiplicity into a system of fixed and representable differences. It produces Man and an opposite Other whose characteristics are defined in contrasting relation to those claimed for the dominant subjects. This Other of colonial representation conceals the singularity of the human persons thus marked. However, every system of representation, no matter how successful it might be, is always haunted by the heterogeneity that it suppresses. The unrepresentable Otherness of its subjects shows through the cracks of its structures and threatens to dis-close the logic of its controlling apparatus. The Other is irreducible to any system. The Other is, Spivak provocatively insists, *wholly Other*.[30] It lies beyond, "on the other side of *différance*," transcending not only our space, but also our time.[31]

What is the relationship between Spivak's wholly Other and real people, with faces and bodies, whom we can and do meet in our daily lives? To address this controversial question we must first consider Spivak's methodology and her relation to deconstruction.[32] I begin with a word on method. Spivak's multidimensional methodological approach has led to her being (im)possibly characterized as a "feminist Marxist decon-structivist."[33] Her writing hovers between interrogating conceptual cate-gories and assumptions, and critiquing sociopolitical structures. She does not attempt, however, to provide a systematic scheme of the relation between the different scenes that she invites us to observe. "There is something like a relationship between [them]" may be as close as she gets to describing this link.[34]

Spivak's writing is intentionally interruptive. For instance, she intro-duces a particular sociopolitical situation in order to disclose its hidden relations to a philosophical definition, but also to show the limits of its conceptual universe. A narrative is introduced to interrupt the coher-ence of another framework. This accounts for much of the feeling of dis-orientation that her writing induces. This is more than the result of a confusion of "Others"—the Other of a philosophical concept and the Other of a philosophical community, for instance. Rather, these ambigu-ities, she suggests, mirror the conditions of the world in which one has to make conceptual and ethical decisions, where the social and the philo-sophical inhabit the same space. Writing, she argues, "should reflect the contradictory and overdetermined character of social and geopolitical relations rather than obscuring them."[35] If we feel confused about whether Spivak's wholly Other is a person, a thing, or a concept, it is per-haps because that uncertainty necessarily inhabits our encounters with whatever the wholly Other might be. If it can be fixed into unequivocal categories, it is no longer the wholly Other.

The wholly Other cannot be accessed directly. "[W]e cannot—no self can—reach" the wholly Other.[36] Time and again Spivak repeats her ver-sion of "Levinas' warning: the wholly Other, *le tout-autre*, cannot be selved or samed. It is not susceptible to *ipseité* or *mêmeté*. The face of the wholly-other is without a name."[37] The wholly Other cannot be assimilated within the limits of the system's structures of representation. The appro-priating moves of any system of power can never reduce all reality to a function of itself. There is always an excess that the system cannot accom-modate. The system is inescapably inadequate for the wholly Other.

Spivak's project does not end with this negative assertion—that we cannot access the wholly Other—but rather seeks to work in what she calls the affirmative mode of deconstruction. In this mode, she explains, deconstruction no longer limits itself to pointing out that each discourse is haunted by an Other that it cannot grasp—a "methodologi-cally necessary presupposition." In its affirmative mode, deconstruction deliberately blurs "the category of presupposition" and makes it "more vulnerable as 'experience.'"[38] In its affirmative mode, Spivak explains, deconstruction would not only say that there is an Other, but also utter a "call to the wholly other."[39] Philosophy thus opens itself to being affected by the Other.

We can now return to the question posed before: what is the relationship between the wholly Other and real people? This wholly Other is not to be identified with the figure of the narcissistic inverted Other produced to consolidate an authoritative self. The wholly Other is not the same as "the colonized," "the poor," or the "stranger." Such identification would imply fixing the transcendence of the Other in a category of sociopolitical systems. Reconceiving the interhuman encounter to account for the emergence of subjectivity as always already marked by historical relations precludes us from identifying transcendence with the difference with which the Other is marked. This identification is not necessarily assumed in Levinas's or Irigaray's models of transcendence, but, as we have seen, their naming of the Other as "the stranger, the foreigner" or "the Other of sexual difference" may and has led to this problematic reading.[40]

The differentiation between our categories of difference and the wholly Other has crucial ethical implications for a model of relational transcendence. I have argued that we always arrive too late to the inter-human encounter. "[T]he project of imperialism has always already his-torically refracted what might have been the *absolutely other* into a *domesticated other* that consolidates the imperialist self."[41] If we are not mindful of this historical masking of the heterogeneity of the absolutely Other and identify those domesticated images with transcendence, our encounter may collude with the imperialist project. And indeed, "It is the very kind of colonized-anthropo-logized difference the master has always happily granted his subordinates," as Trinh Minh-Ha observes.[42] Simply claiming this kind of othering as identity may even end up tran-scendentalizing certain cultural distinctions—a problem we have observed in descriptions of gender roles.

Attending to past encounters cannot bring about the resurrection of others, if that means to bring them back in full presence. Therefore, those of us who trace our history to those excluded in past colonial encounters are warned against the illusion of bringing our excluded (or even killed) ancestors back to life. We are reminded of the impossibility of representing them. Colonizer and colonized were inextricable terms. Attempts to become the Other of the imperialist self, to become the "true" native, the "real" Indian or Latina, which characterized many nationalist projects, fail to account for and problematize the relation between these categories and the definition of the colonizer's self. They rely on the assumption that one can access the Other through representation, and reappropriate her/him as a source of authentic identity and authority—an assumption that lies at the heart of the colonial project. Too many expulsions from nationalist definitions of Man have been authorized by such "resurrections." Instead of crossing over the limits of time, to be attentive to past encounters is to witness that foreclosure of an Other and, perhaps, to mourn those possibilities that died. The burial rituals of many of these others—of those Native Peoples, languages, cultures that are no more—have yet to be performed.

For Spivak, the wholly Other is ungraspable and yet somehow present in the human Other. And yet her reliance on the term "wholly"—or "absolutely"—Other tends to convey the very idea that her work so forcefully rejects: that of an otherworldly reality, completely removed from experience. I interpret Spivak's use of "the wholly Other" as a catachresis—a deliberate misuse of the term, to tap into the power of the traditional image of transcendence to turn it a different direction.[43] The aims of this work are nonetheless better served if we move away from terms that might invoke absolute separation. Still, what Spivak says of the wholly Other can be faithfully and fruitfully adapted to further develop the notion of relational transcendence. I thus adopt the insights of her analysis of the wholly Other for transcendence.

Spivak's elusive image of the wholly Other—the transcendence in the flesh of the Other—alludes to an unnamable reality which we cannot quite demonstrate, but to which many testify. It points toward that indescribable aspect of Patricia Williams's great-great-grandmother which the slaveholder, despite his power, could not own—which, indeed, "no person can own." The Other's transcendence is, I suggest, that aspect of the Other which is always beyond our grasp. That excess of the Other is not an exclusive property of some kinds of Others, nor is it a relation across definable traits of difference. And yet the Other's transcendence is never found outside the encounter with particular human beings. We shall not identify transcendence with victimization. As we explained before, we shall work to end victimization, not transcendence. However, inasmuch as the exclusion of some persons is an overt attempt to objectify them, a tacit denial of their transcendence, the manifestation of transcendence in the bodies of those excluded—the poor, the stranger, the proletarian, women, the subaltern, the queer, and so on—offers unique testimony to the deceptiveness of totalities.[44] Encountering these Others breaks the illusions created by our sociopolitical systems of providing adequate representations of everything and everyone. The Other's transcendence manifests itself most dramatically precisely where the system fails, where it cannot accomplish what it claims to do. The lives of excluded Others escape the system's most forceful attempts to fully grasp them.

Transcendence is not absence; it inhabits the system otherwise. The Other's transcendence can thus disrupt the seeming inevitability of social structures. To imagine this experience requires a peculiar mind-set, indeed a different spatiality, that allows us to think beyond straight lines and between dichotomies of accessible/inaccessible, inside/outside, continuous/discontinuous. We need to be able to picture an embrace. The image of the "deconstructive embrace" appears in one of Spivak's often fleeting elucidations of radical alterity, and yet it is especially help-ful for illustrating the peculiar mind-set for which she strives in thinking about the relation to alterity, or transcendence.

Spivak names a series of pairs that are in a "deconstructive embrace." "Justice and law, ethics and politics, gift and responsibility are structure-less structures because the first item of each pair is neither available nor unavailable."[45] The first term of each pair occupies the space of "radical alterity"—which I am arguing is the space of transcendence. The second term inhabits the realm of calculus. The relation between them is an aporia—a distance that cannot be crossed in a straight line.[46]

Ethics as incalculable and "politics as the calculus of action" are in a deconstructive embrace. Calculus is "imperative for responsible action," but "if responsible action is fully formulated or justified within the system of calculus, it cannot retain its accountability to the trace of the other"; it closes around itself.[47] The image of the embrace alludes to this peculiar relationship: justice "cannot pass in a direct line to law . . . Yet justice is dis-closed in law."[48] In other words, that which occupies the space of radical alterity becomes manifest in that which necessarily compromises it. To appropriate Levinas's words, the infinite manifests itself in the finite.

In a move that is typical of her approach to deconstruction, Spivak attempts to push this analysis beyond the limits of academic or philo-sophical discourse. She applies the figure of the "deconstructive embrace" to describe the relationship between other pairs, for example, the rela-tionship between Derrida's *arrivant* (a figure of radical alterity) and the "calculable diaspora" to which it relates; between the pre–New World "Africa" and contemporary Afro-American communities; between mar-ginalized people (or the subaltern) and the wholly Other. In their embrace, the distinction between the terms in each of these pairs should not be collapsed, but their relation is inextricable and productive.

The image of the deconstructive embrace thus suggests a relationship between the ethicopolitical realm and the realm of transcendence which avoids the identification of transcendence with sociopolitical distinctions and yet affirms their constitutive relation. Always already in relation to that which transcends them, social positions are deemed as always open to transformation. Suggesting a more complex spatiality between the finite and that which transcends it than the face-to-face, the embrace may allow us to envision each social position as embracing both its opposite finite-universals (e.g., femininity and masculinity) and, simultaneously, other competing axes of difference (e.g., sexual and ethnic). A model of relational transcendence inspired by the image of an embrace avoids imagining the other person as absolutely exterior to or unmarked by the system, or as simply contained within it. In such a model the transformation that emerges from the encounter with the Other, with all its ethical shortcomings, may and often does embrace that which is "on the other side of *différance*."

TRANSCENDENCE OF THE OTHER

The Other's transcendence should not be identified with a given quality in relation to which I can compare myself to the Other. Spivak's work helps us explore the distinction between the categories of otherness within a particular sociopolitical system and the Other's transcendence. Transcendence is not a particular position in regards to the system, but what exceeds all the categories with which we attempt to characterize otherness. This does not imply, however, that a person's transcendence is independent of the social conditions in which she or he develops and encounters others. Instead, a person's transcendence is an incalculable dimension that we nonetheless encounter in the realm of calculation.

This chapter began examining the dynamics of foreclosure and worlding to call attention to the fact that a person's otherness is never absolutely external to the system. All of us develop in relation to sociopolitical systems. To realize and to take responsibility for the unrepresented past, I have argued, requires a departure from self-enclosed notions of subjectivity to become mindful of the intricate relationships between our own subjectivities and the system. That is, it requires bringing to the fore our own inextricability from the realm of calculation—from this side of *différance*. Our engagement with Spivak's wholly Other suggests additional dimensions (or re-linkings) of subjectivity.

While a human person is never absolutely external to the system, she/he is always irreducible to it. She is the "existent" whom we encounter as the Other and as something more, which is nonetheless inextricable from her particular existence. Both aspects must be maintained. On the one hand, to deny the Other's excess in regard to the system is to reduce him/her to the same, something Levinas forcefully denounced. On the other hand, the moment we imagine her/his excess as an external universal with no relation to the sociopolitical realities in which we encounter one another, we see transcendence detach itself from ethics. How then can we imagine the Other's transcendence which is neither available nor unavailable, "disclosed in effacement"?

Adapting Spivak's image of the embrace, we can say that each and every person embraces and is embraced by realities that transcend her/him. Each aspect of a person's identity develops in relation to realities that transcend her/his particularity—community, country of origin, sexual identity—but which she or he also transcends. The realities of my own community—its past history, its language, the geography in which I feel most at home—all embrace me, not only as a past reality, but as something that I continue to relate to, be transformed by, and transform. And yet I never grasp it, just as it never completely defines me. These transcending realities take place only in particular persons; that is to say, they are never fully present, as such, and never appear in isolation from other aspects of a person's life. In each person different realities meet and transform each other in unique ways. The unique outcome of these multiple relations accounts for each person's radical singularity—*a function of relations rather than of exteriority.*

Some of the transcending realities that we embrace precede us; indeed, they choose us before birth. The epigraphs to this chapter testify to that calling of the Other beyond time to whom the writers were always already in relation. But our relations to those realities evolve through our encounter with Others and in relation to their own transcendence. In our encounter with the transcendent Other, we have said, we rememorate our becoming in the flesh, the "awakening to another birth." New conception, rebirth, regeneration: in each of our encounters with a transcendent Other we open ourselves and are reborn. This transformation always takes place within the folds of interhuman relations, from which desire and need, identification and representation, are ineradicable. The other person may be thought of as *irreducibly*, rather than *absolutely*, transcendent to me.

Encounters co-constitute who we are. The transcendent Other leaves her trace in our flesh. The traces of Others whom we have encountered in the past are thus also present in our subsequent encounters with other Others. In each encounter, the self and the Other find themselves in indirect relation to multiple Others and thus with other times and places that are not fully present, here and now. All of those times and places meet, as it were, in today's encounter. They constitute the material forces and resources of any single encounter. Our encounter with the Other touches and is touched by realities that transcend us both: the traces of other Others and the communal realities that we embrace. In each encounter we open ourselves to new incarnations of their transcendence.

Each Other is singular, but always already in relation to multiple Others. Each encounter is a unique beginning, but never a self-enclosed origin. The self and the Other both transcend the here and now. Not only are the differences with which we are marked the product of a history of other encounters in which we are both implicated, but the otherness of the Other is also constituted in relation to other peoples, other places, and other times which transcend us both. *We encounter more in less.*

The logic of the self-Other dyad is thus disrupted. Multiple Others are implicated in the face-to-face encounter. We may say that each encounter, each person, is like a "garden of forking paths"—to borrow Jorge Luis Borges's intriguing metaphor—extending in time as well as in space. In a very concrete and contextual sense, a person's relations to Others— past and present, human or not—is *in-fini,* unfinished.

The depiction of the body-to-body encounter, as suggested in the previous chapter, leads us to imagine transcendence taking place in the curving space that envelops bodies—within and without. The motions of transcendence involve both repetition and difference, retaining and changing, dancing to the rhythms of a cosmic co-creation. In the encounters we now observe with Spivak's help, we see bodies branching out in time and space, even as they become one. We catch a glimpse of the multiplicity that, by virtue of one's historicity, each human being incarnates in irreducible singularity. We may now see the spiraling patterns of transcendence in relation not only to one's cosmic ground, but also to the motions of history—always retaining as it advances. A model of the interhuman encounter that attends to the historicity of subjects and their inextricable relation to multiple Others offers a ground for a model of transcendence consonant with Levinas's own assertion: "transcendence is a relation. . . ."

PREPARING TO ENCOUNTER THE (WHOLLY) OTHER

I maintain that she would come if we worked for her, and that so to work, even in poverty and obscurity, is worth while.

—*Virginia Woolf*

I pray only for the courage to remember what I may never have the chance to live. And in remembering may I know and in knowing may I teach.

—*Cherríe Moraga*

We constantly fail to encounter the other as Other. Time and again we ignore or deny the singularity of the Other—we don't see even when the face stands in front of us. We still need, it seems, "eyes to see and ears to hear"—and bodies capable of embracing without grasping. Are we not confronting a paradox here? The possibility of transformation lies in the encounter with the transcendence in the flesh of the Other, and yet how can we meet the other as Other—as transcendent to us—if we are not ourselves transformed?

Undoubtedly, the encounter with the Other's transcendence entails preparation. To prepare for the coming of the Other does not imply determining how, when, or even if the Other will come. It does not entail defining the proper place for her/his coming, but instead preparing a better place, or making a place more suitable for the coming. "The other may come, or he may not. I don't want to programme him, but rather to leave a *place* for him [or her], if he [or she] comes," writes Derrida.[49] We must leave a place for the Other in a world that is still inadequate to it, in a world that her coming will transform. But how or where does one leave (or prepare) such a place for the Other?

Spivak guides us in a few different directions. On the one hand, she insists on the need to meet, face-to-face, those in subaltern communities—as a "training ground" for "learning to learn from below." Yet even that commitment demands preparation; it entails *work.*[50] One must practice critique and self-critique—"not accusing, not excusing"—and imagine.[51] One must develop new habits of the mind.

To seek to uncover the traces of the Others foreclosed from history is part of this preparation. It is an exercise in listening to that which lies beyond—that which, from the past, affects the present. This is the delicate discipline that Patricia Williams exercises in her attentive look at the violent encounters of slavery. "I track meticulously the dimension of meaning in my great-great-grandmother as chattel," she explains. She attempts to learn to see in the dark "her shape and his hand in the vast networking of our society, and in the evils and oversights that plague our lives and laws." Tracing an absent presence is not to recover the past; "the story will never replace" the lost Other.[52] But it opens the way for rethinking the present: "the meaning of money; the power of consumerist world view, the deaths of those we label the unassertive and the inefficient. . . . To *imagine* where and who she would be today."[53]

In an effort to develop "the habit of the mind that can be open to experience ethics," Spivak turns to texts, including the archives of history and works of fiction.[54] For the wholly Other "must be thought and must be thought through imagining."[55] In fiction Spivak seeks accounts of that experience of "an inadequation or an incalculable disproportion" that may motivate a turn toward justice.[56] A number of images appear as figures of the unnamable wholly Other. The wholly Other is figured as a native person, an extinct pterodactyl, as "curious," even strange, guardians appearing from beyond—"strange guardians in the margin."[57] In the struggles, shortcomings, and hopes of these texts to encounter the Other, Spivak finds lessons for our own encounters with the Other. Figures are unverifiable.[58] Constantly reminding her readers of this, through style and content, Spivak attempts to cross out the unavoidable tendency to find certainties in the name (or the face) of the Other. But "[i]f a figure makes visible the impossible, it also invites the imagination to transform the impossible into an experience, a rôle."[59]

This undecidability of imagination is intensified in the elusive figure of the ghost. Spivak's allusions to "haunting" are few and cryptic, but they are for me an irresistible provocation to pursue some understated aspects of the work of preparation in its relation to the messianic.

Ghostly appearances are, according to Derrida, an implication of Levinas's assertion that the Other must be welcomed before assimilating him within our conceptual frameworks. "The absence of determinable properties, of concrete predicates, of empirical visibility, is no doubt what gives to the face of the other the spectral aura." According to this "profound necessity" for indeterminacy, the Other would have "at least the face of a spirit or phantom (*Geist, ghost*)."[60] Those experiences of being faced by something for which there is no concept within our systems of thought, or of encountering someone or something out of its proper place or time, have the quality of haunting.

For both Derrida and Spivak, however, the figures of ghosts, phantoms, and specters evoke not only this absence of determinable properties, but more particularly the appearance of the past in the present, as (well as) the calling of a future-to-come—*porvenir*. I have been arguing that Spivak re-links the encounters and the subjectivity of living persons with their past so that Others are never fully in the present. But Derrida and Spivak typically use "haunting" to allude to encounters with "certain others who are not present, nor presently living, either to us, in us, or out-side us" or "not yet there . . . whether they are already dead or not yet born."[61] Such haunting, or more accurately, responding to such haunting is indispensable for justice. Indeed, Derrida argues, "It is necessary to speak *of the* ghost, indeed *to the* ghost and *with it.*" This type of encounter with those no longer living is indispensable—a preparation, we may say—for the becoming possible of the future. For "no ethics, no politics," Der-rida adds, "seems possible and *thinkable* and just that does not recognize in its principle the respect for those others who are not yet there."[62] Mak-ing ethics and politics possible and thinkable, haunting takes place—not in an Other's face or body, but in the self. Each is a mind-changing event.

No ethics or politics seems possible or thinkable, Derrida continues, "without the principle of some *responsibility,* beyond all living present." To speak to the ghost is a response to those to whom we are *responsible,* whose call we cannot avoid. The "ghosts of those who are not yet born or who are already dead" have, in Derrida's mind, strong ethical claims, for they are the "victims of wars, political or other kinds of violence, nation-alist, racist, colonialist, sexist, or other kinds of exterminations, victims of the oppressions of capitalist imperialism or any forms of totalitarism."[63]

The living victims of totalitarism have for a long time sought to speak of, to, and with ghosts—of, to, and with those who are no longer—in an effort to welcome a different *porvenir.* They have prayed to be haunted by the ghosts of those who were silenced too soon, whose transcendence was violated, their possible contributions foreclosed. Images of ghosts haunt the literature of subaltern peoples, notably among Latin American writers like Juan Rulfo, Gabriel García Márques, Isabel Allende, and Luisa Valenzuela, and African American writer Toni Morrison, to name just a few. These ghosts mark the irruption of the social conscience into the individual and also the call for decisions—for a *"politics of mem-ory."*[64] These writings depict a peculiar kind of knowledge obtained through unusual kinds of perceptions—neither properly seeing nor touching, but somewhat related to both. In *Ghostly Matters,* Avery Gor-don explores the testimonies of haunting in Valenzuela's and Morrison's novels to call attention to the importance of hauntings for theorizing the social and its potential for changing how and what we know."[65]

The "ghost imports a charged strangeness into the place or sphere it is haunting."[66] We have said that preparing for the coming of the Other requires leaving a place for her/him. In a totality, that means calling soci-ety's organizing systems into question—"to *reactivate* the moment of decision that underlies any *sedimented* set of social relations," as Ernesto

Laclau describes it.[67] Can this reactivation happen at the level of a subject encountering an Other, without the import of a "charged strangeness"?[68] Do the images of the shape described by an absence, or the name of an América, whose tortured body is yet to be found, describe this kind of haunting? "Noisy silences and seething absences"—these are symptoms of the haunting of Others beyond the present, but always already in it, with all the uncertainties that it implies. [69]

A ghost "is a symptom of what is missing." It holds the place, as it were, of "a possibility not taken":[70] "an unfinished, unheard history, which cannot be fully presented."[71] Haunting disrupts the stability between the "there" and the "not there," between the past and the present. By witnessing to the space of the no-longer-living Other, a haunting signals to a not-yet. To attend to a possibility not realized is simultaneously to contemplate the possibility of a different future. Commenting on Toni Morrison's *Beloved*, Gordon observes that the ghost is "pregnant with unfulfilled possibility," with "something to be done"; the ghost is "connected to the labor aimed at creating in the present a place."[72] Those who are haunted by and who speak to the ghost "recover the evidence of things not seen."[73] They seek to "allow what cannot be spoken or voiced in the present, *to be opened, or reopened,* as that which remains ungrasped and unrealized, as an approach that is always *yet to be taken*."[74]

Reckoning with ghostly presences demands a peculiar perception—not only a way of seeing, but also a way of feeling. "Being haunted draws us *affectively,* sometimes against our will and always a bit magically, in a structure of *feeling* of a reality we come to experience." If it constitutes a kind of training or preparation for ethical decisions, it is "not as cold knowledge, but as *transformative recognition*."[75] Haunting calls our attention to elements of undecidability, fear, desire, and love, of which ethics is never devoid and on which transformation hinges. For ethics is a "problem of *relation* rather than . . . a problem of knowledge" in the modern sense of the term, Spivak observes.[76] The encounter with the transcendence of the human Other might or might not be sexual. But it is impossible without love.

These invocations of a mind-changing love that opens the way to transformative relations bring these accounts of ethics close to theology. And so do Spivak's acceptance of an element of uncontrollability inherent in a haunting. For the provenance of the desire that haunting evokes is difficult to locate: it is simultaneously a symptom of haunting and a desire to experience that haunting. This desire moves a person to call out, even beg, to experience the Other. Yet this longing for the Other would be impossible were the Other not in a sense already experienced. Should we be surprised if this kind of desire is identified with prayer? The specter of theology might have a deep affinity with Spivak's recurring confession: I "*pray* to be haunted by her ghost."[77]

TRANSCENDENT PLANETARITY

Thus far, we have observed the workings of transcendence in Spivak's depiction of interhuman encounters as well as its ghostly presence in the mind-changing love that makes ethics possible. Now we turn to an additional *affirmative* step. Here Spivak takes us to the unmemorable past to imagine a beginning of ethical responsibility that may lead us to envision a ground where collective hopes and responsibility may take place.

"To be born human," Spivak asserts, "*is* to be born angled toward an other and others." Thus, she proceeds to offer what comes close to a metaphysical explanation of the philosophical need for the Other. "To account for [the fact that we are 'born angled toward an other and others'], the human being presupposes the quite-other. This is the bottom line of being-human as being-in-the-ethical-relation."[78] But how does she account for this fact of birth, for this fact that is the bottom line of being human?

Faced with the threats of a control- and consumption-oriented world, Irigaray takes us back to the fact of our birth in the womb as a reminder of our beginning in an empathy that abides by the outlines of the Other. "Caressing me, he bids me neither to disappear nor to forget, but to rememorate the place where, for me, the most secret life holds itself in reserve."[79] This figure of an originary intimate otherness informs Spivak's view. Like Irigaray, Spivak wants to take us back to our very origin for which we cannot account—which irreducibly transcends us. Spivak invites us to imagine that welcome which always precedes us and makes possible our own welcoming of Others. In her reading of Irigaray's "Fecundity of Caress," Spivak hints at her interpretation of Irigaray's rhetoric in relation to her own thinking on alterity, the wholly Other, and so on. Irigaray's move beyond Levinas is to offer another figuration for the boundary across which ethics must work. "Their faces are not the only ethical surfaces. Their hands take part in *shaping otherness*." Spivak's own work offers multiple figurations of ethical surfaces and a variety of ways in which human beings participate in shaping each other's otherness toward new births. Like Irigaray, she grounds those encounters in an "original" otherness. As "a pre-appropriative site, the impossible origin of the ethical that can only be figured, *falsely,* as the subject as child-in-mother."[80] But Spivak then moves on to link this to other figurations of that "impossible origin." "We provide for ourselves transcendental figurations of what we think is the origin of this animating gift: mother, nation, god, nature," Spivak explains. "These are names of alterity, some more radical than others." She brings together this disjointed multiplicity in the thought of that which gathers us all. "Planet-thought opens up to embrace an inexhaustible taxonomy of such names, including but not identical with the whole range of human universals: aboriginal animism as well as the spectral white mythology of postrational science."[81]

"To be human is to be intended toward the other," Spivak repeats as she begins to expound this vision of a planetary humanity.[82] In response to the increasing abstraction promoted by globalization, and the resulting attempt to reduce the planet to a singular economic value system, Spivak proposes that human beings reimagine themselves in relation to alterity. This time the figure for that alterity is the planet. This alternative is, of course, not to be imagined as directly accessible outside the "globe." Neither is it exclusive of humanity or the political. On the contrary, it appeals to a radically inclusive reality. It is indeed a case of an alterity that, while inextricable from our very existence, remains unmistakably "underived from us." "And yet we inhabit it, on loan."

Although Spivak would not expound a Christian cosmological transcendence based on human-divine participation in creation, she might be closer to such theological anthropology than she would admit. "If we imagine ourselves as planetary subjects rather than global agents, planetary *creatures* rather than global entities, alterity remains underived from us." This view of the planet, she adds, "is not our dialectical negation, it contains us as much as it flings us away."[83] It is an alterity not only underived from us, but also sacred. "Sacred," she quickly adds, "need not have a religious sanction, but simply a sanction that cannot be contained within the principle of reason alone."[84]

A thought of the "experience of ethics as the impossible figure of a founding gap, of the quite other," thus leads Spivak to a sacred planetarity.[85] The deconstructive embrace—the image of an individual's relation to transcendent realities—finds its mirror in this cosmology, where humans are embraced by the planet. Is a reading of Spivak's proposal as posing an intracosmic transcendence as the ground of interhuman transcendence (im)possible? My intention in raising this question is not to literalize or Christianize Spivak's figure—an absurd strategy for encountering texts that insist on taking the "figure" as their guide.[86] Instead I want to explore the ends to which we could deploy these figures in the service of the "large-scale mind change" for which Spivak prays. "We are talking about using the strongest mobilizing discourse in a certain way. . . ."[87] "What we are dreaming of here is . . . how to construct a sense of sacred Nature which can help mobilize a general ecological mindset beyond the reasonable and self-interested grounds of longterm global survival."[88]

If Spivak believes the "name of theology is alien to this thinking," indeed the name of any religion, it is perhaps because she assumes the God of theology is alienated from the planet.

> It is a *curious fact* that many so-called ethno-philosophies (such as Tao, Zen, Sunyāvada, the philosophy of Nāgārjuna, varieties of Sufi, and the like) show affinities with parts of deconstruction. This may relate to their critique of the intending subject. Insofar as they transcendentalize extra-subjective authority, they are not quite "the same thing" as deconstruction. But insofar as they locate agency in the radically other . . . the exorbitancy of the sphere of work in the ethical as figured by Derrida has something like a relationship with them.[89]

Spivak is careful not to "transcendentalize" the wholly Other, to make it into a super-being. Further, she assumes that this establishes a stable border between her work and religions, even between her and Christian liberation theologies—whose "powerful and risky role" she admits fed her own dreams of an "animist liberation theology."[90] "No individual transcendence theology, of being just in this world in view of the next, however the next is underplayed, can bring us to this."[91] I would also worry about such a transcendence theology—and so would other liberation theologians. As Catherine Keller observes in her challenge to Spivak's exclusion of the subversive forces within the "great religions," "liberation theologians such as Leonardo Boff and Ivonne Gebara, and European American ecotheologians such as Rosemary Ruether, Sallie McFague, Jay McDaniel, and John Cobb, have long moved . . . close to the proposed 'animist liberation theology,' and . . . far from any dichotomy of nature/supernature."[92] But Spivak's curiosity—may we say "wonder"?—remains. Despite the repeated setting-off gestures by which Spivak distances her work from it, theology will keep haunting planetarity:[93] that sacred alterity which is always underived from us that marks us as planetary creatures.

TRANSCENDENCE BETWEEN CREATURES

In the previous chapters we explored the characteristics of the interhuman encounter to ground a model of relational transcendence. I have highlighted the ethical significance of respecting each person's singularity while avoiding the temptation to abstract otherness from the complex relations—sexual, social, political, and so forth—through which subjectivity is formed, and suggested an interpretation of transcendence as relation. Adapting Levinas's definition, I proposed that transcendence designates a relation with a reality irreducibly different from my own reality, yet without the difference destroying this relation and without the relation destroying this difference. The difference of the other person marks an epistemological limit of the self. However, the Other's transcendence denotes more than a limit to the self. The Other's difference is inseparable from her/his relations to other Others: other persons, other places, others who are no longer living and not yet living, with the cosmos. In her relations to Others, a person's boundaries extend in-finitely. I have proposed that this web of relations constitutes each person's concrete and particular in-finity.

Deconstructive feminism, whether Irigaray's philosophical or Spivak's postcolonial version, provides a phenomenological ground for the interpretation of relations I have just summarized. But the works we have examined rely also on an unstated metaphysics—a ground that they tend to foreclose. The events that constitute humanity and their relations are joined by a third reality that exceeds them: an Other that cannot be accounted for and which "can only be figured *falsely*."[94] Spivak names this radically inclusive reality "the planet." Irigaray calls it "God."

"The transcendence of 'God' can help in the discovery of the other as other," Irigaray says, "a locus where expectation and hope hold themselves in reserve."[95] Whether or not Irigaray's God is a Christian God is a matter of debate. In Spivak's (non-Christian) opinion, it certainly is. Irigaray's is "not just philosophical or literary talk, but Christian talk, of incarnation," Spivak observes, intuiting the potential of Irigaray's metaphors for a Christian dialogue on ethics—a dialogue that Spivak assumes she cannot enter.[96] However, whether or not these thinkers could be Christianized is not the line of inquiry I wish to pursue. Instead, I would like to think of God as wholly Other—through imagining.

Theology may offer us a language to say what Spivak seems to desire, but cannot quite say, even when she ventures into the affirmative mode.

We have observed that while the Other is implicated in the construction of the self, the Other's transcendence escapes the grasp of any concept. Our relation to the Other is intrinsic to our very humanity—"that which we already are through no choice of our own."[97] Being in relation to the Other is the mark of the beginning of our very life in a reality underived from us. Theology names that reality God—as that which exceeds all names and with which our very existence is related. We thus turn to the name of God to conclude this theological interpretation of the excess of the Other in relation to divine transcendence and relationality.

CHAPTER 7

The Touch of Transcendence

Through my relation to the Other, I am in touch with God.
Emmanuel Levinas, Difficult Freedom[1]

The transcendence of "God" can help in the discovery of the other as other, a locus where expectation and hope hold themselves in reserve.
—*Luce Irigaray,* An Ethics of Sexual Difference[2]

Our engagement with the notion of transcendence has taken us from theological depictions of divine transcendence to philosophical, feminist, and postcolonial models of interhuman transcendence. From the image of the face-to-face encounter we have turned to the body-to-body encounter, which reveals sinuous contours of the space between self and Other. We have also noted, however, that human bodies are not self-contained, but diffract in space and time, appearing as nodes in an infinite web of relations. This expansion through relations toward a broader interhumanity brings us now to consider that which gathers it all. The various models of interhuman transcendence we have reviewed lead us back to explicit God-talk, to divine transcendence—which, of course, we never really left behind.

As we moved away from orthodox theological images of transcendence as vertical distance, we observed the emergence of images of a radically inclusive planetarity and of a living cosmic reality in which the interhuman encounter participates. Images of transcendence as linear progress were gradually displaced by metaphors of transformation in relation to past experiences—a transcendence that retains even as it moves beyond. The fact that these cosmological images emerge from within nontheological models of interhuman transcendence is theologically significant, for it suggests the desire for an embracing reality, one in which the multiplicity of our singular ethical encounters may be welcomed—an elusive but fecund ground upon which interhumanity takes place.

The metaphors and images used in discourses of interhuman transcendence and in those of divine transcendence converge and intertwine. Our images of divine transcendence inform our constructions of interhuman otherness. Ideas about the divine Other are always related to our perceptions of and relationships with the human Other. Indeed, the otherness of God may be interpreted as the conceptual limit of interhuman otherness, yet we have also suggested that theologically God's transcendence is inseparable from theological anthropology. This chapter further develops this connection, by exploring the Christian affirmation that the cosmos, and thus human beings, emerge from and participate in the divine. Whereas in the previous chapters we have seen images of interhuman transcendence touch lightly upon theological ones, here we follow these images to the point where they embrace each other. Responding to Irigaray's implicit challenge, I offer a model of divine transcendence that "can help in the discovery of the other as other."

A theology of relational transcendence is necessarily and self-consciously metaphorical. Theology cannot encompass the divine Other, and yet, divine transcendence "must be thought and must be thought through imagining."[3] This theology thus hopes to "touch upon" the experiences of the divine in the flesh. It is mindful that to invoke God's transcendence, like that of the human Other, is never to claim access to absolute certainty. Quite the contrary: a theology of transcendence can never close around itself, never rest assured in its own knowledge. The truth of the Other—divine or human—will never be ours to possess. A theology of relational transcendence constantly opens itself to the possibility of the coming of the new: "the unknown, the as-yet-unthought, or even the nonexistent."[4] For "no matter what one gets, no matter how delighted and secure one may be in one's faith, there is always more."[5] Theology shall seek to be touched by that which transcends it and, in the process, transform itself.

After briefly rehearsing the role of planetarity and the cosmos in the accounts of interhuman transcendence as described in chapters 5 and 6, I turn to certain recent theological cosmologies. Among Latin American eco-theologians we find Christian cosmologies that thematize the intrinsic connections between the ethical relations among human beings, the cosmic reality which we all share, and what theology calls God. Drawing from these theo-cosmological visions, along with biblical images of creation, we imagine creation as the place of transcendence—the site where we encounter the glory of God.

RELATIONAL TRANSCENDENCE

In the accounts of interhuman transcendence we have examined, we have found not only self and Other, but an elusive "third." This third reality is figured variously as a mother's womb, as the planet, as the cosmos, sometimes as God. In their different figurations, the third serves at least two functions. On the one hand, it locates the relation to the Other at the very origin of the human being. This other reality is prior to and underived from any of us, and yet it is in and through our intimate relation to it that we become. On the other hand, that immemorial relation to the Other marks our subjectivity: we are always already beings-in-relation-to-the-Other. "To be born human *is* to be born angled toward an other and others," Spivak states.[6]

Our birth inscribes us as beings-in-relation to others. But we do not always honor that birth or those relations. Historically we have tended to ignore that "debt toward that which gives and renews life,"[7] and approached others as mere objects to be appropriated for ourselves. Indeed, the immaterial separate God of many Christian theologies has helped conceal the infinite debt of our irreducibly material livelihood.[8] Thus, we are called back to the beginning, as it were, in the hope that we will remember that originary gift and reconceive ourselves as responsible subjects.

As the nurturing ground of our lives and the space where ethical encounters take place, the third connects the multiplicity of interhuman relations. To be human is to participate in one living cosmic reality, which "contains us as much as it flings us away."[9] The ethical responsibility to other humans is inextricable from our relation to the rest of the natural world. The gift of life derives from the material nourishment of the planet or even of the entire cosmos. Thus, our ethical responsibility is always already marked by the trace of that originating gift, and conversely our ethical responses also leave their traces in that cosmic space. For while this living cosmos exceeds, it is never exterior to the world we live in, with all the sociopolitical and economic divisions that we have historically inscribed on it. Ethical responsibility only bears the fruits of transcendence when the interhuman encounter takes place. It is thus only in the flesh that we encounter transcendence. Only in particular spaces can the encounter with the Other take place. Only in singular encounters do our relations bring forth transcendence. Interhuman transcendence takes place in and contributes to cosmic co-creation. The interhuman, the cosmic, and the social converge.

If interhuman encounters are to bring forth transcendence, rather than the appropriation or consumption of the Other, each woman and each man must have her/his own space. "I will never occupy the space of the Other." Yet the distance marked by the spaces between us is not a barrier. It is a dynamic interval "subtended" "toward and into infinity"— by the cosmos, or maybe by Godself? Irigaray muses. A dynamic interval between us protects both the relationship with and the infinity of the Other, infinity-in-relation to the Other.

Space is thus depicted as the site of the originary intimate embrace, the continuing source of livelihood, the shared place of our ethical actions, and the interval that protects the otherness of the Other. This space certainly invites theological interpretation. In these depictions, "space" evokes images of the intrinsic relations between materiality and the creating/transforming/uniting energies of life. Is this not what theology calls "creation"?

CREATION: THE PLACE OF TRANSCENDENCE

Creation is the extension of God.
Creation is God encountered in time and space.
Creation is the infinite in the garb of the finite.

To attend to creation is to attend to God.
To attend to the moment is to attend to eternity.
To attend to the part is to attend to the whole.
To attend to Reality is to live constructively.
—*Pirke Avot 6.2*

But the finitude and multiplicity of the creature cannot be just finitude and nothing more, and lack of perfection. They unfold God's infinitude.
—*Nicholas of Cusa*

In many of its Christian versions, transcendence draws a rift between cosmos and God, equating divine transcendence with exteriority. But this hardly exhausts Christian interpretations of the relation between God and the cosmos. The verses above—the first from a section of the Talmud titled "Ethics of our Ancestors" (200 CE), the second from a medieval church cardinal (b. 1400)—give voice to a vision of the cosmos as a divine reality. They proclaim that the potentially infinite transformation of the universe is the outcome of the unfolding of God in creation. Creation is figured as the "infinite in the garb of the finite," as a divinely embraced multiple singularity. For human beings, remarks Ellacuría, creation is "the dual unity of God in humanity and humanity in God."[10] It is a physical matrix of complexity and differentiation where "every real thing . . . is intrinsically and constitutively" linked "to every other."[11] "Creation" here names the space of divine transcendence. "The world is not only a bridge to God. It is also *the place* where . . . we meet God," Boff observes.[12]

It is thus within creation that we find transcendence. When the transcendence of God refers to the inexplicable gift and infinite creativity of life, to that which moves us toward transformation, it is no longer an exclusive "attribute" of a "Father" God eternally removed from creation. The divine invites us, Ivone Gebara notes, "to commune with the earth, with all peoples, and with all living things, and to realize that transcendence is not a reality 'out there,' isolated, 'in itself.' . . ." The transcendence of God "within us, among us; in the earth, in the cosmos, and everywhere," summons us to individual and collective ethical responses, to open ourselves and "reach beyond the limits of our selfishness and respond to our call to a new collective ethical behavior . . ." Thus Gebara imagines divine transcendence calling forth and joining together the cosmic multiplicity as "a symphony unceasingly played by the infinite creativity of *life*."[13]

The beginning of creation in God constitutes a theological figure for that immemorial event by virtue of which we are essentially angled toward the Other, in a similar way as the womb and the planet served Irigaray and Spivak as figures of the immemorial "origin" of ethics. Christian eco-theology has sought to articulate how the doctrine of creation may indeed help reconnect God-talk with ethical and ecological concerns. For instance, Leonardo Boff proposes a reading of the Genesis creation narrative that links creation-as-gift to our emergence from the cosmos. Boff observes that in the creation story, human beings are created last. The world is already there to witness the becoming of the first human beings. "Humanity did not see the beginning." This fact of birth is the ground of our responsibility, which does not derive from human choice. Responsibility to the Other, not least to the cosmic Other, is essential to being human. In Christian parlance, to ignore this responsibility is sin. "The responsibility is anterior to [human] freedom and is inscribed in its creational liberty," Boff concludes.[14] Thus described, creatureliness—the fact that we are "planetary creatures," as Spivak would say—entails a structure of responsibility.

Irigaray and Spivak would be leery, however, of theological allusions to "creation," because of theology's tendency to abstract that immemorial gift of life from materiality by positing an immaterial creator God outside the cosmos. The originary inclination of human beings toward the Other is then directed to that external Other rather than (or at best only secondarily) to other creatures; the relation to God is thus seen as something other than relationships among creatures. Human participation in the divine, or getting closer to God, is imagined as a movement away from creatures. Even if the goodness that radiates from a human's closeness to God is eventually beneficial to others, the orientation of such transformation, of human transcendence, lies still outside creation. Prevalent conceptions of creation by the word (based on Gen. 1 and the prologue of John) tend to reinforce the image of the exteriority of God to creation, and collude with the dominant dualistic metaphysics that sets intelligibility over and against the sensible, just as it sets spirit over and against matter. Keeping God untouchable, these models of creation tend to obliterate the transcendence of touchable creatures. We have already observed the traces of this mind-set in Levinas's depiction of ethics as being over and against the erotic, and the related attempt to extricate the desire from need.

At the same time, the depictions of the act of creation as external to Godself—out of a nothingness that is the radically nondivine—lead to theological anthropologies that place the human being perilously close to the void. We observed how this vision, which undergirds radical orthodoxy's cosmology, opens a gap between the divine and the human that in turn decouples divine transcendence from social processes, human needs, liberation—in short, from ethics. We also noted that, as transcendence becomes abstracted from human history, representations of human otherness become detached from their historicity.

The "hard boundary between heaven and earth" on which this cosmology rests emerged in the context of late antiquity, and is inscribed in the Nicene Creed. "The father begets the Son out of his own essence, but makes the world out of nothing" is how Virginia Burrus succinctly articulates it.[15] The world and its creatures fall on the side of (almost) nothing. The creed thus "came to function as the touchstone of a newly crystallizing orthodoxy that would eventually both fix the masculine terms of theological language and pull down the cosmic veil separating the transcendental triad of Father, Son, and Spirit from material creation."[16] To stabilize the boundary between divinity and the created cosmos demanded the disavowal of maternal birth—indeed, its foreclosure. The "originary womb, the first nourishing earth, first waters, first sheaths, first membranes" all had to be excluded from representation in order for the separation between material and divine creation to hold.

This separation further entails the assimilation of its generativity to a "radically sublimated paternity" to be accomplished by fixing the Trinity in strictly patriarchal terms.[17] This exclusion never fully succeeds. Thus, the attempts to replace an irreducible material birth with an absolute act of creation—out of nothing—must always repeat this impossible foreclosure. When Pickstock declares that the names "Father," "Son," and "Holy Spirit" "are really one name"—indeed "an *essential* name *commensurate* with the existential space of the Trinitarian journey"—she replays once more this fourth-century articulation.[18]

This model of relational transcendence refuses the "hard boundary" between the divine and the created. Instead it affirms that the beginning, sustenance, and transformation of the cosmos are intrinsically divine. This theology professes that the human responsibility implied in our creatureliness is ethical responsibility to the created Others. Intracosmic and inter-creaturely transcendence are thus inherently linked; both are theologically grounded in an assertion of the beginning of creation in God. The doctrine of creation may indeed help us to reconceive ourselves as subjects in responsibility with other creatures. However, the doctrine of creation may ground inter-creaturely transcendence only if it resists the theological tendencies to extricate "that which gives and renews life" from the irreducible materiality of life, the enlivening spirit from the living flesh.

The Judeo-Christian tradition offers resources for rethinking creation—and consequently God and creature—in ways that honor the memory of the flesh. Although the idea of creation by word seems to work against this effort to overcome the break between matter and spirit, between transcendence and creatureliness, the creative Word has not always been untouchable; words have not always been uprooted from bodies and matter. The Jewish culture from which these images of creation emerge did not subscribe to the platonic idea that "the words are bodies and the meanings, souls"—the word's rulers and masters.[19] Although the prologue of John is most frequently construed as a narrative of the triumph of a (disembodied) Word over incarnate love, it may be read as part of a tradition in which creation is depicted using suggestively carnal metaphors.

> 22 The Lord *begot me*[20] at [as] the beginning of his work,
>   the first of his acts long ago.
> 23 Ages ago I was *poured out* [as from the waters of the womb][21]
>   at the first,
>   Before the beginning of the earth.

²⁴ When there were no depths I was *brought forth,*[22]
when there were no springs abounding of water.
²⁵ Before the mountains had been shaped,
before the hills I was *brought forth.*[23]

Proverbs 8

In the beginning, the ancient cosmogony recounts, Sophia is brought forth. Envisioned as that prior reality that inscribes us as beings-in-relation-to-Others, God is not just creating, but begetting—not just saying, but bringing forth from within Godself.[24] This beginning, like our beginning in the womb, evokes an encounter before any encounter in which shared intimacy brings forth otherness, difference, beginnings.

As Daniel Boyarin has shown, this cosmogony, while not found in the actual prologue of John, is nonetheless its inspiration. From his exploration of Jewish sources that associate Sophia with the Word of God (*Memra*), Boyarin concludes that the prologue of John was a midrash on the opening verses of Genesis, implicitly invoking Proverbs 8 as its hermeneutic intertext. "The primacy of Genesis as exegeted text explains why we have here 'Logos' and not 'Sophia,' without necessitating the assumption of a 'Word' tradition of Genesis in alleged conflict with a 'Wisdom' tradition. . . . The preacher of the Prologue of John had to speak of Logos here, because his homiletical effort is directed at the opening verses of Genesis, with their majestic: 'And God said: Let there be light, and there was light.'"[25]

In Proverbs' account of beginning, Sophia is poured out of the depths of Godself. Through those images God is depicted as intimately related to the maternal and the material, with Sophia "serving as active memory" of God's embrace.[26] Our readings of John's prologue, however, have tended to hide the traces of Sophia and its cosmogony and the primordial intimacy of the creating God. Read in isolation from its Jewish background, John's Logos has *lost touch* with the suggestive images of Proverbs. We no longer perceive the intimate contact or the intense delight that were at the heart of this story. In fact, there is only a Father and a Son-Word; no wombs are in sight. If we lose the prologue's textual debt to the tradition of Sophia, Logos seems to lose its own ties to the flesh. No longer do we see creatures as finite fragments of divine matter or, as Ellacuría puts it, as "limited way[s] of being divine." For if this Son-Word has no memory of God's begetting, if he/it has forgotten the material debt to the womb, how could he bear witness to the beginning? To any beginning?

To remember the material/maternal images of Proverbs' cosmogony may help us recover from our own tradition the proclamation of the essential link between God and creature, divinity and flesh, which is invaluable for a theology of inter-creaturely transcendence. Retrieving the crucial insight of a creation that emerges out of Godself and the primacy of tactile images that it evokes allows us to reconceive our religious responsibility, re-linking (*religare*) our becoming to creation. It also leads us to a theological anthropology that affirms that creatures are finite fragments of divine matter. As Ellacuría puts it, "each thing, within its own limits, is a limited way of being God. This limited way is precisely the *nature* of each thing."[27] It is not "simply that God is in all things, as essence, presence, and potential," but that the Trinitarian life is "*intrinsic* to all things."[28] Furthermore, as Sophia/Logos, the Word who was in the beginning is perceived not as an image of the power of the intelligible over the sensible, but quite to the contrary, as the very figure of God's originary embrace of creation within Godself. May we find in the memory of our flesh the traces of creation that echo the statement, "In the beginning was touch"?[29]

DIVINE TOUCH

Latin American liberation theology, which is based on the search for the materiality of transcendence, knows how God is to be found in the presence of the untouchables. . . . [Transcendence] is God touching its own limits in the untouchables.

Marcella Althaus-Reid, "El Tocado"[30]

Divine touch and cosmic creation are, to be sure, not only conditions of a historical past, but the continuing reality of the world in which we live and encounter one another. The originary embrace of God and creation may serve as a figure for the intimate relation through which God transcends in creation and creation transcends in God. "To deny God a boundary is to suggest that he has no understanding of himself or of his creation," Origen protests (*First Principles*, 3.5.2). It is to say that God does not *embrace* creation.

How could God be denied an embrace? The boundary, the envelope of God, allows God to touch creation, to envelop its dwelling places in a nonconfining embrace. To embrace, enfold, is "never quite to grasp securely . . . ; to wrap around still somehow . . . respects those edges, those surface limits."[31] "It is by touching the other that the body is a body, absolutely separated and absolutely shared."[32] Touch reveals the simultaneity of transcendence and intimacy, a divine enveloping through which God may caress creation and feel its joy and suffering. As in the embrace between self and Other, the communal and the individual, past and present, distinctions are not erased. One is wrapped around the other while sharing space—"[e]ach at the boundary of the other."[33] Like a lover caressing the cosmos, God calls it "to rememorate the place where . . . the most secret life holds itself in reserve," to awaken it to another birth.[34] God calls it to new beginnings, as cosmos in symphonic harmony. Again and again and again.

God is "over all," we might say, following Irenaeus.[35] Not above all, but over all, I suggest. God is over all—as one who envelopes the immense organism of which we are all part, a divine envelope through which God and creation touch each other. Not a rigid impermeable barrier, but a "confirmation of a limit without imposing upon the other any form."[36] Where the cosmos meets the mystery, the untotalizable excess, of the divine as its limit, which is also the potentiality beyond all conceivable possibilities. Not even the cosmos is limitless, not even all-there-is is actually *All*. Here lies the significant difference between pantheism and panentheism. The latter remains open to mystery and unpredictable possibilities: to the ineffable, unnameable, and unutterable. In this ultimate openness we find a model for the personal openness to the human Other and the collective openness of sociopolitical systems. "[W]e should not build a closed discourse," declares Gebara, "a discourse in which the unknown, the as-yet-unthought, or even the nonexistent has no chance to be included."[37] This openness is critical for all theology.

As the all-embracing reality of a cosmos which is never pure immanence but the site of transcendence in the flesh. "God brings together the world," Origen explains in *First Principles* (2.1.2).[38] By his power—the boundary through which God is present to all things—and by God's Word and Wisdom, God is in all things "as if they were *joined in one*" (1.2.9). God joins the irreducible multiplicity of creation, of its past and potential future, in God's own infinite singularity. Christianity was forged by a witness to the transfigured and transforming presence of the crucified one—"pregnant with unfulfilled possibility," and with the message of "something to be done."[39] This tradition sustains "the hope that the memories of suffering will be told and not go unredeemed, the hope that personal and social existence can and will be transformed." The multiplicities of past encounters that co-constitute our subjectivities are gathered in God; process theologians would say that they are received in God's consequent nature.[40] "God as the term of transcendence allows for the remembering of the dead and of those who survive, the critique of the present, the creative naming of possibilities for the future."[41]

A theology that grounds the ethical relations between creatures cannot stop at an outer boundary of the universe. To do so would reinforce the image of a relation between God and a creation imagined as one self-enclosed thing in relation to the one God. It may lead us to lose sight of the transcendence of the created Other, of the Other's "limited way of being divine." A God who knows (in the broadest sense of the term) each and every creature, as Origen suggests, embraces each one of them and is touched by each one in her/his own singularity—caressing and calling the particularity of each and every creature to its new births.[42]

God is thus seen as that multiple singularity that joins together all creatures—creatures that are themselves irreducible in the infinite multiplicity of their own singularity. In God is the beginning of diversity as well as their joining together, that which makes possible and receives the outcome of each inter-creaturely encounter—past and present. This radically inclusive reality relates us to one another while maintaining a space of difference between us. "*Approaching* involves an irreducible *distancing*," Irigaray states in her depiction of the interhuman encounter. As we have seen, the distance that she imagines is not antithetical to the touch. It is rather the protection of a space of difference between humans "in order that desire *unfold* toward a blossoming"—that is, toward transcendence.[43] The space between us would not be emptiness, where life cannot subsist. Instead, Irigaray proposes that this space of the interval be imagined as material. Rather than a void, the space between us is envisioned as that element that nurtures each one of us, that which is "left in common between subjects living in different worlds."[44] Air, Irigaray proposes, "is the elemental of the life starting from which it is possible to elaborate the transcendental."[45]

That reality in which, like in air, "we dwell and which dwells in us"[46] —is, we may say, divine. The dynamic interval between us, Irigaray realizes, must be subtended "toward and into infinity," perhaps by Godself, she adds. "The *irreducible*."[47] In this theology of transcendence, the intimate and yet insurmountable space between our differences would be divine. Like sap or placenta, what flows in and between us and nurtures us all is God among us, a living and dynamic, fluid envelope that both links—within and throughout—and subtends the space of difference and thus opens creatures to a relational infinity. Through it the Other's demands reach me and call me into responsibility. Through it the needs of the Other touch me.

"Through my relation to the Other I am in touch with God," Levinas proposes, without ever fully welcoming the wisdom of the sensible intimacy that the statement insinuates. If God is to be found in the Other, in "the presence of the untouchables," if God links us to the Other and embraces the very otherness of the Other, ethics becomes a central concern of theology. Theology shall help us develop the habits of the mind that will prepare us for the coming of the Other. It shall call us to transform our bodies so that they become capable of embracing without grasping, to transform our eyes to see and ears to hear. Theology shall encourage us to perceive the transcendence of the Other as the glory of God.

THE GLORY OF GOD

The glory of God is the human being fully alive.
                              —*Irenaeus of Lyons*, Against Heresies

Creatures are the very brilliance of God's coming to presence.
                              —*Jean Luc Nancy*, Being Singular Plural

A turning on the basis of the face of the other, in which, at the very heart of the phenomenon, in its very light, a surplus of signification is signified that could be designated as *glory*.
                              —*Emmanuel Levinas*

Human beings, we have been saying, are never fully present to us. There is always more to the Other. We do encounter Others: we hear their voices, see their faces, and touch their bodies, and yet in the very encounter we also hear, see, and feel that there is more. The gleam of transcendence in the flesh of the Other, an "elusive mystery" that envelops the other person, evokes that which cannot be made present. The experience of that mystery goes beyond the recognition of some strangeness that merely compares differences and calculates their threats. It induces in us a feeling of wonder, surprise, and astonishment in the flesh of the unknowable, which is also quite ordinary. Theologically, we may imagine this brilliance as manifestation of the divinity of creation, "the love and the glory of God . . . deposited right at the level of what is created."[48] Not something *through* which an external divinity shows itself, but the very brilliance of God. The glory of God may be seen as the manifestation of the intrinsic transcendence of creatures. A sign of the luring excess of the Other, as well as of his/her unappropriable otherness, glory "crosses the divide between aesthetics and ethics."[49]

What does it mean to see the glory of God, to see a thing or a person illuminated—while realizing that there is much that one cannot see? The glory of God reveals while concealing—or rather makes visible something while signaling that something else escapes that vision, that there is always more that has passed by. The glory of God manifests the divine presence here and now, in the flesh, as well as the fact that there is always more, a surplus that overflows every here and now.

The glory of God shines in the bodies of all created beings, as a sign of their participation in God. "The heavens are telling the glory of God," celebrates the psalmist. "Day to day pours forth speech, and night to night declares knowledge." And yet as Wisdom and Word flow incessantly from the created world, "There is no speech, nor are there words; their voice is not heard; yet their voice goes out through all the earth, and their words to the end of the world."[50] Biblical references to glory frequently allude to the transfiguration of the ordinary in its encounter with the divine. Recall the burning bush or Moses' own illumined face. The metaphors of light used for glory imply that, like light, glory is "not the visible thing, but that by virtue of which visibility may be."[51] MacKendrick calls attention to the interrelation between word, light, and flesh in the Gospel of John. Word is also light and flesh, she observes. Just as word must become flesh, light must also become flesh for us to see the glory, for "flesh makes possible the shining of light." Thus the glory of God is always encountered as flesh. Whether it is human or nonhuman, flesh "seems to be *essential* to the glory of Word and of Light."[52]

The body of the Other makes possible the shining of light, while simultaneously revealing the unsurpassable mystery of creatureliness. This mystery encompasses the complex history and multiple relations through which a person branches out to other times and places, forming an infinite, irreducible web of relations-across-difference that constitute the living creation. In Jesus' transfiguration, the disciples behold both the brilliance of Jesus' glory and his relationship to those prophets who preceded him: Elijah and Moses. Past relations leave their marks in our bodies. The Other's face, her/his skin, indeed her/his whole body bears the marks of past encounters—signs of renewal as well as scars. These scars are never absent from our encounters. When we see, hear, or touch the Other, we touch upon the Other's scars. As self and Other emerge from the interhuman encounter, as they come forth as new creatures, scars become transfigured in the divine embrace. Again, and again, and again.

Each creature's glory is thus a manifestation of divinity enveloping its unique transcendence: its brilliance tailored to the creature's shape. In its own singularity, a creature's glory does not cover over its history and relations, but it transfigures them.[53] In Christ's glorification "those most material marks, the wounds in his hands and his side, become most evident. They too are glorified."[54] Similarly, God envelops each and every one of our new births with divine glory, transfiguring, without obliterating the marks of their passions. It is a transfiguration that never bypasses the body in its complex historicity, but transubstantiates matter into divine flesh: "into a more subtle, spiritual, even divine, matter. To illuminate it so that it enlightens he, or she, who gazes upon it, who contemplates it."[55]

In our glorified singularity we encounter the Other, as persons already blessed by divine love, without which we could not love the Other in her or his transcendence.[56] Enveloped by God, "illuminated-illuminating," we seek that contact with the Other. We aspire to give and receive that which may open for us new paths for continuous liberation: a love that renounces its consuming impulses while opening itself to be touched by the Other. "[O]verflowing" our own worlds "in order to taste another brightness."[57] Glowing with the touch of transcendence.

Notes

CHAPTER 1—INTRODUCTION

1. The use of the term "transcendence" appears here in close correlation with the term "the Other." As in the case of transcendence, we will gradually discover the various connotations of each theorist's use of this term through our close readings of the texts. A few clarifying remarks are nonetheless in order. There is a widespread convention for capitalizing the term except when it refers to another person. However, this practice is not common to all the discourses with which we will be dealing. On the one hand, translations of Levinas's works usually capitalize "Other" when translating the French term *autrui*, which refers to the personal other. On the other hand, in discourses working out of the psychoanalytic tradition, such as postcolonial theory, the capitalized "Other" alludes to the image of authority against which identity is measured. In the latter sense, "the Other" may refer to an idea such as a stereotype, rather than to a person. I have here adhered to the conventions followed by each of the discourses with which I am engaging. In my own use of the term, I employ capitalization to distinguish it from nontechnical uses of the word.

2. Luce Irigaray, *I Love to You: Sketch of a Possible Felicity in History*, trans. Alison Martin (New York and London: Routledge, 1996), 124–25.

3. *Against Heresies* 4.20.7.

4. Elizabeth A. Johnson, *She Who Is: The Mystery of God in Feminist Theological Discourse* (New York: Crossroad, 1992).

5. Drawing from Paul Ricoeur's thought, Rebecca Chopp describes the imaginative mode of theology as follows: "The poetics of theological discourse is about the conversion of the imaginary, which works not only by stirring up 'the sedimented universe of conventional ideas,' but by shaking up 'the order of persuasion'" (Chopp, "Theology and the Poetics of Testimony," in *Converging on*

Culture: Theologians in Dialogue with Cultural Analysis and Criticism, ed. Delwin Brown, Sheila Greeve Davaney, and Kathryn Tanner, The American Academy of Religion Reflection and Theory in the Study of Religion Series [Oxford and New York: Oxford University, 2001], 66).

6. Karl Barth, *Epistle to the Romans,* trans. Edwyn C. Hoskyns (New York: Oxford University Press, 1991), 10.

7. Ibid., 31.

8. Ibid., 30; italics added.

9. Ibid., 100–101.

10. This concern is still central to feminist critiques of the predominant notions of the divine. Grace Jantzen claims, for instance, that the "present construction of Western symbolic [is] based on the Name of the Father and guaranteed ... by the concept of the divine as radically other than the material world in a cosmic dualism which validates and underwrites the whole system of binary polarities" (Jantzen, *Becoming Divine: Towards a Feminist Philosophy of Religion* [Bloomington: Indiana University Press, 1999], 268).

11. Mary Daly, *Beyond God the Father: Toward a Philosophy of Women's Liberation* (Boston: Beacon Press, 1973).

12. Simone de Beauvoir, *The Second Sex,* trans. H. M. Parshley (New York: Alfred A. Knopf, 1953), lix.

13. Even after abandoning the use of "God" in *Gyn/Ecology* and *Pure Lust,* "transcendence" and the "intimate ultimate reality" remained central concepts in Daly's articulation of women's liberation.

14. Ruether contended that Daly's separatist vision is "built on the dualism of transcendent spirit world of femaleness over against the deceitful anticosmos of masculinity" (Rosemary Radford Ruether, *Sexism and God-talk: Towards a Feminist Theology* [Boston: Beacon Press, 1983], 230). For a recent feminist theological critique of de Beauvoir's (and Levinas's) notion of transcendence, see Catherine Keller, "Rumors of Transcendence: The Movement, State, and Sex of 'Beyond,'" in John D. Caputo and Michael J. Scanlon, eds., *Transcendence and Beyond: A Postmodern Inquiry* (Bloomington and Indianapolis: Indiana University Press, forthcoming, 2007).

15. Catherine Keller, *From a Broken Web: Separation, Sexism and Self* (Boston: Beacon Press, 1986).

16. Ibid., 27.

17. Keller explores these connections in subsequent works. See Catherine Keller, *Apocalypse Now and Then: A Feminist Guide to the End of the World* (Boston: Beacon Press, 1996).

18. Ruether, *Sexism and God-talk,* 269.

19. Cf. Sallie McFague, *The Body of God: An Ecological Theology* (Minneapolis: Fortress Press, 1993); Jantzen, *Becoming Divine*; Catherine Keller, *Face of the Deep: A Theology of Becoming* (London and New York: Routledge, 2003).

20. Walter Benjamin, "Theses on the Philosophy of History," in *Illuminations: Essays and Reflections,* ed. Hannah Arendt (New York: Schocken Books, 1986), 261. Benjamin is here addressing specifically the notion of progress as pictured by Social Democrats, but his observations apply more generally to predominant ideas of development and history.

21. Ibid., 260.

22. Ibid., 259.

23. For the details of the public policies through which this was accomplished in Puerto Rico, which included starvation as a mechanism of coercion, see Kevin A. Santiago-Valles, *"Subject People" and Colonial Discourses: Economic Transformation and Social Disorder in Puerto Rico, 1898–1947* (Albany: State University of New York Press, 1994).

24. Keller, *Apocalypse Now and Then,* 119.

25. Otto Maduro has put the power of the geographical imaginary to the test on several occasions, flipping the map before an audience so that the South is "up." Despite his attempts to explain that the orientation is arbitrary (what would "up" be in open space?), many listeners are invariably appalled by the idea (personal communication).

26. Brian Jarvis, *Postmodern Cartographies: The Geographical Imagination in Contemporary American Culture* (New York: St. Martin's Press, 1998), 52.

27. That faith in the self's capacity for comprehending others also affected modern humanism. For instance, Jean-Paul Sartre expressed his progressive commitment as follows: "And, diverse though man's projects may be, at least none of them is wholly foreign to me. . . . Every project, even that of a Chinese, an Indian or a Negro, can be understood by a European. . . . There is always some way of understanding an idiot, a child, a primitive man or a foreigner *if one has sufficient information*" (quoted in Gayatri Chakravorty Spivak, *A Critique of Postcolonial Reason: Toward a History of the Vanishing Present* [Cambridge, MA, and London: Harvard University Press, 1999], 171).

28. Robert McLean, *Old Spain in New America* (New York: Association Press, 1916), 134.

29. Homi K. Bhabha, *The Location of Culture* (London and New York: Routledge, 1994), 4.

30. Ibid., 1.

31. Walter Mignolo proposes a different configuration for the relationship between "post" in postcoloniality and postmodernity. He points out that "the very idea of the 'post' is entrenched within the logic of the 'modern' side of the [modern/colonial] imaginary, since 'modernity' has been conceived in terms of progress, chronology, and superseding a previous stage." "Beyond," on the other hand, "has a spatial connotation that underlines the side of coloniality." This might be the reason that Latin American thinkers Enrique Dussel and Fernando Coronil prefer "beyond" to "post," Mignolo speculates (Walter D. Mignolo, *Local*

Histories/Global Designs: Coloniality, Subaltern Knowledges, and Border Thinking [Princeton, NJ: Princeton University Press, 2000], 91).

32. Cf. Jacques Derrida, "Violence and Metaphysics: An Essay on the Thought of Emmanuel Levinas," in *Writing and Difference*, ed. Jacques Derrida (Chicago: University of Chicago Press, 1978); Jacques Derrida, "Sauf le Nom," in *On the Name*, ed. Thomas Dutoit (Stanford, CA: Stanford University Press, 1995).

33. Kevin Hart, *The Trespass of the Sign: Deconstruction, Theology, and Philosophy* (Cambridge and New York: Cambridge University Press, 1989); John D. Caputo and Michael J. Scanlon, eds., *God, the Gift, and Postmodernism* (Bloomington and Indianapolis: Indiana University Press, 1999).

34. Jacques Derrida, *The Gift of Death*, trans. David Wills (Chicago and London: University of Chicago, 1995), 78.

35. Ibid. Derrida states thrillingly the ethical implications of this challenge for God-talk. Claiming to be absolutely responsible to the divine wholly Other, this is paradoxically also "irresponsible because it is guided neither by reason nor by an ethics justifiable before men or before the law of some universal tribunal." "Abraham is a murderer." However, this intolerable murder "is at the same time the most common event in the world." Indeed, "the smooth functioning of [our] society, the monotonous complacency of its discourses on morality, politics, and the law, and the exercise of rights . . . are in no way impaired by the fact that, because of the structure of the laws of the market that society has instituted and controls, because of the mechanisms of external debt and other similar inequities, the same 'society' puts to death or . . . [a]llows to die of hunger and disease tens of millions of children . . . without any moral or legal tribunal ever being considered competent to judge such a sacrifice, the sacrifice of others to avoid being sacrificed oneself" (Derrida, *The Gift of Death*, 86).

36. Bhabha, *The Location of Culture*, 5.

37. Ibid., 173.

38. Mignolo, *Local Histories/Global Designs*.

39. Bhabha, *The Location of Culture*, 4.

40. Ibid., 4, 7.

41. Ibid., 4.

42. Ibid., 7.

CHAPTER 2—RADICAL TRANSCENDENCE?

1. Augustine, Sermon 52, c. 1, n. 16.

2. Michael A. Sells, *Mystical Languages of Unsaying* (Chicago and London: University of Chicago, 1994), 11. Dietrich Bonhoeffer coined the phrase "cheap grace" to refer to grace that does not entail discipleship.

3. Merold Westphal identifies three interrelated ways of construing transcendence: cosmological, epistemological, and ethical/religious transcendence

(Westphal, *Transcendence and Self-Transcendence: On God and the Soul* [Bloomington and Indianapolis: Indiana University Press, 2004]). In most theological articulations of divine transcendence, all these aspects are present although the emphasis given to each varies greatly.

4. John Milbank, *Being Reconciled: Ontology and Pardon*, ed. Milbank, Pickstock, and Graham Ward (London and New York: Routledge, 2003), 194; italics added.

5. Ibid., italics added. Milbank is referring to Gilles Deleuze's and Félix Guattari's notion of the "plane of immanence": an "unlimited One-All" that gathers all philosophical concepts, which they contrast with the exterior transcendence of classical theology and philosophy (Deleuze and Guattari, *What Is Philosophy?* ed. Lawrence D. Kritzman, trans. Hugh Tomlinson and Graham Burchell [New York: Columbia University, 1994]).

6. Milbank, *Being Reconciled*, 194.

7. Ibid.

8. See Anne McClintock, *Imperial Leather: Race, Gender and Sexuality in the Colonial Contest* (New York: Routledge, 1995).

9. Zygmunt Bauman, "Living and Dying in the Planetary Frontier-Land," *Tikkun* 17, no. 2 (2002).

10. Milbank, *Being Reconciled*, 194. Similarly, Pickstock mourns Western thought's departure from its ancient Athens roots, which has led to a new version of immanentism, "immanentist modernity," with similar social consequences.

11. Ibid.

12. Ibid., 187.

13. Ibid., 207.

14. Ibid., 189.

15. One would need to analyze the consequences of this historical depiction, not only for its assumption of the inherent goodness of Christian empires, but also for its reliance on a logic of fall—the inverted mirror of the myth of progress—which fails to problematize a basic assumption of that myth: the primacy of the West as the gauge of world history.

16. For a discussion of different reactions to the postmodern and a development of a position that welcomes the dissolution of structures for its democratic potential, see Michael Hardt and Antonio Negri, *Multitude: War and Democracy in the Age of Empire* (New York: Penguin Press, 2004), and Chela Sandoval, *Methodology of the Oppressed* (Minneapolis and London: University of Minnesota Press, 2000).

17. Milbank, *Being Reconciled*, 175; italics added.

18. In the introduction to *Radical Orthodoxy*, the editors state: "[Radical orthodoxy] does not, like liberal theology, transcendentalist theology and even certain styles of neo-orthodoxy, seek in the face of [the nihilistic drift of postmodernism] to shore up [modern] universal accounts of immanent human

value (humanism) nor defenses of supposedly objective reason." It also differs from those theologies that "indulge . . . in the pretence of a baptism of nihilism in the name of a misconstrued 'negative theology'"—radical orthodoxy's typical characterization of postmodern theology. Instead, they argue that radical orthodoxy seeks to respond to "the secular demise of truth" by seeking "to reconfigure theological truth." The latter may seem surprisingly "close to nihilism," because "it, also, refuses a reduction of the indeterminate." Yet that theological truth differs from nihilism in "its proposal of the rational possibility, and the faithfully perceived actuality, of an indeterminacy that is not impersonal chaos but infinite interpersonal harmonious order in which time participates" (John Milbank, Catherine Pickstock, and Graham Ward, *Radical Orthodoxy* [London and New York: Routledge, 1999], 2; italics added).

19. Ibid., 3; italics added.

20. Transcendence is an infinite reservoir of meaning that assures "that that which is communicated and circulated may assume new meanings which can blend seamlessly with the old" (Milbank, *Being Reconciled*, 171).

21. Milbank, Pickstock, and Ward, *Radical Orthodoxy*, 2; Milbank, *Being Reconciled*, 175.

22. Milbank, *Being Reconciled*, 175.

23. Ibid., 174.

24. Ibid., 171; italics added.

25. Ibid., 179; italics added.

26. Ibid.; italics added.

27. Milbank, Pickstock, and Ward, *Radical Orthodoxy*, 3.

28. Milbank, *Being Reconciled*, 210. This is also reflected in Catherine Pickstock's description of the liturgy as revealing "the merely (or empirically) 'present' to be that which, without this relation with the apparent 'absent,' constitutes the ultimate absence" (Pickstock, *After Writing: On the Liturgical Consummation of Philosophy* [Oxford, UK, and Madel, MA: Blackwell Publishers, 1998], 197; italics added).

29. Aquinas, *Summa Theologica* 1a.104.1.

30. Jacques Derrida, "Faith and Knowledge," in *Religion* (Stanford, CA: Stanford University Press, 1998), 50.

31. Milbank, *Being Reconciled*, 177.

32. Although the use of spatial language is almost unavoidable, as we habitually depict differences using spatial language, beyond is not a simple location in space (outside) or in time (before or after the present). The spatial tendencies of our language emerged from philosophical and scientific views that are not irrelevant for our discussion of transcendence. In *The Domestication of Transcendence*, William C. Placher traces the literalization of spatial language about God—distance, separation, etc.—to the homogenization of space produced by modern sciences (Placher, *The Domestication of Transcendence: How Modern*

Thinking about God Went Wrong [Louisville, KY: Westminster John Knox Press, 1996]).

33. Milbank, *Being Reconciled*, 177.

34. Homi K. Bhabha, *The Location of Culture* (London and New York: Routledge, 1994), 4.

35. Ibid., 7.

36. Milbank, *Being Reconciled*, 180.

37. Ibid.

38. Ibid.

39. Ibid.

40. *First Principles* 4.1.36.

41. Thomas Aquinas developed this idea to assert that the goals (*telos*) for each creature is contained in it and thus final causation is the divine actualization of the potential that is already in the creature—adding a deterministic emphasis not evidenced in Origen's work.

42. Placher, *Domestication of Transcendence.*

43. Xavier Zubiri observes the beginnings of this development in Galileo's work, where, as he puts it, "the cause of inertial movement is left out of the meaning of physics." This exclusion has grave consequences for the notion of causality, he argues (Zubiri, *Estructura dinámica de la realidad* [Madrid: Alianza Editorial and Fundación Xavier Zubiri, 2006], 75).

44. Milbank, *Being Reconciled*, 211.

45. Ibid., 174.

46. Ibid.

47. Ibid.; italics added.

48. I am grateful to Trish Sheffield for bringing Durkheim's distinction to my attention. Cf. Trish Sheffield, "Totemic Desires: The Religious Dimensions of Advertising in the Culture of Consumer Capitalism" (PhD dissertation, Drew University, 2004); see especially chaps. 1 and 2.

49. Luce Irigaray, *This Sex Which Is Not One*, trans. Catherine Porter and Carolyn Burke (Ithaca, NY: Cornell University Press, 1977), 86.

50. Ibid., 74.

51. Milbank, *Being Reconciled*, 176; italics added.

52. Pickstock, *After Writing*, 183; italics added.

53. The use of apostrophic language—the words addressed to an absent God as if God were present—is not completed "with the first utterance of an invocation. . . . Rather, our utterance must give rise to further speaking" (ibid., 197).

54. Ibid., 173.

55. Milbank, *Being Reconciled*, 177.

56. Ibid., 179.

57. Ibid.

58. Ibid., 180.

59. Pickstock, *After Writing*, 182; italics added.

60. Ibid.; italics added. Pickstock is here arguing against postmodern philosophy's emphasis on the incidental relation between the signs and the signified.

61. Ibid., 259, xv.

62. Ibid., 262; italics added.

63. Ibid., 259.

64. Ibid., 262.

65. It is precisely this leap of the signifier toward the signified that Derrida criticizes in his challenges to onto-theology—as distinct from the denial that there is a reference, a world, etc., that he is often accused of espousing.

66. Pickstock notes that "however much a particular finite relationship might seem to have the quality of destiny, it ultimately remains fortuitous and is at most transitory, since one I-Thou relationship can be followed by a second and a third, and in each case, the new 'Thou' will be endowed with a new and different name" (*After Writing*, 197).

67. "[One soul] clinging to God from the beginning . . . in a union inseparable and indissoluble . . . was made with him in a pre-eminent degree one spirit. . . . This soul acting as a medium between God and the flesh . . . there is born . . . the God-man, the medium being that existence to whose nature it was not contrary to assume a body" (Origen, *On First Principles*, 2.6.3).

68. Milbank, *Being Reconciled*, 204.

69. Ibid., 203.

70. Ibid.

71. Ibid., 201.

72. Judith Butler, *Gender Trouble: Feminism and the Subversion of Identity* (New York and London: Routledge, 1999), 43.

73. Milbank, *Being Reconciled*, 210; italics added.

74. Ibid., 203.

75. Ibid., 206; italics added. Milbank claims that while race is a cultural construction, gender is not.

76. Ibid., 207.

77. Ibid.; italics added.

78. Ibid.

79. Luce Irigaray, "Each Transcendent to the Other," in *To Be Two* (New York: Routledge, 2001).

80. Milbank, *Being Reconciled*, 207.

81. Ibid., 196, 197.

82. Irigaray, "Each Transcendent to the Other," 90.

83. Irigaray also observes the anxiety that the givenness of the body and nature provokes in a capitalist society. "It is because the same, and the Other's relation to it, is priceless that it unquestionably poses the greatest danger we face today" (Luce Irigaray, *An Ethics of Sexual Difference* [New York: Cornell University Press, 1993], 99).

84. Milbank, *Being Reconciled,* 5.

85. Irigaray, "Each Transcendent to the Other," 92.

86. E.g., some examples of Pickstock's formulations that show these associations are: "immanentist modernity," "spatialization [of modernity] constitutes a bizarre kind of immanentist ritual," "the nihilism of immanent presence" (Pickstock, *After Writing,* 239, 198).

87. Milbank, *Being Reconciled,* 5.

88. Ibid. For him, however, the term "secular immanence" might be tautology, as his definition of both "secular" and "immanence" emphasize their lack of reference to transcendence. Right after defining "secular" as, among other things, lacking reference to transcendence, he asserts that postmodernity is "not more open to religion than modernity," but indeed "more emphatically immanentist" (195).

89. Pickstock, *After Writing,* 48; italics added.

90. Milbank, *Being Reconciled,* 195.

91. Ibid.

92. Deleuze and Guattari, *What Is Philosophy?* 43.

93. Milbank, *Being Reconciled,* 209.

94. Jung Mo Sung, "Human Being as Subject," in *Latin American Liberation Theology: The Next Generation,* ed. Ivan Petrella (Maryknoll, NY: Orbis Books, 2005), 13.

CHAPTER 3—INTRACOSMIC TRANSCENDENCE: LIBERATION THEOLOGY

1. Gustavo Gutiérrez, *A Theology of Liberation: History, Politics and Salvation,* trans. Sister Claridad Inda and John Eagleson (Maryknoll, NY: Orbis Books, 1973), 194.

2. Roberto S. Goizueta, "Locating the Absolutely Absolute Other: Toward a Transmodern Christianity," in *Thinking from the Underside of History: Enrique Dussel's Philosophy of Liberation,* ed. Linda Martín Alcoff and Eduardo Mendieta (New York: Rowman & Littlefield Publishers, 2000), 183; italics added. Similarly, Michael E. Lee explains, "The most significant charge leveled against Latin American Liberation theologies in this period [last decade of the past century] concerned the proper articulation of the relationship between the transcendent and the material or historical. . . . Recent critiques, though articulated in a different theological milieu, bear an underlying resemblance to the older suspicions; namely, that liberation theologies are reductionist . . ." (Lee, "Liberation Theology's Transcendent Moment: The Work of Xavier Zubiri and Ignacio Ellacuría as Noncontrastive Discourse," *Journal of Religion* 83, no. 2 [2003]: 227).

3. Goizueta, "Locating the Absolutely Absolute Other," 183.

4. Manuel J. Mejido, "The Fundamental Problematic of U.S. Hispanic Theology," in *New Horizons in Hispanic/Latino(a) Theology*, ed. Benjamín Valentín (Cleveland: Pilgrim Press, 2003).

5. Enrique Dussel, *1492: El encubrimiento del otro: Hacia el origen del mito de la modernidad* (Madrid: Nueva Utopía, 1993). This challenge to constructions of "modernity" has been further developed by other Latin American philosophers such as Eduardo Mendieta and Walter Mignolo. Radical orthodoxy's fall narrative (a fall from premodernity to modernity to postmodernity) has also been challenged for its homogenizing tendency even by scholars closely related to radical orthodoxy, such as Rowan Williams.

6. Homi K. Bhabha, *The Location of Culture* (London and New York: Routledge, 1994), 241.

7. Eduardo Mendieta, "From Christendom to Polycentric Oikonumé: Modernity, Postmodernity, and Liberation Theology," in *Liberation Theologies, Postmodernity, and the Americas*, ed. David Bastone et al. (London and New York: Routledge, 1997).

8. Enrique Dussel, "The 'World-System': Europe as 'Center' and Its 'Periphery' beyond Eurocentrism," in *Beyond Philosophy: Ethics, History, Marxism, and Liberation Theology*, ed. Eduardo Mendieta (Oxford, UK: Rowman & Littlefield Publishers, 2003), 81n81.

9. Ignacio Ellacuría, "The Historicity of Christian Salvation," in *Mysterium Liberationis: Fundamental Concepts of Liberation Theology*, ed. Ignacio Ellacuría and Jon Sobrino (Maryknoll, NY: Orbis Books, 1993), 254.

10. Ignacio Ellacuría, "Historia de la salvación y salvación en la historia," in *Escritos Teológicos* (San Salvador: UCA Editores, 2000), 528.

11. For a detailed analysis of the relation between Ellacuría and Zubiri, focusing on its impact on Ellacurías's notion of transcendence, see Lee, "Liberation Theology's Transcendent Moment."

12. Ignacio Ellacuría, *Filosofía de la realidad histórica* (San Salvador: UCA Editores, 1990), 31; all translations from this work are mine.

13. To avoid the implication that things exist and then relate to one another, Zubiri does not use the term "relationality" but the neologism "respectivity." "Es el carácter en virtud del cual ninguna cosa empieza por ser ella lo que es y luego se pone en relación con otras, sino justamente al revés: lo que cada cosa es, es constitutivamente función de las demás" (Zubiri, *Estructura dinámica de la realidad* [Madrid: Alianza Editorial and Fundación Xavier Zubiri, 2006], 56).

14. The fact that Zubiri emphasizes the oneness of history tends to convey the image of a totalizing system. Although he uses the term "totality," his use does not follow Levinas's description of totality (which I discuss in the next chapter) and which is challenged by postmodern thinkers because it is predicated on the exclusion of the other. Instead, it refers to an open unity that is more akin to Irigaray's cosmos or Spivak's planetarity, presented later in this work.

15. Ellacuría, *Filosofía de la realidad histórica*, 522.

16. Ibid., 121–22.

17. Ellacuría, "The Historicity of Christian Salvation," 254.

18. Ibid., 264.

19. Ibid., 254; italics added.

20. Mary Daly suggested a consonant reinterpretation of final causes that would move away from Thomistic "enthelechy" (the "indwelling of the goal as yet unattained, but unfolding itself") which is limited by the "nature" of things. Instead, she proposes the more open definition of final causality as "Be-ing" (Daly, *Beyond God the Father: Toward a Philosophy of Women's Liberation* [Boston: Beacon Press, 1973]).

21. James K. A. Smith, *Speech and Theology* (London and New York: Routledge, 2002), 160.

22. Ibid., 126; italics added. Marking his disagreement with Milbank's and Pickstock's readings of Plato, though not with their proposals, Smith argues that this condescension is not an extension, but an inversion of Platonic participation, as it implies not the finite participation in the infinite, but the infinite's participation in the finite.

23. For a discussion of the relationship between the idea of condescension in ancient Christology and the then emerging model of imperial society that combined fellow feeling toward the poor "with the exercise of absolute power," see Peter Brown, *The Making of Late Antiquity* (Cambridge, MA: Harvard University Press, 1978), 155.

24. Ellacuría, "Historicity of Christian Salvation," 266. Ellacuría clarifies, however, that this does not imply the "subjection of profane history to the specificity of Christ as head of the church, and therefore to the church as continuation of the work of Christ," but to the "historical-cosmic Christ" (273). Nonetheless, Ellacuría does not explore the effects of this distinction for the anthropocentrism of his own proposal.

25. Ellacuría, "Historicity of Christian Salvation," 276; italics added. See also Xavier Zubiri, *El hombre y Dios* (Madrid: Fundación Xavier Zubiri and Alianza Editorial, 2003), 307–24.

26. Ellacuría, "Historicity of Christian Salvation," 277; italics added.

27. Zubiri, *El hombre y Dios*, 183.

28. Ellacuría, *Filosofía de la realidad histórica*, 590.

29. Ellacuría, "Historicity of Christian Salvation," 259.

30. Ibid., 263; italics added.

31. Graham Ward, *Barth, Derrida, and the Language of Theology* (Cambridge: Cambridge University Press, 1995).

32. Ellacuría, "Historicity of Christian Salvation," 259.

33. Juan Luis Segundo, "Revelation, Faith, Signs of the Times," in *Mysterium Liberationis: Fundamental Concepts of Liberation Theology*, ed. Ignacio Ellacuría and Jon Sobrino (Maryknoll, NY: Orbis Books, 1993), 330.

34. Ibid., 332.

35. Ellacuría, "Historicity of Christian Salvation," 259.

36. Ibid.

37. Kevin Burke, *The Ground Beneath the Cross: The Theology of Ignacio Ellacuría* (Washington, DC: Georgetown University Press, 2004), 126.

38. Ellacuría, quoted in ibid., 135.

39. Marcella Althaus-Reid, *Indecent Theology: Theological Perversions in Sex, Gender and Politics* (New York: Routledge, 2000), 148; italics added.

40. Ibid., ; italics added.

41. John Milbank, *Being Reconciled: Ontology and Pardon* (London and New York: Routledge, 2003), 195.

42. John Milbank, "Founding the Supernatural: Political and Liberation Theology in the Context of Modern Catholic Thought," in *Theology and Social Theory: Beyond Secular Reason*, ed. Milbank (Oxford, UK, and Cambridge, MA: Blackwell, 1993). Milbank challenges liberation theology on a number of fronts, which, although not reducible to the question of divine transcendence, do seem to converge in a concern about its perceived failure to assert a theological foundation comprehensive enough to subordinate the social sciences. Unfortunately, Milbank does not offer the textual basis for most of his contentions, frequently not even referring to any particular theologian or text, and thus he precludes the reader from engaging him at specific points. Furthermore, for many of his points he refers to Karl Rahner, or to "Rahner and his followers," arguing that it is from him that liberation theology gets its problematic version of integralism.

43. Milbank, *Theology and Social Theory*, 243; italics added.

44. In contrast to his description of liberation theology, Milbank argues that "every discipline must be framed by a theological perspective" (*Being Reconciled*, 3).

45. Milbank, *Theology and Social Theory*, 209.

46. Milbank, *Being Reconciled*, 27.

47. Milbank, *Theology and Social Theory*, 229. It is not clear whether the characterization of liberation as "purely human" or of the needs as "immanently met" are presented as Milbank's opinion or as his representation of liberation theology's stance. If the latter is assumed, one would have to contend that neither "purely human" (as opposed to divine) nor immanent (as opposed to transcendent) fit easily with the historical transcendence proposed by Ellacuría, Sobrino, or Dussel, for instance.

48. Lee, "Liberation Theology's Transcendent Moment," 230.

49. Ibid., 241. Drawing from Xavier Zubiri's philosophy, Ellacuría calls the "rooted dimension of reality" in God its "theologal" dimension—in distinction to the *theological* reflections on that reality (ibid., 234).

50. Ellacuría, "Historicity of Christian Salvation," 255.

51. Ibid., 258; italics added.

52. Walter Benjamin, "Theses on the Philosophy of History," in *Illuminations: Essays and Reflections*, ed. Hannah Arendt (New York: Schocken Books, 1968), 264.

53. Jon Sobrino, "Central Position of the Reign of God in Liberation Theology," in *Mysterium Liberationis: Fundamental Concepts of Liberation Theology*, ed. Ignacio Ellacuría and Jon Sobrino (Maryknoll, NY: Orbis Books, 1993), 382.

54. Ibid. For an argument in favor of the definition of divine transcendence as that which relativizes all created reality and establishes a "reference point for critique beyond" social structures, see Kathryn Tanner, *The Politics of God: Christian Theologies and Social Justice* (Minneapolis: Fortress Press, 1992).

55. Sobrino, "Central Position of the Reign of God in Liberation Theology," 382.

56. Ibid.

57. "Utopía y Profetismo," quoted in Burke, *Ground Beneath the Cross*, 132.

58. Milbank, *Theology and Social Theory*, 251.

59. Althaus-Reid, *Indecent Theology*, 5.

60. Ivone Gebara, *Longing for Running Water: Ecofeminism and Liberation* (Minneapolis: Fortress Press, 1999), 35.

61. Althaus-Reid, *Indecent Theology*, 22.

62. Ibid., 149.

63. Milbank, *Being Reconciled*, 203.

CHAPTER 4—TRANSCENDENCE IN THE FACE OF THE OTHER

1. Ofelia Schutte, "Origins and Tendencies of the Philosophy of Liberation in Latin American Thought: A Critique of Dussel's Ethics," *The Philosophical Forum* 22, no. 3 (1991): 270–95.

2. For Levinas, the Other is always imagined as male, as we shall see in detail in the following chapter. Through my discussion of his work, I use masculine pronouns to reflect this crucial aspect of Levinas's thought.

3. Emmanuel Levinas, *Otherwise Than Being* (Pittsburgh, PA: Duquesne University Press, 1998).

4. A statement by Shlomo Malka in a 1982 radio interview with Levinas and Alain Finkielkraut, quoted in Claire Elise Katz, *Levinas, Judaism, and the Feminine: The Silent Footsteps of Rebecca* (Bloomington and Indianapolis: Indiana University Press, 2003), 1.

5. Mary Doria Russell, *A Thread of Grace: A Novel* (New York: Random House, 2005), 120.

6. Jacques Derrida, "Violence and Metaphysics: An Essay on the Thought of Emmanuel Levinas," in *Writing and Difference*, ed. Derrida (Chicago: University of Chicago Press, 1978), 83.

7. Ibid.

8. Emmanuel Levinas, *Totality and Infinity: An Essay on Exteriority* (Pittsburgh, PA: Duquesne University Press, 1969), 25, 24.

9. Ibid., 52.

10. Ibid.

11. Ibid., 24.

12. Marilynne Robinson, *Gilead* (New York: Farrar Straus Giroux, 2004), 66.

13. Levinas, *Totality and Infinity*, 43.

14. Ibid., 34.

15. Ibid., 300.

16. Edith Wyschogrod, *Emmanuel Levinas: The Problem of Ethical Metaphysics* (New York: Fordham University Press, 2000), xii.

17. Matt. 25:35–38.

18. Levinas, *Totality and Infinity*, 78.

19. Emmanuel Levinas, *Alterity and Transcendence* (New York: Columbia University Press, 1999), 35. "An un-known God who does not take a body . . . ," Levinas clarifies, as if to guard God from the (Christian) image (35). But can he relate to an other bereft of an image, however provisional? Is Christianity not a suppressed Other?

20. Levinas, *Totality and Infinity*, 38. Hardt and Negri highlight this distinction using otherness to name a difference defined in relation to the same in contrast with "singularity," their term for a difference that is underived from the self (Hardt and Negri, *Multitude*, 125). While I find this terminology helpful, I will keep here Levinas's language.

21. Levinas, *Totality and Infinity*, 39.

22. Ibid., 194.

23. Ibid., 41.

24. Ibid., 25; italics added.

25. Levinas, *Totality and Infinity*, 41.

26. Ibid., 34. I wonder if, like Milbank, who faults liberation theology for associating transcendence with the satisfaction of "immanent" human needs, Levinas is also relegating needs to something other than transcendence—even while calling attention to the needs of the Other. We address this in the next chapter.

27. Ibid., 26; italics added. "The presence of a being not entering into, but overflowing, the sphere of the same determines its 'status' as infinite" (195).

28. Ibid., 26–27.

29. Adriaan Peperzak, *To the Other: An Introduction to the Philosophy of Emmanuel Levinas* (West Lafayette, IN: Purdue University, 1996), 161.

30. Levinas, *Totality and Infinity*, 251. Yet "the closedness of the separated being" is "ambiguous." On the one hand, the subject must be "a *separated being* fixed in its identity, the same, the I" (26–27). On the other hand, "this closedness must not prevent" the appearance of the Other (148). But only a separated, autonomous, already happy "I" can respond to the Other. Metaphysical desire is "the misfortune of the happy" (62).

31. Conversation "maintains the distance between me and the Other, the radical separation asserted in transcendence," Levinas explains (ibid., 40). Tracing

the changes in Levinas's notion of transcendence from *Time and the Other* to *Totality and Infinity*, Diane Perpich observes that in the latter, Levinas depicts the ethical relation in terms of discourse precisely to protect the separation of transcendence. Significantly, Perpich argues, this development in Levinas's notion of transcendence also marks a turning point at which, departing from his previous assessments, intimate physical contact—particularly the caress— comes to be seen as a lapse into immanence (Diane Perpich, "From the Caress to the Word: Transcendence and the Feminine in the Philosophy of Emmanuel Levinas," in *Feminist Interpretations of Emmanuel Levinas*, ed. Tina Chanter [University Park: Pennsylvania State University, 2001], 44).

32. Ibid., 36.

33. Ibid., 77.

34. Levinas, *Alterity and Transcendence*, 101.

35. Levinas, *Totality and Infinity*, 75; italics added. Levinas continues, "The strangeness that is freedom is also strangeness-destitution."

36. Sara Ahmed, *Strange Encounters: Embodied Others in Post-Coloniality* (London and New York: Routledge, 2000). See also David Wood, *The Step Back: Ethics and Politics after Deconstruction* (Albany: State University of New York, 2005).

37. Ahmed, *Strange Encounters*, 142.

38. Ibid., 143; first italics added. Levinas attempts to avoid such implications. He explains that the Other's "formal characteristic, to be other, makes up its content" (Levinas, *Totality and Infinity*, 35).

39. Ahmed, *Strange Encounters*. Similarly, Cathryn Vasseleu points out that "Derrida challenges the proposition that alterity of the non-thematizable of the singular can be thematized in the face. As the experiencing of a presence of any kind, the presence of the face is textually defined. The unthematizable expresses itself as a figure which is always already thematized" (Vasseleu, *Textures of Light: Vision and Touch in Irigaray, Levinas and Merleau-Ponty* [London and New York: Routledge, 1998], 90).

40. Levinas's critics observe that his emphasis on asymmetry locks the excluded person in a passive role. David Wood argues that this is based on Levinas's unacknowledged ontology, which turns out to precede rather than follow his ethics (Wood, *The Step Back*).

41. Enrique Dussel and Daniel E. Guillot, *Liberación latinoamericana y Emmanuel Levinas* (Buenos Aires: Editorial Bonum, 1975), 7; my translation. That first encounter, initially reflected in his work *Towards an Ethics of Latin American Liberation* (1973), still characterizes his most recent work. In *Ética de la liberación*, Dussel argues, "la dialéctica de Totalidad (de 'lo Mismo') y el Otro nos abre camino desde donde deberemos reconstruir todo el discurso hasta ahora avanzado" (Enrique Dussel, *Ética de la liberación: En la edad de la globalización y de la exclusión* [Madrid: Trotta, 2002], 359). Eduardo Mendieta observes that although he differs from him in very significant ways, Levinas's model is definitive through Dussel's works (Mendieta, "Introduction," in Enrique

Dussel, *Beyond Philosophy: Ethics, History, Marxism, and Liberation Theology* [Lantham, MD: Rowman & Littlefield Publishers, 2003], 9).

42. I borrow the phrase "setting to work" from Spivak, who espouses a *setting to work* of deconstruction. Spivak draws from Derrida's use. Derrida attributes the phrase to Levinas and quotes his definition: "A work radically conceived is a movement of the same into the other which never returns to the same" (Levinas, quoted in Jacques Derrida, *Adieu to Emmanuel Levinas*, trans. Pascale-Anne Brault and Michael Naas [Stanford, CA: Stanford University Press, 1997]).

43. For a critique of Dussel's ontologization of social location, see Schutte, "Origins and Tendencies," and Ofelia Schutte, *Cultural Identity and Social Liberation* (Albany: State University of New York Press, 1993), 175–205.

44. Dussel, *Ética de la liberación*, 359; my translation.

45. Dussel and Guillot, *Liberación latinoamericana*, 23; Enrique Dussel, *The Invention of the Americas: Eclipse of "the Other" and the Myth of Modernity*, trans. Michael D. Barber (New York: Continuum, 1995). Dussel comments that Levinas himself told him he had never thought of the Indian, the African, or the Asian as an Other (Dussel and Guillot, *Liberación latinoamericana*, 8).

46. Dussel, *Invention of the Americas*, 12. For a more recent analysis of the role of the colonization of America in the constitution of modernity, see Walter D. Mignolo, *Local Histories/Global Designs: Coloniality, Subaltern Knowledges, and Border Thinking* (Princeton, NJ: Princeton University Press, 2000).

47. Dussel, *Invention of the Americas*, 12.

48. Ibid. "The Indian was not discovered as Other, but subsumed under categories of the Same. This Indian was known beforehand as Asiatic and reknown in the face-to-face encounter and so denied as other, or covered over (encubierto)" (ibid). In his use of revelation, Dussel already departs from Levinas, who clarifies that "The relation between the same and the other is not always reducible to knowledge of the other by the same, nor even to the *revelation* of the other to the same, which is already fundamentally different from disclosure" (Levinas, *Totality and Infinity*, 28).

49. Dussel, *Invention of the Americas*, 29. "[Columbus's] hypothesis depended on a priori convictions.... His hypothesis never escaped the *previous* image conditioning it. As a result, when he ran across land in an unexpected site, he was incapable of an *empirical, revelatory* insight into what that land might have been" (Dussel, *Invention of the Americas*, 31).

50. Ibid., 148n1. "The colonizing ego, subjugating the Other, the woman and the conquered male, in an *alienating erotics* and a mercantile *capitalist economics*, follows the route of the conquering ego toward the modern ego cogito."

51. Ibid., 25.

52. Jorge Luis Borges, "La penúltima versión de la realidad," in *Jorge Luis Borges: Obras completas* (Barcelona: Emecé Editores, 1996), 200.

53. Dussel, *Invention of the Americas*, 148n1.

54. Ibid.

55. Roberto S. Goizueta, "Locating the Absolutely Absolute Other: Toward a Transmodern Christianity," in *Thinking from the Underside of History: Enrique Dussel's Philosophy of Liberation,* ed. Linda Martin Alcoff and Eduardo Mendieta (New York: Rowman & Littlefield Publishers, 2000), 184.

56. Roberto S. Goizueta, *Liberation, Method and Dialogue: Enrique Dussel and North American Theological Discourse* (Atlanta: Scholars Press, 1988), 166.

57. Dussel and Guillot, *Liberación latinoamericana,* 26.

58. Enrique Dussel, "An Ethics of Liberation: Fundamental Hypotheses," in *Beyond Philosophy: Ethics, History, Marxism, and Liberation Theology,* ed. Eduardo Mendieta (Lanham, MD: Rowman & Littlefield Publishers, 2003).

59. Dussel offers "Anglo-Saxon capitalism," sexism, and "ideological domination in education" as examples of contemporary "systems" (ibid., 139).

60. Ibid.

61. Ibid., 142; italics added.

62. Ibid., 139.

63. Dussel and Guillot, *Liberación latinoamericana,* 25–26.

64. Goizueta, *Liberation, Method and Dialogue,* 148.

65. Dussel, "Ethics of Liberation," 139.

66. Ibid.

67. Dussel and Guillot, *Liberación latinoamericana,* 23–24.

68. Dussel, "An Ethics of Liberation," 144.

69. Goizueta, "Locating the Absolutely Absolute Other," 184.

70. Significantly, Goizueta explains the metaphorical nature of "exteriority" in contradistinction from God's exteriority. He writes, "Dussel does not mean to say that the Other exists really outside the world—that would be a natural impossibility, unless one were God" (Goizueta, *Liberation, Method and Dialogue,* 117). The assumption seems to be that whereas the poor person is metaphorically exterior, God is literally so.

71. For a careful look at the effects of this naming process on "entitled advocates" and the ways to avoid its dangers, see Mark Lewis Taylor, "Subalternity and Advocacy as *Kairos* for Theology," in *Opting for the Margins: Postmodernity and Liberation in Christian Theology,* ed. Joerg Rieger (New York: Oxford University Press, 2003).

72. Marcella Althaus-Reid, "Feetishism: The Scent of a Latin American Body Theology," in *Toward a Theology of Eros: Transfiguring Passion at the Limits of Discipline,* ed. Virginia Burrus and Catherine Keller (New York: Fordham University Press, 2006), 144.

73. Dussel and Guillot, *Liberación latinoamericana,* 9. "El Otro se presenta como absolutamente otro, al fin es equívoco, es absolutamente incomprensible, es incomunicable, es irrecuperable, no puede liberárselo (salvarlo). El pobre pro-voca, pero al fin es para siempre pobre, miserable."

74. A similar difficulty is found in Dussel's treatment of the relation to the past. Dussel brings in an important dimension of the human encounter that

Levinas's face-to-face does not consider: that of encountering those who are no longer living. But in doing so, he seems to open the possibility for crossing boundaries of space and time to irrupt, in full presence. "In Latin America an oppressed people will emerge again as new. We thus recuperate all those murdered in the history of totality. The emergence of the murdered is resurrection" (ibid., 26). This encounter with the past and the possibility of tapping into its unrealized possibilities is a crucial element in the liberation of oppressed peoples—a subject to which we will return in chap. 6. But the repetition is never without a difference, and failure to recognize the difference can easily lead to appropriation.

75. Ibid., 43, 28. "[E]l hombre inequívoco," "es el que anuncia lo Nuevo que se revela en la alteridad."

76. Ibid., 38.

77. Ibid., 43; italics added. "Cuando se llega a este momento, al límite, en que se *quiere* abandonar la Totalidad, y constituirse como un Otro, y le saca la colaboración al Todo, la guerra comienza."

78. Dussel, *Ética de la liberación*, 311.

79. Ibid.

80. Ibid., 298; italics added. "Lo que permite situarse desde la alteridad del sistema, en el mundo de la vida cotidiana del sentido común pre-científico, pero no cómplice éticamente, es el saber adoptar la perspectiva de las víctimas del sistema de eticidad dado."

81. Schutte, *Cultural Identity and Social Liberation*, 179. See also Schutte, "Origins and Tendencies."

82. Schutte, *Cultural Identity and Social Liberation*, 179.

83. A notable postcolonial deployment of Caliban is Roberto Fernández Retamar's *Calibán: Apuntes sobre la cultura en nuestra América* (México: Diogenes, 1971).

84. Gayatri Chakravorty Spivak, *A Critique of Postcolonial Reason: Toward a History of the Vanishing Present* (Cambridge, MA, and London: Harvard University Press, 1999), 118.

85. Spivak, *Critique of Postcolonial Reason*.

86. See Derrida's assessment of Levinas's reliance on exteriority in Jacques Derrida, "Violence and Metaphysics: An Essay on the Thought of Emmanuel Levinas," in *Writing and Difference*, ed. Derrida (Chicago: University of Chicago Press, 1978).

87. Fernando F. Segovia, "Toward a Hermeneutics of the Diaspora: A Hermeneutics of Otherness and Engagement," in *Reading from This Place: Social Location and Biblical Interpretation in the United States*, ed. Fernando F. Segovia and Mary Ann Tolbert (Minneapolis: Fortress, 1995).

88. Ibid., 58n2.

89. Ibid., 63.

90. Fernando F. Segovia, "Two Places and No Place on Which to Stand," in *Mestizo Christianity*, ed. Arturo J. Bañuelas (Maryknoll, NY: Orbis Books, 1995), 36–37.

91. Segovia, "Toward a Hermeneutics," 67; italics added.

92. For an elucidation of the contours of Latina theological anthropology, see Michelle Gonzalez, "Who Is Americana/o? Theological Anthropology, Postcoloniality, and the Spanish-Speaking Americas," in *Postcolonial Theologies: Divinity and Empire*, ed. Catherine Keller, Michael Nausner, and Mayra Rivera (St. Louis: Chalice, 2004). The implications of the use of *mestizaje* as a model of identity for constructions of subjectivity have not always been reflected in this literature. The need to resist the negative definitions of U.S. Hispanics as "the other" have frequently led to a use of *mestizaje* as a stable trait of identity that provides an epistemological advantage. *Mestizaje* thus ceases to allude to complex otherness.

93. Roberto Goizueta explains that identity, as inextricable from community, extends "not only spatially but also temporally: that community includes my ancestors as well as my progeny and their progeny" (Roberto S. Goizueta, *Caminemos con Jesús: Toward a Hispanic/Latino Theology of Accompaniment* [Maryknoll, NY: Orbis Books, 1995], 52).

94. Ahmed, *Strange Encounters*, 151.

95. Goizueta, *Caminemos con Jesús*, 50.

96. Ibid.

97. Ibid., 64.

98. Ibid., 179.

99. Ibid., 195, 191.

100. Such a model would also need to struggle to take account of others that the geopolitical distribution of power renders truly invisible—lest we ignore, for instance, our own ties to Latin America, which is now U.S. Hispanics' other.

101. Levinas, *Totality and Infinity*, 23.

102. Ibid., 27.

CHAPTER 5: TRANSCENDENCE IN THE FLESH OF THE OTHER

1. An earlier version of this chapter was published in Virginia Burrus and Catherine Keller, *Toward a Theology of Eros: Transfiguring Passion at the Limits of Discipline* (New York: Fordham University Press, 2006).

2. Hélène Cixous, *Manna: For the Mandelstams for the Mandelas*, trans. Catherine A. F. MacGillivray (Minneapolis: University of Minnesota, 1994), 70.

3. Ibid.

4. Ibid.; italics added.

5. Luce Irigaray, "Each Transcendent to the Other," in *To Be Two* (New York: Routledge, 2001).

6. Ibid., 86.

7. Ibid.

8. Ibid., 88.

9. Luce Irigaray, *An Ethics of Sexual Difference* (Ithaca, NY: Cornell University Press), 17, 12.

10. Luce Irigaray, *I Love to You: Sketch of a Possible Felicity in History,* trans. Alison Martin (New York and London: Routledge, 1996), 104.

11. *An Ethics of Sexual Difference* closes with an essay on Levinas, but the influence of his work can be seen throughout the volume, as well as in other of her essays. Irigaray refuses to be described as a disciple of Levinas, however. In fact, she explains that when she "sought dialogue with Levinas" through her reading of his texts and the publication of "The Fecundity of Caress," "[e]ach time, it was a failure" (Luce Irigaray, "What Other Are We Talking About?" in *Encounters with Levinas,* ed. Thomas Trezise, Yale French Studies [New Haven, CT: Yale University Press, 2004], 68). For a detailed analysis of Irigaray's rewriting of Levinas, see Tina Chanter, *Ethics of Eros: Irigaray's Rewriting of the Philosophers* (New York and London: Routledge, 1995), 170–214.

12. Emmanuel Levinas, *Totality and Infinity: An Essay on Exteriority* (Pittsburgh, PA: Duquesne University Press, 1969), 43, 41.

13. Jacques Derrida, "Violence and Metaphysics: An Essay on the Thought of Emmanuel Levinas," in *Writing and Difference,* ed. Derrida (Chicago: University of Chicago Press, 1978), 92.

14. Levinas, *Totality and Infinity,* 34.

15. The structure of this outward-moving ethics is replayed in the unreturnability of the gift as described by Derrida.

16. Levinas, *Totality and Infinity,* 254.

17. Levinas's depiction of the feminine has been the subject of much feminist scholarship. See, for instance, Tina Chanter, ed., *Feminist Interpretations of Emmanuel Levinas* (University Park: Pennsylvania State University, 2001); Stella Sandford, *The Metaphysics of Love: Gender and Transcendence in Levinas* (London and New Brunswick, NJ: Athlone, 2000); and Claire Elise Katz, *Levinas, Judaism, and the Feminine: The Silent Footsteps of Rebecca* (Bloomington and Indianapolis: Indiana University Press, 2003).

18. For an appreciative note on the distinction between erotic love and ethical love, see, for instance, Katz's insightful reading of Levinas's portrayal of the feminine against the backdrop of Jewish thought (*Levinas, Judaism, and the Feminine*).

19. Emmanuel Levinas, *Nine Talmudic Readings,* trans. Annette Aronowicz (Bloomington and Indianapolis: Indiana University Press, 1990), 76. Significantly, the images of creation over a reviled chaos are evoked here. For an assessment of the influence and ethical repercussions of this theological trope see Catherine Keller, *Face of the Deep: A Theology of Becoming* (London and New York: Routledge, 2003).

20. Levinas, *Totality and Infinity,* 264.

21. Levinas, *Nine Talmudic Readings*, 76.

22. Enrique Dussel and Daniel E. Guillot, *Liberación latinoamericana y Emmanuel Levinas* (Buenos Aires: Editorial Bonum, 1975), 8.

23. Enrique Dussel, *Filosofía ética latinoamericana*, vol. 3 (1977), 60.

24. Enrique Dussel, *Liberación de la mujer y erótica latinoamericana* (Bogotá: Editorial Nueva América, 1990), 26.

25. Ibid.

26. Ofelia Schutte, *Cultural Identity and Social Liberation* (Albany: State University of New York Press, 1993), 201–4. That text also develops Schutte's critique of Dussel's position regarding feminism. It shall be noted too that, in his early works, Dussel describes feminism as a totalitarian ideology, problematically interpreting it as a pursuit of sameness (*Liberación de la mujer*, 25).

27. Levinas, *Totality and Infinity*, 39.

28. Levinas, *Alterity and Transcendence*, 27; italics added.

29. Luce Irigaray, *The Way of Love*, trans. Heidi Bostic and Stephen Pluhácek (New York: Continuum, 2002), 131; italics added.

30. Irigaray, *Ethics of Sexual Difference*, 193.

31. Irigaray remarks that the world of the womb "is not to be confused with her. It is destroyed forever at birth and it is impossible ever to return to it. All kinds of veils may claim to take its place, seek to repeat it, but there can be no return to that first dwelling place" (Irigaray, *Sexes and Genealogies* [New York: Columbia University Press, 1993], 33).

32. Irigaray, *Ethics of Sexual Difference*, 186.

33. Ibid., 187.

34. "Union-in-touch, parting, and reunion constitute a different rhythm," Ofelia Schutte observes, "for lovers whose touch is an incarnation of the other's alterity" (Schutte, "A Critique of Normative Heterosexuality: Identity, Embodiment, and Sexual Difference in Beauvoir and Irigaray," *Hypatia* 12, no. 1 [1997]: 53).

35. Luce Irigaray, "Questions to Emmanuel Levinas: On the Divinity of Love," in *Re-Reading Levinas*, ed. Robert Bernasconi and Simon Critchley, Studies in Continental Thought (Bloomington and Indianapolis: Indiana University Press, 1991), 110–11.

36. Ibid., 110.

37. Gayatri Chakravorty Spivak, "French Feminism Revisited," in *Outside in the Teaching Machine*, ed. Spivak (New York and London: Routledge, 1993), 171.

38. Luce Irigaray, "Sexual Difference," in *French Feminist Thought: A Reader*, ed. Toril Moi (New York: Basil Blackwell, 1987), 124.

39. Irigaray, "Questions to Emmanuel Levinas," 111.

40. Levinas, *Totality and Infinity*, 36. See discussion in chap. 4.

41. Dussel and Guillot, *Liberación latinoamericana*, 9.

42. Irigaray, "What Other Are We Talking About?" 69.

43. Irigaray, *Ethics of Sexual Difference*, 13. Similarly she states, "One of the dangers of love between women is the confusion of their identities, the lack of

respect for or of perception of their differences" (63). Other readers contend that Irigaray's privilege of sexual difference should be read only "in the context of a culturally specific situation," and not as a universally applicable principle; see Tamsin Lorraine, *Irigaray & Deleuze: Experiments in Visceral Philosophy* (Ithaca, NY, and London: Cornell University Press, 1999), 21. (See also my discussion of Spivak's reading of Irigaray in chap. 6.)

44. Amy Hollywood, *Sensible Ecstasy: Mysticism, Sexual Difference, and the Demands of History* (Chicago and London: University of Chicago Press, 2002), 210. Although she alludes to the naturalization and depolitization of difference that the "restriction of difference to sex" fosters, Hollywood's main concern is Irigaray's replacement of God by sexual difference. "Irigaray reifies sexual difference as the essential difference that replaces the universal human possibility or actuality represented by Feuerbach's notion of the species being. . . . Sexual difference is the locus for finite human beings' desire for infinite possibility. Irigaray may safeguard against the reification of female (or male) divinities, but in order to accomplish this task she must put sexual difference in the place once occupied by God. It is, she argues, the universal and objective difference through which subjectivity can be discovered . . ." (232).

45. See chap. 2.

46. Irigaray, *Ethics of Sexual Difference*, 12.

47. Ibid.

48. John Milbank, *Being Reconciled: Ontology and Pardon* (London and New York: Routledge, 2003), 207.

49. Irigaray, *Ethics of Sexual Difference*, 12.

50. Irigaray, "Questions to Emmanuel Levinas," 111.

51. Levinas proposed that the third is the beginning of justice, but excluded it/him from the sexual encounter. His third may suggest a God-like principle or the community.

52. Challenging the common confusion of ground with "fixity, the self-present, the changeless . . . the Same," Catherine Keller proposes thinking of the metaphor of ground not as something that discourses provide, but which they "variously inhabit and honor." Concepts "will either attend to their own 'ground,' the earthly habitat that endlessly and differently gives rise to thought, or they will drift in the conventional groundlessness that has provided the very foundation for *classical* metaphysics" (Keller, "Introduction," in Catherine Keller and Anne Daniell, eds., *Process and Difference: Between Cosmological and Poststructuralist Postmodernisms* [Albany: State University of New York, 2002], 13).

53. Irigaray, *Ethics of Sexual Difference*, 100.

54. Chanter, *Ethics of Eros*, 219.

55. Irigaray, *Ethics of Sexual Difference*, 195.

56. Ibid., 48; italics added.

57. Ofelia Schutte argues that Irigaray's challenge is not to discard heterosexuality, but "to unlink the notion of sexual difference from the normative understanding of heterosexuality—that is, to rethink and re-symbolize sexual difference" (Schutte, "Critique of Normative Heterosexuality," 52).

58. Luce Irigaray, *This Sex Which Is Not One,* trans. Catherine Porter and Carolyn Burke (Ithaca, NY: Cornell University Press, 1977), 279.

59. Irigaray's single focus has been strategically crucial for challenging the ubiquitous erasure of the female subject in Western thought. However, the urgent need for resisting the global forms of imperialism demands attention to other Others also forcefully excluded from Western thought.

60. Luce Irigaray, *This Sex Which Is Not One,* 272. "The work of mestiza consciousness is to break down the subject-object duality which keeps her prisoner and to show in the flesh and through images in her work how duality is transcended" (Gloria Anzaldúa, *Borderlands/La Frontera: The New Mestiza* [San Francisco: Aunt Lute Books, 1999], 151).

61. Anzaldúa, *Borderlands/La Frontera,* 104.

62. Irigaray, *Ethics of Sexual Difference,* 193.

63. Yvonne Yarbro-Bejarano, *The Wounded Heart: Writing on Cherríe Moraga* (Austin: University of Texas, 2001), 19.

64. Ibid., 92.

65. Do "we need to think this body as quite so pure, so new-born as Irigaray's woundless utopia of the flesh," Catherine Keller wonders. "I suspect," Keller proposes, "that the deep flesh, even in its resurrection, will carry the redemptive scars" (Keller, *Face of the Deep,* 221).

CHAPTER 6: TRANSCENDENCE OF PLANETARY CREATURES

1. Rubén Blades, *Buscando América* (New York: Elektra Records, 1984), my translation.

2. Quoted in Avery F. Gordon, *Ghostly Matters: Haunting and the Sociological Imagination* (Minneapolis and London: University of Minnesota Press, 1997), 5–6. "Patricia Williams is a commercial lawyer and professor of contract and property law. . . . Her great-great grandmother's owner and the father of her children was Austin Miller, a well-known Tennessee Lawyer and jurist" (5).

3. For Levinas, the relation between the singularity of the encounter and the generality of politics is the presence of the third; see Jacques Derrida, *Adieu to Emmanuel Levinas,* trans. Pascale-Anne Brault and Michael Naas (Stanford, CA: Stanford University Press, 1997), 30ff.

4. Emmanuel Levinas, *Totality and Infinity: An Essay on Exteriority* (Pittsburgh, PA: Duquesne University Press, 1969), 25; italics added.

5. Ibid., 24.

6. Jacques Derrida, "Violence and Metaphysics: An Essay on the Thought of Emmanuel Levinas," in *Writing and Difference,* ed. Derrida (Chicago: University of Chicago Press, 1978), 103.

7. Homi K. Bhabha, *The Location of Culture* (London and New York: Routledge, 1994), 4.

8. Ibid., 7.

9. Ibid., 171.

10. Ibid., 12.

11. Levinas, *Totality and Infinity,* 75.

12. Toni Morrison, *Playing in the Dark: Whiteness and the Literary Imagination* (New York: Vintage Books, 1992), 48. "Africanism is the vehicle by which the American self knows itself as not enslaved, but free; not repulsive, but desirable; not helpless, but licensed and powerful; not history-less, but historical; not damned, but innocent; not a blind accident of evolution, but a progressive fulfillment of destiny" (52).

13. See Walter D. Mignolo, *Local Histories/Global Designs: Coloniality, Subaltern Knowledges, and Border Thinking* (Princeton, NJ: Princeton University Press, 2000).

14. Cf. Edward Said, *Orientalism* (New York: Vintage Books, 1994).

15. I am not yet talking about the wholly other. I am instead attempting to call attention to the historicity of our representations of the world, ourselves, and others.

16. Levinas, *Totality and Infinity,* 75; italics added.

17. Gayatri Chakravorty Spivak uses Heidegger's "concept-metaphor of earth and world" to describe the "imperialist project" and uncover the "multifarious thingliness . . . of a represented world on a map." The "necessary yet contradictory assumption of an uninscribed earth that is the condition of possibility of the worldling of a world generates the force to make the 'native' see himself as 'other'" (Spivak, *A Critique of Postcolonial Reason: Toward a History of the Vanishing Present* (Cambridge, MA, and London: Harvard University Press, 1999), 212). These processes affect the subject-constitution of the colonized subject and thus must be reckoned with in any treatment of (post)colonial identity (Spivak, *The Post-colonial Critic: Interviews, Strategies, Dialogues* [New York and London: Routledge, 1990], 129).

18. Spivak borrows the term "foreclosure" from Jacques Lacan's psychoanalytic theory, where it is defined as an "energetic and successful kind of defense" where the "ego rejects the incompatible idea *together with the affect* and behaves as if the idea had never occurred to the ego at all" (Lacan, quoted in Spivak, *Critique,* 4).

19. Ibid., 9.

20. Ibid., 6.

21. Ibid.

22. Bhabha, *Location of Culture,* 12.

23. Levinas states, for instance, "For the presence before a face ... can lose the avidity proper to the gaze only by turning into generosity incapable of approaching the Other with empty hands" (Levinas, *Totality and Infinity,* 50).

24. The similarities between this description of the workings of colonial discourse and *différance* betrays postcolonial thinkers' dependence on Derrida. This dependence in turn responds to an important premise of postcolonial criticism: that the apparent opposition between conceptual knowledge and political practice, like the other pair of opposites described above, depends on the suppression of an economy that produces and destabilizes both terms.

25. Spivak does not differentiate between these terms, and sometimes refers simply to "the other" or even "the quite-Other."

26. Ernesto Laclau, *Emancipation(s)* (London and New York: Verso, 1996), 78.

27. Ibid.

28. Spivak, "French Feminism Revisited," in *Outside in the Teaching Machine,* 165.

29. Ibid.

30. Spivak's use of the term "wholly other" in conjunction with the subaltern has been criticized for supposedly reopening a gap, reducing the effectiveness of the Others' intervention. For Bhabha, the representation of the Other as unrepresentable is part of Western theory's "strategy of containment where the other text is forever the exegetical horizon of difference, never the active agent of articulation" (Bhabha, *Location of Culture,* 31). "[T]he more the subaltern is seen as wholly other, the more Spivak seems to construct the subaltern's identity neither relationally nor differentially, but in essentialist terms ..." (Bart Moore-Gilbert, *Postcolonial Theory: Context, Practices, Politics* [London and New York: Verso, 1997], 102). For a similar critique, see Asha Varadahrajan, *Exotic Parodies: Subjectivity in Adorno, Said, and Spivak* (Minneapolis and London: University of Minnesota Press, 1995), xvi. However, rather than reducing the subaltern to a given category, Spivak is, in my opinion, attempting to find a way in which the subaltern can be perceived as a disruption of the normative truths without relying on an assumption of presence and availability of the other. Moore-Gilbert contends that in such model, "the nonsubaltern must either maximally respect the Other's radical alterity, thus leaving the status quo intact, or attempt the impossible feat of 'opening up' to the Other without in any way 'assimilating' the Other to his/her own subject position, perspectives or identity" (103). In her most recent work, Spivak has clarified that she uses the subaltern to refer to those others whose voice is not heard within "the system." She has also been careful to distinguish between the wholly Other "as such," who strictly speaking is unrepresentable, and the figures through which she attempts to allude to its effects, its traces. My discussion of Spivak's use of deconstruction attempts to clarify her admittedly cryptic and controversial use of the term.

31. "The alterity of history [is] a line we cannot cross" (Spivak, *Critique,* 189).

32. In my opinion, many accusations that Spivak in effect denies the agency of subaltern communities seem to collapse the related but distinct modes of her

critique: the critique of theoretical categories and her analyses of strategies for social change. Ignoring the interruptive strategy, some critics assume an identity between the figure of the wholly other and a describable subaltern community.

33. Colin MacCabe, "Forward," in Spivak, *In Other Worlds.*

34. Spivak, *Critique,* 175.

35. Spivak avoids making a single case representative of the appearance of otherness. "The Indian case cannot be taken as representative of all countries, nations, cultures, and the like that may be invoked as the Other of the European Self" (ibid., 209). "[D]ealing with the position of the other as an implied 'subject'(ive) position, must also vary our assumptions depending upon the text with which we are dealing" (ibid., 9).

36. Gayatri Chakravorty Spivak, "A Moral Dilemma," in *What Happens to History? The Renewal of Ethics in Contemporary Thought,* ed. Howard Marchitello (New York and London: Routledge, 2001), 215.

37. Spivak, *Outside in the Teaching Machine,* 212.

38. Spivak, *Critique,* 426.

39. Ibid., 425.

40. In contrast to those readings that completely identify transcendence with difference, also drawing from the work of Levinas, Richard Kearney proposes a model of subjectivity where finitude and in-finity are inextricable from each other within any human being. Kearney uses *person* to designate that which appears *as if* fully present to me, *as if* within my grasp. *Persona,* on the other hand, alludes to the otherness of the Other. It "is all that in others exceeds my searching gaze, safeguarding their inimitable and unique singularity" (Richard Kearney, *The God Who May Be: A Hermeneutics of Religion* [Bloomington and Indianapolis: Indiana University Press, 2001], 10). The persona of the Other does not appear as such, its time is the "futural horizon" and the no-place of the person. It is eschatological, never fully present. "The eschaton, as *persona,* is precisely the Other's future possibilities which are impossible for me" (12). "[T]he *persona* never actually appears at all, as such, in that it has *already come and gone,* leaving only its traces; or is *still to come,* outstripping every figuration on my past. The *persona* hails and haunts me *before* I even begin to represent it *as if* it were present before me" (16). Yet the persona takes place in the person, from which it is inextricable. The *infinite in the finite, the more in the less,* as Levinas would say. "[T]he *persona* in the face of ther person" "transcends us" (11). The excess of the face is what Kearney calls the *persona* of a person.

Kearney's use of the terms *person* and *persona* brings to the fore the difference and inextricability between the conceptual categories with which we define otherness and which influence our encounters with another person at any given moment, on the one hand, and the singularity and infinity of each creature which is implied in the transcendence of the Other. Although we will not adopt Kearney's terminology, we keep this distinction in mind as we continue to probe the relation between social-production of otherness and what we might call *transcendence.*

41. Ibid., 130.

42. Trinh T. Minh-Ha, *Woman Native Other* (Bloomington and Indianapolis: Indiana University Press, 1989), 101.

43. "Catachresis" is a critical strategy that Spivak frequently analyzes and deploys. It involves "wrenching particular images, ideas or rhetorical strategies out of their place within a particular narrative and using them to open up new arenas of meaning" (Moore-Gilbert, *Postcolonial Theory*, 84).

44. This is reminiscent of the way in which liberation theologies have explained the "preferential option for the poor"; their poverty shows the absence of the reign of God.

45. Spivak, *Critique*, 427.

46. Ibid.

47. Ibid., 428.

48. Ibid., 427.

49. Jacques Derrida and Maurizio Ferraris, *A Taste for the Secret*, trans. Giacomo Donis (Cambridge, UK: Polity, 2001), 83; italics added.

50. Derrida, *Adieu*, 129n12.

51. Gayatri Chakravorty Spivak, *Death of a Discipline* (New York: Columbia University Press, 2003), 36.

52. Danna Nolan Fewell, *The Children of Israel: Reading the Bible for the Sake of Our Children* (Nashville: Abingdon Press, 2003), 69.

53. Patricia Williams, quoted in Gordon, *Ghostly Matters*, 5–6.

54. Spivak, "Moral Dilemma," 228. Spivak explains, for instance, that "reading literature, we learn to learn from the singular and the unverifiable" (Spivak, *Critique*, 145n49).

55. Spivak, "Moral Dilemma," 215.

56. Spivak, *Death of a Discipline*, 13.

57. Spivak, *Critique*, 175–76.

58. "Imagination is structurally unverifiable" (Spivak, "Moral Dilemma," 221).

59. Spivak, *Critique*, 394.

60. Derrida, *Adieu*, 111. Derrida adds, "When someone once expressed concern to Levinas about the 'phantomatic character' of his philosophy, especially when it treats the 'face of the other,' Levinas did not directly object. Resorting to what I have just called the 'Pascalian' argument ('it is necessary that the other be welcomed independently of his qualities'), he clearly specified 'welcomed,' especially in an 'immediate,' urgent way, without waiting, as if 'real' qualities, attributes, or properties (everything that makes a living person into something other than a phantom) slowed down, mediatized, or compromised the purity of this welcome. It is necessary to welcome the other in his alterity, without waiting, and thus not to pause to recognize his real predicates. It is thus necessary, beyond all perception, to receive the other while running the risk, a risk that is always troubling, strangely troubling, like the stranger (*unheimlich*), of a hospitality offered to the *guest* as *ghost* or *Geist* or *Gast*." I have been arguing, however,

that Levinas does not heed (cannot heed) his own warning, that he did move into conceptualizing the Other as the stranger.

61. Jacques Derrida, *Specters of Marx: The State of Debt, the Work of Mourning, and the New International,* trans. Peggy Kamuf (New York and London: Routledge, 1994), xix.

62. Ibid.

63. Ibid., xix.

64. Ibid.

65. Gordon, *Ghostly Matters.*

66. Ibid., 63.

67. Laclau, *Emancipation(s),* 78.

68. "I should have liked to establish a transferential [self-consolidating] relationship. I pray instead to be haunted by her slight ghost" (Spivak, *Critique,* 207). "Haunting for transference, the unconscious as interruption" (Spivak, *Critique,* 209).

69. Gordon, *Ghostly Matters,* 200.

70. Ibid., 63.

71. Sara Ahmed, *Strange Encounters: Embodied Others in Post-Coloniality* (London and New York: Routledge, 2000), 156.

72. Gordon, *Ghostly Matters,* 183.

73. Ibid., 195.

74. Ahmed, *Strange Encounters,* 156.

75. Gordon, *Ghostly Matters,* 8; italics added.

76. Spivak, "Moral Dilemma," 221; italics added.

77. See, for instance, Spivak, *Critique,* 207; Spivak, *Death of a Discipline,* 50, 53.

78. Spivak, "Moral Dilemma," 215.

79. Luce Irigaray, *An Ethics of Sexual Difference* (Ithaca, NY: Cornell University Press, 1993), 232.

80. Spivak, "French Feminism Revisited," 167; italics added.

81. Spivak, *Death of a Discipline,* 73.

82. Ibid., 72.

83. Ibid., 73.

84. Donna Landry and Gerald MacLean, eds., *The Spivak Reader: Selected Works of Gayatri Chakravorty Spivak* (London and New York: Routledge, 1995), 275.

85. Spivak, "Moral Dilemma," 228.

86. Spivak, *Death of a Discipline,* 71.

87. Spivak, *Critique,* 383.

88. Landry and MacLean, eds., *The Spivak Reader,* 275.

89. Spivak, *Critique,* 429.

90. Ibid., 382.

91. Ibid.

92. Catherine Keller, "The Love of Postcolonialism: Theology in the Interstices of Empire," in *Postcolonial Theologies: Divinity and Empire*, ed. Catherine Keller, Michael Nausner, and Mayra Rivera (St. Louis: Chalice, 2004), 238.

93. This is perhaps another risk of affirmative deconstruction. Spivak, *Critique*, 430.

94. Spivak, "French Feminism Revisited," 167; italics added.

95. Luce Irigaray, "The Fecundity of Caress: A Reading of Levinas, *Totality and Infinity*, 'Phenomenology of Eros,'" in *An Ethics of Sexual Difference*, ed. Irigaray (Ithaca, NY: Cornell University Press, 1993), 204.

96. Spivak, "French Feminism Revisited," 168. Although Spivak is understandably hesitant to inhabit Irigaray's Christian-inflected narrative world, that does not preclude her from tapping into its energies to develop her own planetarity. Furthermore, Spivak suggests the possibility of a dialogue between Irigaray and other activists among the "peoples of the book," whose work she also engages (ibid., 169).

97. Roberto S. Goizueta, *Caminemos con Jesús: Toward a Hispanic/Latino Theology of Accompaniment* (Maryknoll, NY: Orbis Books, 1995), 179.

CHAPTER 7: THE TOUCH OF TRANSCENDENCE

1. Emmanuel Levinas, *Difficult Freedom: Essays in Judaism*, trans. Seán Hand (Baltimore: Johns Hopkins University Press, 1990).

2. Luce Irigaray, "The Fecundity of Caress: A Reading of Levinas, *Totality and Infinity*, 'Phenomenology of Eros,'" in *An Ethics of Sexual Difference*, ed. Irigaray (Ithaca, NY: Cornell University Press, 1993), 204.

3. Gayatri Chakravorty Spivak, "A Moral Dilemma", in *What Happens to History? The Renewal of Ethics in Contemporary Thought*, ed. Howard Marchitello (New York and London: Routledge, 2001), 215.

4. Ivone Gebara, *Longing for Running Water: Ecofeminism and Liberation* (Minneapolis: Fortress Press, 1999), 124.

5. Karmen MacKendrick, *Word Made Skin: Figuring Language at the Surface of Flesh* (New York: Fordham University Press, 2004), 41.

6. Spivak, "Moral Dilemma", 215; italics added.

7. Irigaray, *Ethics of Sexual Difference*, 100.

8. Cf. Virginia Burrus, *Begotten, Not Made* (Stanford, CA: Stanford University Press, 2000).

9. Spivak, *Death of a Discipline* (New York: Columbia University Press, 2003), 73.

10. Ignacio Ellacuría, "The Historicity of Christian Salvation," in *Mysterium Liberationis: Fundamental Concepts of Liberation Theology*, ed. Ignacio Ellacuría and Jon Sobrino (Maryknoll, NY: Orbis Books, 1993), 264.

11. Following Xavier Zubiri, Ellacuría describes reality in relation to two powers: "relegation," which "bind[s] reality to its ground"; "respectivity," which "links any real thing to every other thing in the cosmos" (Kevin Burke, *The Ground beneath the Cross: The Theology of Ignacio Ellacuría* [Washington, DC: Georgetown University Press, 2004], 55).

12. Leonardo Boff, *Ecology and Liberation: A New Paradigm,* trans. John Cumming (Maryknoll, NY: Orbis Books, 1995), 51; italics added.

13. Gebara, *Longing for Running Water,* 167.

14. Boff, *Ecology and Liberation,* 46.

15. Virginia Burrus, "The Sex Life of God: Divine Begetting and Creativity in Ancient Christian Texts," paper presented at The Language of Bodily Processes: Sensual and/or Metaphorical, University of Oslo, Norway, November 8–9, 2004.

16. Burrus, *Begotten, Not Made,* 37. Peter Brown develops the argument of the closing of the heavens in his *Making of Late Antiquity,* from which Burrus draws for her study on manhood and the Nicene Trinitarian formula.

17. Ibid.

18. Catherine Pickstock, *After Writing: On the Liturgical Consummation of Philosophy* (Oxford, UK, and Model, MA: Blackwell Publishers, 1998), 182; italics added.

19. Daniel Boyarin, "Midrash and the 'Magic of Language': Reading without Logocentrism", in *Derrida and Religion: Other Testaments,* ed. Yvonne Sherwood and Kevin Hart (New York and London: Routledge, 2005), 132.

20. The translation "begot" me is well supported among biblical scholars. See, for example, Carol R. Fontaine, "The Social Role of Women in the World of Wisdom," in Carol A. Newsom, *Women's Bible Commentary* (Louisville, KY: Westminster John Knox Press, 1998); Roland E. Murphy, *The Tree of Life: An Exploration of Biblical Wisdom Literature* (Grand Rapids: William B. Eerdmans, 1996), 136; William McKane, *Proverbs: A New Approach* (Philadelphia: Westminster, 1970); and Leo G. Perdue, *Proverbs* (Louisville, KY: Westminster John Knox Press, 2000).

21. See Perdue, *Proverbs,* 144. See also McKane, *Proverbs,* 352: "I was hidden in the womb in antiquity."

22. "Literally, 'was given birth'" (Perdue, *Proverbs,* 143). See also McKane, *Proverbs,* 352.

23. See n. 22.

24. Tellingly, the second-century Christian apologist Theophilus seems to have resisted the idea of God's labor, replacing the image of delivery for a no less material one. "God, having his own Logos innate in his bowels, generated him together with his own Sophia, vomiting him forth before everything else" (2.10).

25. Daniel Boyarin, "The Gospel of the Memra: Jewish Binitarianism and the Prologue to John," *Harvard Theological Review* 94 no. 3 (2001): 269.

26. I borrow the phrase "serving as active memory" from Irigaray (Luce Irigaray, *Sexes and Genealogies* [New York: Columbia University Press, 1993], 40).

27. Ignacio Ellacuría, "The Historicity of Christian Salvation," in *Mysterium Liberationis: Fundamental Concepts of Liberation Theology*, ed. Ellacuría and Jon Sobrino (Maryknoll, NY: Orbis Books, 1993), 276; italics added.

28. Ibid., 277; italics added.

29. See chap. 5.

30. Marcella Althaus-Reid, "El Tocado (Le Toucher): Sexual Irregularities in the Translation of God (the Word) in Jesus", in *Derrida and Religion: Other Testaments*, ed. Yvonne Sherwood and Kevin Hart (New York: Routledge, 2004), 394.

31. MacKendrick, *Word Made Skin*, 92.

32. Nancy, quoted in ibid., 45.

33. MacKendrick, *Word Made Skin*, 162.

34. Irigaray, *Ethics of Sexual Difference*, 187.

35. "Well also does Paul His apostle say: One God, the Father, who is over all and through all and in us all (Eph 4:6). For *over all* is the Father; and *through all* is the Son, for through him all things were made by the Father; and *in us* all is the Spirit" (Irenaeus of Lyons, *Apostolic Preaching*).

36. Luce Irigaray, *The Way of Love*, trans. Heidi Bostic and Stephen Pluhácek (New York: Continuum, 2002), 171.

37. Gebara, *Longing for Running Water*, 124.

38. "[T]he whole world . . . ought to be regarded as some huge and immense animal, which is kept together by the power and reason of God as by one soul" (*First Principles*, 2.1.3).

39. See chap. 6.

40. For an interpretation of ancestral immortality in process-metaphysical terms, see Anita Coleman, "Walking in the Whirlwind: A Whiteheadian-Womanist Soteriology" (PhD thesis, Claremont University, 2004).

41. Rebecca S. Chopp, "Theology and the Poetics of Testimony," in *Converging on Culture: Theologians in Dialogue with Cultural Analysis and Criticism*, ed. Delwin Brown, Sheila Greeve Davaney, and Kathryn Tanner (Oxford and New York: Oxford University Press, 2001), 66–67.

42. Serene Jones draws from Irigaray's work to propose an interpretation of the doctrine of grace as a God-given "'envelope' of identity that fragmented women can inhabit and thereby use to claim their embodied agency." My own proposal is perhaps an elaboration of this vision, which nonetheless resists the logic of justification and sanctification, inasmuch as it tends to reinscribe the idea of an alienated creature who God embraces only *a posteriori* (Serene Jones, *Feminist Theory and Christian Theology: Cartographies of Grace* [Minneapolis: Fortress Press, 2000], 64).

43. Irigaray, *Way of Love*, 131; italics added.

44. Ibid., 66–67.

45. Ibid., 67.

46. Ibid.

47. Irigaray, *Ethics of Sexual Difference*, 48; italics added.

48. Jean-Luc Nancy, *Being Singular Plural,* trans. Robert D. Richardson and Anne E. O'Brien, Crossing Aesthetics (Stanford, CA: Stanford University Press, 2000), 17.

49. Serene Jones, "Creation and Imagination: Reflections on Language, Law, and Beauty" (paper presented at the Transdisciplinary Theology Colloquium, Drew University, Madison, NJ, September 30–October 1, 2001).

50. Ps. 19:1–4.

51. MacKendrick, *Word Made Skin,* 76.

52. Ibid., 27.

53. Mark 9:2–8.

54. MacKendrick, *Word Made Skin,* 36.

55. Irigaray, *Way of Love,* 173.

56. Jesus refers to "My glory which you have given me because you loved me," in John 17:24. Similarly, in his love, he gives the glory to the disciples, "that they may be one, as we are one, I in them and you in me, that they may become completely one, so that the world may know that you have sent me and have loved them even as you have loved me" (John 17:22–23).

57. Irigaray, *Way of Love,* 174.

Bibliography

Ahmed, Sara. *Strange Encounters: Embodied Others in Post-Coloniality.* London and New York: Routledge, 2000.

Althaus-Reid, Marcella. "El Tocado (Le Toucher): Sexual Irregularities in the Translation of God (the Word) in Jesus." In *Derrida and Religion: Other Testaments,* edited by Yvonne Sherwood and Kevin Hart, 393–406. New York: Routledge, 2004.

———. "Feetishism: The Scent of a Latin American Body Theology." In *Toward a Theology of Eros: Transfiguring Passion at the Limits of Discipline,* edited by Virginia Burrus and Catherine Keller, 134–52. New York: Fordham University Press, 2006.

———. *Indecent Theology: Theological Perversions in Sex, Gender and Politics.* New York: Routledge, 2000.

Anzaldúa, Gloria. *Borderlands/La Frontera: The New Mestiza.* San Francisco: Aunt Lute Books, 1999.

Barth, Karl. *Epistle to the Romans.* Translated by Edwyn C. Hoskyns. New York: Oxford University Press, 1991.

Benjamin, Walter. "Theses on the Philosophy of History." In *Illuminations: Essays and Reflections,* edited by Hannah Arendt, 253–64. New York: Schocken Books, 1986.

Bhabha, Homi K. *The Location of Culture.* London and New York: Routledge, 1994.

Blades, Rubén. *Buscando América.* New York: Elektra Records, 1984.

Boff, Leonardo. *Ecology and Liberation: A New Paradigm.* Translated by John Cumming. Maryknoll, NY: Orbis Books, 1995.

Borges, Jorge Luis. "La penúltima versión de la realidad." In *Jorge Luis Borges: Obras completas,* 198–201. Barcelona: Emecé Editores, 1996.

Boyarin, Daniel. "The Gospel of the Memra: Jewish Binitarianism and the Prologue to John." *Harvard Theological Review* 94, no. 3 (2001): 243–84.

———. "Midrash and the 'Magic of Language': Reading without Logocentrism." In *Derrida and Religion: Other Testaments,* edited by Yvonne Sherwood and Kevin Hart, 131–40. New York and London: Routledge, 2005.

Brown, Peter. *The Making of Late Antiquity.* Cambridge, MA: Harvard University Press, 1978.

Burke, Kevin. *The Ground beneath the Cross: The Theology of Ignacio Ellacuría.* Washington, DC: Georgetown University Press, 2004.

Burrus, Virginia. *Begotten, Not Made.* Stanford, CA: Stanford University Press, 2000.

———. "The Sex Life of God: Divine Begetting and Creativity in Ancient Christian Texts." Paper presented at The Language of Body and Bodily Processes: Sensual and/or Metaphorical? Conference. University of Oslo, Norway, November 8–9, 2004.

Burrus, Virginia, and Catherine Keller. *Toward a Theology of Eros: Transfiguring Passion at the Limits of Discipline.* New York: Fordham University Press, 2006.

Butler, Judith. *Gender Trouble: Feminism and the Subversion of Identity.* New York and London: Routledge, 1999.

Caputo, John D., and Michael J. Scanlon, eds. *God, the Gift, and Postmodernism.* Bloomington and Indianapolis: Indiana University Press, 1999.

Chanter, Tina. *Ethics of Eros: Irigaray's Rewriting of the Philosophers.* New York and London: Routledge, 1995.

———, ed. *Feminist Interpretations of Emmanuel Levinas.* University Park: Pennsylvania State University, 2001.

Chopp, Rebecca S. "Theology and the Poetics of Testimony." In *Converging on Culture: Theologians in Dialogue with Cultural Analysis and Criticism,* edited by Delwin Brown, Sheila Greeve Davaney, and Kathryn Tanner, 56–70. Oxford and New York: Oxford University Press, 2001.

Cixous, Hélène. *Manna: For the Mandelstams for the Mandelas.* Translated by Catherine A. F. MacGillivray. Minneapolis: University of Minnesota, 1994.

Coleman, Anita. "Walking in the Whirlwind: A Whiteheadian-Womanist Soteriology." PhD thesis, Claremont University, 2004.

Daly, Mary. *Beyond God the Father: Toward a Philosophy of Women's Liberation.* Boston: Beacon Press, 1973.

De Beauvoir, Simone. *The Second Sex.* Translated by H. M. Parshley. New York: Alfred A. Knopf, 1953.

Deleuze, Gilles, and Félix Guattari. *What Is Philosophy?* Translated by Hugh Tomlinson and Graham Burchell. New York: Columbia University Press, 1994.

Derrida, Jacques. *Adieu to Emmanuel Levinas.* Translated by Pascale-Anne Brault and Michael Naas. Stanford, CA: Stanford University Press, 1997.

———. "Faith and Knowledge." In *Religion.* Stanford, CA: Stanford University Press, 1998.

———. *The Gift of Death.* Translated by David Wills. Chicago and London: University of Chicago, 1995.

———. "Sauf le Nom." In *On the Name,* edited by Thomas Dutoit, 35–85. Stanford, CA: Stanford University Press, 1995.

———. *Specters of Marx: The State of Debt, the Work of Mourning, and the New International.* Translated by Peggy Kamuf. New York and London: Routledge, 1994.

————. "Violence and Metaphysics: An Essay on the Thought of Emmanuel Levinas." In *Writing and Difference*, edited by Jacques Derrida, 79–153. Chicago: University of Chicago Press, 1978.

Derrida, Jacques, and Maurizio Ferraris. *A Taste for the Secret.* Translated by Giacomo Donis. Cambridge, UK: Polity, 2001.

Dussel, Enrique. *Beyond Philosophy: Ethics, History, Marxism, and Liberation Theology.* Lanham, MD: Rowman & Littlefield Publishers, 2003.

————. "An Ethics of Liberation: Fundamental Hypotheses." In *Beyond Philosophy: Ethics, History, Marxism, and Liberation Theology,* edited by Eduardo Mendieta, 135–48. Lanham, MD: Rowman & Littlefield Publishers, Inc., 2003.

————. *Ética de la liberación: En la edad de la globalización y de la exclusión.* Madrid: Trotta, 2002.

————. *Filosofía ética latinoamericana: De la erótica a la pedagógica de la liberación.* México: Editorial Edicol, 1977.

————. *1492: El encubrimiento del otro: Hacia el origen del mito de la modernidad.* Madrid: Nueva Utopía, 1993.

————. *The Invention of the Americas: Eclipse of "the Other" and the Myth of Modernity.* Translated by Michael D. Barber. New York: Continuum, 1995.

————. *Liberación de la mujer y erótica latinoamericana.* Bogotá: Editorial Nueva América, 1990.

————. "The 'World-System': Europe as 'Center' and Its 'Periphery' beyond Eurocentrism." In *Beyond Philosophy: Ethics, History, Marxism, and Liberation Theology,* edited by Eduardo Mendieta, 53–81. Oxford, UK: Rowman & Littlefield Publishers, 2003.

Dussel, Enrique, and Daniel E. Guillot. *Liberación latinoamericana y Emmanuel Levinas.* Buenos Aires: Editorial Bonum, 1975.

Ellacuría, Ignacio. *Filosofía de la realidad histórica.* San Salvador: UCA Editores, 1990.

————. "Historia de la salvación y salvación en la historia." In *Escritos Teológicos,* 519–33. San Salvador: UCA Editores, 2000.

Ellacuría, Ignacio, and Jon Sobrino, eds. "The Historicity of Christian Salvation." In *Mysterium Liberationis: Fundamental Concepts of Liberation Theology.* 251–89. Maryknoll, NY: Orbis Books, 1993.

Fernández Retamar, Roberto. *Cáliban: Apuntes sobre la cultura en nuestra América.* México: Diogenes, 1971.

Fewell, Danna Nolan. *The Children of Israel: Reading the Bible for the Sake of Our Children.* Nashville: Abingdon Press, 2003.

Gebara, Ivone. *Longing for Running Water: Ecofeminism and Liberation.* Minneapolis: Fortress Press, 1999.

Goizueta, Roberto S. *Caminemos con Jesús: Toward a Hispanic/Latino Theology of Accompaniment.* Maryknoll, NY: Orbis Books, 1995.

————. *Liberation, Method and Dialogue: Enrique Dussel and North American Theological Discourse.* Atlanta: Scholars Press, 1988.

————. "Locating the Absolutely Absolute Other: Toward a Transmodern Christianity." In *Thinking from the Underside of History: Enrique Dussel's Philosophy of Liberation,* edited by Linda Martín Alcoff and Eduardo Mendieta, 181–93. New York: Rowman & Littlefield Publishers, 2000.

Gonzalez, Michelle. "Who Is Americana/o? Theological Anthropology, Postcoloniality, and the Spanish-Speaking Americas." In *Postcolonial Theologies: Divinity and Empire,* edited by Catherine Keller, Michael Nausner, and Mayra Rivera, 58–78. St. Louis: Chalice, 2004.

Gordon, Avery F. *Ghostly Matters: Haunting and the Sociological Imagination.* Minneapolis and London: University of Minnesota Press, 1997.

Gutiérrez, Gustavo. *A Theology of Liberation: History, Politics and Salvation.* Translated by Sister Claridad Inda and John Eagleson. Maryknoll, NY: Orbis Books, 1973.

Hardt, Michael, and Antonio Negri. *Multitude: War and Democracy in the Age of Empire.* New York: Penguin Press, 2004.

Hart, Kevin. *The Trespass of the Sign: Deconstruction, Theology, and Philosophy.* Cambridge and New York: Cambridge University Press, 1989.

Hollywood, Amy. *Sensible Ecstasy: Mysticism, Sexual Difference, and the Demands of History.* Chicago and London: University of Chicago Press, 2002.

Irigaray, Luce. "Each Transcendent to the Other." In *To Be Two,* 85–93. New York: Routledge, 2001.

————. *An Ethics of Sexual Difference.* Ithaca, NY: Cornell University Press, 1993.

————. *I Love to You: Sketch of a Possible Felicity in History.* Translated by Alison Martin. New York and London: Routledge, 1996.

————. "Questions to Emmanuel Levinas: On the Divinity of Love." In *Re-Reading Levinas,* edited by Robert Bernasconi and Simon Critchley, 109–18. Studies in Continental Thought. Bloomington and Indianapolis: Indiana University Press, 1991.

————. *Sexes and Genealogies.* New York: Columbia University Press, 1993.

————. "Sexual Difference." In *French Feminist Thought: A Reader,* edited by Toril Moi, 118–30. New York: Basil Blackwell, 1987.

————. *This Sex Which Is Not One.* Translated by Catherine Porter and Carolyn Burke. Ithaca, NY: Cornell University Press, 1977.

————. *The Way of Love.* Translated by Heidi Bostic and Stephen Pluhácek. New York: Continuum, 2002.

————. "What Other Are We Talking About?" In *Encounters with Levinas,* edited by Thomas Trezise, 67–81. Yale French Studies. New Haven, CT: Yale University Press, 2004.

Jantzen, Grace M. *Becoming Divine: Towards a Feminist Philosophy of Religion.* Bloomington: Indiana University Press, 1999.

Jarvis, Brian. *Postmodern Cartographies: The Geographical Imagination in Contemporary American Culture.* New York: St. Martin's Press, 1998.

Johnson, Elizabeth A. *She Who Is: The Mystery of God in Feminist Theological Discourse.* New York: Crossroad, 1992.

Jones, Serene. "Creation and Imagination: Reflections on Language, Law, and Beauty." Paper presented at the Transdisciplinary Theology Colloquium, Drew University, Madison, NJ. September 30–October 1, 2001.

———. *Feminist Theory and Christian Theology: Cartographies of Grace.* Minneapolis: Fortress Press, 2000.

Katz, Claire Elise. *Levinas, Judaism, and the Feminine: The Silent Footsteps of Rebecca.* Bloomington and Indianapolis: Indiana University Press, 2003.

Kearney, Richard. *The God Who May Be: A Hermeneutics of Religion.* Bloomington and Indianapolis: Indiana University Press, 2001.

Keller, Catherine. *Apocalypse Now and Then: A Feminist Guide to the End of the World.* Boston: Beacon Press, 1996.

———. *Face of the Deep: A Theology of Becoming.* London and New York: Routledge, 2003.

———. *From a Broken Web: Separation, Sexism and Self.* Boston: Beacon Press, 1986.

———. *God and Power: Counter-Apocalyptic Journeys.* Minneapolis: Fortress Press, 2005.

———. "The Love of Postcolonialism: Theology in the Interstices of Empire." In *Postcolonial Theologies: Divinity and Empire,* edited by Catherine Keller, Michael Nausner, and Mayra Rivera, 221–42. St. Louis: Chalice, 2004.

———. "Rumors of Transcendence: The Movement, State, and Sex of 'Beyond.'" in *Transcendence and Beyond: A Postmodern Inquiry,* edited by John D. Caputo and Michael J. Scalon. Bloomington and Indianapolis: Indiana University Press, forthcoming 2007.

Keller, Catherine, and Anne Daniell, eds. *Process and Difference: Between Cosmological and Poststructuralist Postmodernisms.* Albany: State University of New York, 2002.

Laclau, Ernesto. *Emancipation(s).* London and New York: Verso, 1996.

Landry, Donna, and Gerald MacLean, eds. *The Spivak Reader: Selected Works of Gayatri Chakravorty Spivak.* London and New York: Routledge, 1995.

Lee, Michael E. "Liberation Theology's Transcendent Moment: The Work of Xavier Zubiri and Ignacio Ellacuría as Noncontrastive Discourse." *Journal of Religion* 83, no. 2 (2003): 226–43.

Levinas, Emmanuel. *Alterity and Transcendence.* New York: Columbia University Press, 1999.

———. *Difficult Freedom: Essays in Judaism.* Translated by Seán Hand. Baltimore: Johns Hopkins University Press, 1990.

———. *Nine Talmudic Readings.* Translated by Annette Aronowicz. Bloomington and Indianapolis: Indiana University Press, 1990.

———. *Otherwise Than Being.* Pittsburgh, PA: Duquesne University Press, 1998.

————. *Totality and Infinity: An Essay on Exteriority*. Pittsburgh, PA: Duquesne University Press, 1969.

Lorraine, Tamsin. *Irigaray & Deleuze: Experiments in Visceral Philosophy*. Ithaca, NY, and London: Cornell University Press, 1999.

MacKendrick, Karmen. *Word Made Skin: Figuring Language at the Surface of Flesh*. New York: Fordham University Press, 2004.

McClintock, Anne. *Imperial Leather: Race, Gender and Sexuality in the Colonial Contest*. Routledge, 1995.

McFague, Sallie. *The Body of God: An Ecological Theology*. Minneapolis: Fortress Press, 1993.

McKane, William. *Proverbs: A New Approach*. Philadelphia: Westminster, 1970.

McLean, Robert. *Old Spain in New America*. New York: Association Press, 1916.

Mejido, Manuel J. "The Fundamental Problematic of U.S. Hispanic Theology." In *New Horizons in Hispanic/Latino(a) Theology*, edited by Benjamín Valentín. Cleveland: Pilgrim Press, 2003.

Mendieta, Eduardo. "From Christendom to Polycentric Oikonumé: Modernity, Postmodernity, and Liberation Theology." In *Liberation Theologies, Postmodernity, and the Americas*, edited by David Bastone, Eduardo Mendieta, Lois Ann Lorentzen, and Dwight N. Hopkins, 253–72. London and New York: Routledge, 1997.

Mignolo, Walter D. *Local Histories/Global Designs: Coloniality, Subaltern Knowledges, and Border Thinking*. Princeton, NJ: Princeton University Press, 2000.

Milbank, John. *Being Reconciled: Ontology and Pardon*. London and New York: Routledge, 2003.

————. "Founding the Supernatural: Political and Liberation Theology in the Context of Modern Catholic Thought." In *Theology and Social Theory: Beyond Secular Reason*, edited by John Milbank, 206–55. Oxford, UK, and Cambridge, MA: Blackwell, 1993.

————. *Theology and Social Theory: Beyond Secular Reason*. Oxford, UK, and Cambridge, MA: Blackwell, 1993.

Milbank, John, Catherine Pickstock, and Graham Ward. *Radical Orthodoxy*. London and New York: Routledge, 1999.

Moore-Gilbert, Bart. *Postcolonial Theory: Context, Practices, Politics*. London and New York: Verso, 1997.

Morrison, Toni. *Playing in the Dark: Whiteness and the Literary Imagination*. New York: Vintage Books, 1992.

Murphy, Roland E. *The Tree of Life: An Exploration of Biblical Wisdom Literature*. Grand Rapids: William B. Eerdmans, 1996.

Nancy, Jean-Luc. *Being Singular Plural*. Translated by Robert D. Richardson and Anne E. O'Brien. Stanford, CA: Stanford University Press, 2000.

Newsom, Carol A. *Women's Bible Commentary*. Louisville, KY: Westminster John Knox Press, 1998.

Origen. *On First Principles*.

Peperzak, Adriaan. *To the Other: An Introduction to the Philosophy of Emmanuel Levinas.* West Lafayette, IN: Purdue University, 1996.

Perdue, Leo G. *Proverbs.* Louisville, KY: Westminster John Knox Press, 2000.

Perpich, Diane. "From the Caress to the Word: Transcendence and the Feminine in the Philosophy of Emmanuel Levinas." In *Feminist Interpretations of Emmanuel Levinas,* edited by Tina Chanter. University Park: Pennsylvania State University, 2001.

Pickstock, Catherine. *After Writing: On the Liturgical Consummation of Philosophy.* Oxford, UK, and Madel, MA: Blackwell Publishers, 1998.

Placher, William C. *The Domestication of Transcendence: How Modern Thinking about God Went Wrong.* Louisville, KY: Westminster John Knox Press, 1996.

Robinson, Marilynne. *Gilead.* New York: Farrar Straus Giroux, 2004.

Ruether, Rosemary Radford. *Sexism and God-talk: Towards a Feminist Theology.* Boston: Beacon Press, 1983.

Russell, Mary Doria. *A Thread of Grace: A Novel.* New York: Random House, 2005.

Said, Edward. *Orientalism.* New York: Vintage Books, 1994.

Sandford, Stella. *The Metaphysics of Love: Gender and Transcendence in Levinas.* London and New Brunswick, NJ: Athlone, 2000.

Sandoval, Chela. *Methodology of the Oppressed.* Minneapolis and London: University of Minnesota Press, 2000.

Santiago-Valles, Kevin A. *"Subject People" and Colonial Discourses: Economic Transformation and Social Disorder in Puerto Rico, 1898–1947.* Albany: State University of New York Press, 1994.

Schutte, Ofelia. "A Critique of Normative Heterosexuality: Identity, Embodiment, and Sexual Difference in Beauvoir and Irigaray." *Hypatia* 12, no. 1 (1997): 40–62.

———. *Cultural Identity and Social Liberation.* Albany: State University of New York Press, 1993.

———. "Origins and Tendencies of the Philosophy of Liberation in Latin American Thought: A Critique of Dussel's Ethics." *The Philosophical Forum* 22, no. 3 (1991): 270–95.

Segovia, Fernando F. "Toward a Hermeneutics of the Diaspora: A Hermeneutics of Otherness and Engagement." In *Reading from This Place: Social Location and Biblical Interpretation in the United States,* edited by Fernando F. Segovia and Mary Ann Tolbert, 57–74. Minneapolis: Fortress, 1995.

———. "Two Places and No Place on Which to Stand." In *Mestizo Christianity,* edited by Arturo J. Bañuelas, 28–43. Maryknoll, NY: Orbis Books, 1995.

Segundo, Juan Luis. "Revelation, Faith, Signs of the Times." In *Mysterium Liberationis: Fundamental Concepts of Liberation Theology,* edited by Ignacio Ellacuría and Jon Sobrino, 328–49. Maryknoll, NY: Orbis Books, 1993.

Sells, Michael A. *Mystical Languages of Unsaying.* Chicago and London: University of Chicago, 1994.

Sheffield, Trish. "Totemic Desires: The Religious Dimensions of Advertising in the Culture of Consumer Capitalism." PhD dissertation, Drew University, 2004.

Smith, James K. A. *Speech and Theology*. London and New York: Routledge, 2002.

Sobrino, Jon. "Central Position of the Reign of God in Liberation Theology." In *Mysterium Liberationis: Fundamental Concepts of Liberation Theology*, edited by Ignacio Ellacuría and Jon Sobrino, 350–88. Maryknoll, NY: Orbis Books, 1993.

Spivak, Gayatri Chakravorty. *A Critique of Postcolonial Reason: Toward a History of the Vanishing Present*. Cambridge, MA, and London: Harvard University Press, 1999.

———. *Death of a Discipline*. New York: Columbia University Press, 2003.

———. "French Feminism Revisited." In *Outside in the Teaching Machine*, edited by Gayatri Chakravorty Spivak, 141–71. New York and London: Routledge, 1993.

———. *In Other Worlds: Essays in Cultural Politics*. London and New York: Methuen, 1987.

———. "A Moral Dilemma." In *What Happens to History? The Renewal of Ethics in Contemporary Thought*, edited by Howard Marchitello, 215–36. New York and London: Routledge, 2001.

———. *Outside in the Teaching Machine*. New York and London: Routledge, 1993.

———. *The Post-colonial Critic: Interviews, Strategies, Dialogues*. New York and London: Routledge, 1990.

Sung, Jung Mo. "Human Being as Subject." In *Latin American Liberation Theology: The Next Generation*, edited by Ivan Petrella, 1–19. Maryknoll, NY: Orbis Books, 2005.

Tanner, Kathryn. *The Politics of God: Christian Theologies and Social Justice*. Minneapolis: Fortress Press, 1992.

Taylor, Mark Lewis. "Subalternity and Advocacy as *Kairos* for Theology." In *Opting for the Margins: Postmodernity and Liberation in Christian Theology*, edited by Joerg Rieger. New York: Oxford University Press, 2003.

Trinh, T. Minh-Ha. *Woman Native Other*. Bloomington and Indianapolis: Indiana University Press, 1989.

Varadahrajan, Asha. *Exotic Parodies: Subjectivity in Adorno, Said, and Spivak*. Minneapolis and London: University of Minnesota Press, 1995.

Vasseleu, Cathryn. *Textures of Light: Vision and Touch in Irigaray, Levinas and Merleau-Ponty*. London and New York: Routledge, 1998.

Ward, Graham. *Barth, Derrida, and the Language of Theology*. Cambridge: Cambridge University Press, 1995.

Westphal, Merold. *Transcendence and Self-Transcendence: On God and the Soul*. Bloomington and Indianapolis: Indiana University Press, 2004.

Wood, David. *The Step Back: Ethics and Politics after Deconstruction*. Albany: State University of New York, 2005.

Wyschogrod, Edith. *Emmanuel Levinas: The Problem of Ethical Metaphysics.* New York: Fordham University Press, 2000.

Yarbro-Bejarano, Yvonne. *The Wounded Heart: Writing on Cherríe Moraga.* Austin: University of Texas, 2001.

Zubiri, Xavier. *El hombre y Dios.* Madrid: Fundación Xavier Zubiri and Alianza Editorial, 2003.

———. *Estructura dinámica de la realidad.* Madrid: Alianza Editorial and Fundación Xavier Zubiri, 2006.

Index